Criminal Defence

THIRD EDITION

Other titles available from Law Society Publishing:

Active Defence (2nd edn)
Roger Ede and Eric Shepherd

CLSA Duty Solicitors' Handbook (3rd edn)
Andrew Keogh

Drinking and Driving Offences (2nd edn)
Jonathan Black

Forensic Practice in Criminal Cases
Lynne Townley and Roger Ede

Immigration Advice at the Police Station (3rd edn)
Rosie Brennan

Police Station Skills Kit (3rd edn)
Eric Shepherd

Prison Law (forthcoming)
Margaret Obi

Related Family and Criminal Proceedings
Family-Criminal Interface Committee

Road Traffic Offences Handbook (forthcoming)
Kenneth Carr and Patrick Musters

All books from Law Society Publishing can be ordered from good bookshops or direct from our distributors, Prolog, by telephone 0870 850 1422 or email law.society@prolog.uk.com. Please confirm the price before ordering.

For further information or a catalogue, please contact our editorial and marketing office by email publishing@lawsociety.co.uk.

CRIMINAL DEFENCE

Good Practice in the Criminal Courts

THIRD EDITION

Roger Ede, *District Judge (Magistrates' Courts), Sussex*

Anthony Edwards, *Solicitor, Senior Partner at TV Edwards, solicitors*

The Law Society

Crown copyright material is reproduced with the permission of the Controller of Her Majesty's Stationery Office (Appendix 10). Material in Appendix 16 is reproduced with kind permission of the Bar Council.

ISBN 978-1-85328-924-8

First edition published in 2000
Second edition published in 2002

This third edition published in 2008 by the Law Society
113 Chancery Lane, London WC2A 1PL

Typeset by J&L Composition, Filey, North Yorkshire
Printed by TJ International Ltd, Padstow, Cornwall

Contents

Acknowledgements

We would like to thank the following for their comments and assistance with the text:

Sally Arnold, Neelam Sarkaria, Stephen Cummins, Patrick Lines of the Office for Criminal Justice Reform
Chief Inspector Mark Aslett
Jonny Bugg of the Youth Justice Board for England & Wales
Professor Ed Cape of the University of the West of England
Jane Cosgrove and Gaynor Ogden of the Public Defender Service
Maryvonne Islip of the Criminal Defence Service, Legal Services Commission
Kathryn Lynch of the Sentencing Policy and Penalties Unit, National Offender Management Service
Christopher Murray of Kingsley Napley & Co, solicitors
Jane Brown and Stephen Street of the Secretariat to the Criminal Procedure Rule Committee
Tim Strouts and Andrew Wesson of Her Majesty's Courts Service
Maureen Miller and Joanne Van Zeeland of the Law Society of England & Wales
Teresa Reynolds and Beverley Radcliffe of Victim Support.
We are also indebted to David Roberts and Mike Fitton for their contributions towards the text.

Responsibility for the final text is, however, ours alone.

The law is stated at 1 November 2007.

List of abbreviations

ACPO	Association of Chief Police Officers
Active Defence	R. Ede and E. Shepherd, *Active Defence: A Lawyer's Guide to Police and Defence Investigation and Prosecution and Defence Disclosure in Criminal Cases* (2nd edn, Law Society Publishing, 2000)
AI	advance information
ASBO	anti-social behaviour order
BSS	bail supervision and support
CACDP	Council for the Advancement of Communication with Deaf People
CCPD	Consolidated Criminal Practice Direction
CCRC	Criminal Cases Review Commission
CDA 1998	Crime and Disorder Act 1998
CDS	Criminal Defence Service
CJA 1967	Criminal Justice Act 1967
CJA 2003	Criminal Justice Act 2003
CJPOA 1994	Criminal Justice and Public Order Act 1994
CJS	criminal justice system
CJSSS	Criminal Justice – Simple Speedy Summary
CLS	Community Legal Service
CPIA 1996	Criminal Procedure and Investigations Act 1996
CPR	Criminal Procedure Rules 2005, SI 2005/384
CPS	Crown Prosecution Service
CTM	contact trace material
DPP	Director of Public Prosecutions
DPSI	Diploma in Public Service Interpreting
EAH	early administrative hearing
ECHR	European Convention on Human Rights 1950
EFH	early first hearing
FOA	first officer attending
FPN	fixed penalty notice
FSP	forensic science provider
LPP	legal professional privilege

LSC	Legal Services Commission
MCA 1980	Magistrates' Courts Act 1980
MHA 1983	Mental Health Act 1983
NRPSI	National Register of Public Service Interpreters
OCJR	Office for Criminal Justice Reform
PACE	Police and Criminal Evidence Act 1984
PCC(S)A 2000	Powers of Criminal Courts (Sentencing) Act 2000
PCMH	plea and case management hearing
PND	penalty notice for disorder
POA 1985	Prosecution of Offences Act 1985
RDCO	Recovery of Defence Costs Order
ROTI	record of taped interview
RPSI	Registered Public Service Interpreter
RQSLI	Registered Qualified Sign Language Interpreter
RTSLI	Registered Trainee Sign Language Interpreter
SDN	short descriptive note
SQM	Specialist Quality Mark
TA 2000	Terrorism Act 2000
TIC	taken into consideration
YOI	Young Offenders Institution
YOT	youth offending team

Table of cases

Table of statutes

Table of statutory instruments

Table of international conventions and treaties

CHAPTER 1

The defence solicitor

Objectives of this chapter

- To emphasise the adversarial role of the solicitor in protecting the client
- To show the need for the solicitor to have legal, investigative and management skills
- To explain the part that the solicitor is required to play in criminal proceedings

1.1 THE ADVERSARIAL PROCESS

As a defence solicitor you have a vital and challenging role. You must believe in the adversarial process and the need for the prosecution to prove its case; you must actively investigate and prepare the case for the defence, systematically examining the prosecution case and taking nothing at face value. That process begins with your obtaining details of the prosecution case, advising on the law and allowing your client to give an account of what happened in your client's own words, with the minimum of interruptions. Even if your client admits guilt, you must enquire further and make sure that your client is actually guilty in law and that there is sufficient prosecution evidence to secure a conviction. If your client contests the allegations, you must piece together your client's defence and draw up a case plan. This may involve investigating and recording the scene of the crime, analysing the prosecution witness testimony, tracing and interviewing witnesses, and challenging prosecution forensic evidence by engaging an expert. You must do much more than just speak for your client.

Guidance tells you:

> The primary duty . . . is to protect the interests of the client so far as consistent with any duties owed to the court and any other rules of professional conduct. Subject to this, [you] shall do [your] utmost to promote and work for the best interests of the client and to ensure that the client receives a fair hearing. [You] shall provide the client with fearless, vigorous and effective defence and may use all proper and lawful means to secure the best outcome for the client.[1]

If there is a conflict between your client's instructions and your duties under the Criminal Procedure Rules 2005, SI 2005/384 (CPR), you must not override your instructions but rather withdraw from the case.

You must be prepared to challenge the police if necessary, and not mind being considered 'difficult' by police officers or by the courts when that is unavoidable. Defence solicitors make themselves available to help the client whenever that is necessary: at night in the police station; at court during the day; in prison if the client is in custody.

You must be prepared to stand your ground. In appropriate cases you should consider with your client whether an adjournment should be sought. Do not be pressurised by the court into advising your client to plead guilty against your better judgement. See the checklist 'Considerations before entering a guilty plea' in **Chapter 8**.

1.2 NECESSARY SKILLS AND KNOWLEDGE

Criminal law and procedure has been in a process of continuous change for some years. The battleground in a contested case has to some extent moved from the trial hearing to the police station where the work has become much more complex and demanding. The law on defence and prosecution disclosure may now penalise the client who has failed to give a written statement of the defence and make a focused and specific request for unused material that assists the defence case. This and the law relating to silence demand particular skills from the solicitor and a more thoughtful and planned approach to the preparation of the client's case pre-trial.

Criminal defence is skilled work. For a solicitor's firm to succeed in such work the staff must include solicitors who are competent managers, able to supervise and motivate professional staff and paralegals to whom part of the preparation work may be delegated. Achieving the necessary quality standards requires a careful balance in the use of standardised documents, to ensure nothing is omitted, and advice that is tailored to the needs of the particular client. The Specialist Quality Mark (SQM) of the Legal Services Commission (LSC) is designed to ensure that the firm is successfully run and that it provides a quality service for the firm's clients.[2] Under the preferred supplier initiative the LSC will increasingly allow firms to choose their own quality mark and Lexcel[3] is likely to be accepted in place of the SQM.

It is important that senior and experienced solicitors continue to be involved in the preparation of criminal defence work within the solicitor's firm, and are able to play a significant part in the advice given to the client in the investigation of the defence case before trial, in the training of those who prepare the case, and in file review and supervision. This preparation, and the commitment that goes into ensuring that no stone is left unturned, are the most significant factors in the proper presentation of the case for the client.

Effective supervision and review are essential if good peer review results are to be achieved. A firm is only as strong as its weakest representative. A case may be fought in the courtroom, but the success or failure of the defence will depend largely upon the work done in the police station and on the investigations and preparation undertaken before the trial.

As a defence criminal lawyer you will be an all-rounder:

(a) a legal technician well versed in the relevant law – an advocate for your client's interests;
(b) socially skilled – able to enjoy a working relationship with people who may be difficult and demanding;
(c) assertive – able to stand up for your client;
(d) a negotiator – able to persuade others to see your client's point of view;
(e) an investigator – questioning, challenging and analysing the prosecution and defence case.

1.3   THE OVERRIDING OBJECTIVE OF THE CRIMINAL PROCEDURE RULES 2005

Your responsibility as a defence solicitor is to do what is best for your client, consistent with the client's instructions, while respecting your duties under the CPR.[4] The rules (CPR 1.2) place a personal obligation on you to work in accordance with the 'overriding objective' of acquitting the innocent and convicting the guilty (CPR 1.1) but you require your client's authority for any step you take if you are to continue to work on a case.

The CPR require courts to manage the progression of criminal cases. As part of this, if a plea of not guilty is entered the court will ask the defence:

- the reasons for a plea of not guilty;
- the factual issues in dispute; and
- whether there are any legal issues or points of law that could affect the trial.

Courts will no longer permit the defence to 'ambush' the prosecution by remaining silent about an omission by the prosecution until the defence makes a submission.

In *DPP* v. *Stephens* [2006] EWHC 1860 the court decided that the magistrates should have granted an adjournment to allow the prosecution to serve an analyst's certificate in the manner required by the Road Traffic Act 1988, s.16 – the defence not having objected to the admissibility of the certificate before the trial.

In *Malcolm* v. *DPP* [2007] EWHC 363 (Admin), Stanley Burnton J referred to CPR 1.1, 'the overriding objective', and said:

> criminal trials are no longer to be treated as a game, in which each move is final and any omission by the prosecution leads to its failure. It is the duty of the

defence to make its defence and the issues it raises clear to the prosecution and the court at an early stage . . . to make the real issues clear at the latest before the prosecution closes its case.

In *R. (on the application of DPP)* v. *Chorley Magistrates' Court* [2006] EWHC 1795, Thomas LJ said:

> In our experience, it is very rare in a court, when such a question is asked (what issues were taken by the defence), that parties do not reply. Most people approach a case on the basis that they want justice done as they wish to be acquitted if they are innocent; it is our experience that the case where a defendant refuses to identify the issue is very rare indeed. If a defendant refuses to identify what the issues are, one thing is clear: he can derive no advantage from that or seek . . . to attempt an ambush at trial.

Privilege applies to any information given by a defendant so as to obtain advice or advance his case (see **Chapter 2**). You must decide how much information to release and at which stage.

1.4   THE ADULT CRIMINAL CASE MANAGEMENT FRAMEWORK

The Adult Criminal Case Management Framework[5] covers all adult prosecutions in the magistrates' courts. A further document covering the Crown Court will be issued later. It does not cover cases involving youth offenders. It is intended to provide guidance to those engaged in a criminal case as to their functions and as to what the court will expect from them at the various stages of a case. The Framework complements CPR Part 3 on case management. It sets out the actions that should be taken at each stage by the defence.

The Adult Criminal Case Management Framework (3rd edition) outlines the responsibilities of the defence advocate including responsibilities as to case progression. For example, at 3.6(b):

> The defendant or his advocate should be prepared to indicate to the court that the defendant is aware of the importance of preparing his case, keeping appointments with his solicitor, and attending court (knowing the consequences of not doing so).

This requires the disclosure of confidential information as all dealings between you and the defendant are confidential but the CPR override that. However, you cannot disclose confidential information without the authority of your client if you are to continue to act in the case. Such authority is sought in the standard client care letters in **Appendix 2 (2.18** and **2.19)**.

4

NOTES

1. The Code of Conduct for Employees of the Legal Services Commission Who Provide Services as Part of the Criminal Defence Service, para.2.1 (**www.legalservices.gov.uk**).

2. The LSC SQM requires management standards to ensure a quality assured service of a universal standard. All firms that have a contract with the LSC must meet the requirements stipulated in the SQM. While the LSC is moving towards peer review as its primary audit tool, SQM is still in effect and will be used in an LSC file review and in a management audit.

3. Lexcel is the Law Society's practice management quality mark. It allows any type and size of legal practice to undergo independent assessment to certify that the requirements of the Lexcel standard are being met.

4. Further information about the CPR is given in **Chapter 2**. The Criminal Procedure Rules Committee is chaired by the Lord Chief Justice. The members include a representative of the Home Secretary, two Court of Appeal judges, a High Court judge, two circuit judges, a District Judge, a magistrate, a justices' clerk, the Director of Public Prosecutions (DPP), two barristers, two solicitors, a representative of the Association of Chief Police Officers and representatives of Nacro (the national crime reduction charity) and Victim Support. The CPR are available (updated) on the Ministry of Justice website at **www.justice.gov.uk** (see **Appendix 1**).

5. The Adult Criminal Case Management Framework (3rd edition) was produced by practitioners from Criminal Justice System (CJS) agencies based in the Office for Criminal Justice Reform (OCJR), in consultation with members of the judiciary, the Law Society, the Bar, the Witness Service and CJS agencies including the CPS, the police, Her Majesty's Courts Service) and the National Offender Management Service. The Framework is available on **www.cjsonline.gov.uk/framework**.

CHAPTER 2

Legal and professional duties

Objectives of this chapter

• To show how the solicitor maintains a professional relationship with the client and the court
• To explain how the solicitor should work with prosecution and defence witnesses
• To show how to avoid the pitfalls of criminal practice, including issues of confidentiality, privilege and conflict
• To explain how the solicitor should work within the criminal case process to achieve competence plus at peer review

---

2.1 INTRODUCTION

Your duty to obtain the best result for each client has to be exercised in the context of the criminal law (legal duties) and the professional rules and codes of conduct (professional duties). In general terms you must keep information about your client's affairs confidential unless, by doing so, you would commit a criminal offence or you are required to disclose the information by a valid order of the court or by the CPR. The law in relation to confidentiality and also as to privileged material is considered in detail below.

Your duty to act in your client's best interests is recognised by the peer review criteria established by the Institute of Advanced Legal Studies for the Legal Services Commission.

The criteria are designed to highlight the quality of:

• the information gained from the client and other sources;
• the advice given based on that information;
• the steps taken following that advice.

Indicators of Excellence in the standard of work include ensuring that:

• clients' instructions are fully and appropriately recorded;

- communication, advice and other work are tailored to each individual client's circumstances;
- clients are all advised correctly and in full;
- all issues are progressed comprehensively, appropriately and efficiently;
- there is a demonstration of in-depth knowledge and appreciation of the wider context;
- there is excellent use of tactics and strategies, demonstrating skill and expertise, in an attempt to ensure the best outcomes for clients;
- the supplier adds value to their cases, taking a full proactive approach;
- there are no areas for major improvement.

2.2 YOUR DUTY TO YOUR CLIENT

You are your client's adviser and, if appropriate, his advocate (see Solicitors' Code of Conduct 2007, rule 11 (Litigation and advocacy); **www.sra.org.uk**).

Your client is the principal and you are his agent. Your duties to your client include:

(a) giving independent advice;
(b) not permitting any compromise of your integrity;
(c) acting in your client's best interest;
(d) ensuring the confidentiality of information about your client and his affairs;
(e) using reasonable care and skill, proper diligence and promptness and keeping your client properly informed.

Your objectives include:

(a) seeking relevant information;
(b) considering relevant facts, law and procedure;
(c) advising your client;
(d) preparing your client's case for presentation in court, including as appropriate:

    (i) interviewing and taking a statement from your client and any potential witnesses;
    (ii) investigating the prosecution and defence case, including the scene of the crime;
    (iii) securing documentary evidence;
    (iv) seeking expert assistance;
    (v) passing information when appropriate to the court and Crown Prosecution Service (CPS).

2.3   YOUR DUTY TO THE COURT

While your primary duty is to your client, you have an overriding duty not to deceive or knowingly or recklessly mislead the court (Solicitors' Code of Conduct 2007, 11.01; **www.sra.org.uk**). Your duty to the court is to act in good faith. In the context of preparing a case this means:

(a)   never knowingly or recklessly letting the advocate, your client or his witnesses, by what they say, mislead the court or tell the court facts that you know to be untrue;

(b)   never assisting your client to make a statement to the police that you know to be untrue;

(c)   never inventing a defence or assisting your client to invent one including persuading or attempting to persuade a witness not to give evidence.

The Criminal Procedure Rules 2005 and delay

CPR 3.2 states that active management includes:

> . . . discouraging delay, dealing with as many aspects of the case as possible on the same occasion, and avoiding unnecessary hearings.

CPR 3.8(2) states that, where relevant, at each hearing a court must take a plea or obtain an indication of whether the defendant is likely to plead guilty or not guilty.

You should aim to progress cases speedily within the practice outlined in the CPR, but this must not be at the expense of following proper procedures. Many factors in the criminal justice system can unavoidably contribute to defence delay. It may be necessary to request further disclosure from the prosecutor before advising on plea. It may be difficult to obtain an appointment to take instructions in person or by video link from a client in custody. An adjournment to allow time for discussions with the prosecution to take place may lead to a case being discontinued or a lesser charge being substituted.

Reasons why an adjournment may be necessary are listed below:

(a)   to persuade the CPS to discontinue proceedings (notwithstanding that under the charging arrangements, the CPS will have already reviewed and advised on charge before the case goes to court);

(b)   to persuade the CPS to reduce the charge (see note above);

(c)   to persuade the CPS that a caution should be administered instead of a charge, if a caution is appropriate and can be given (see note above);

(d)   to obtain unused material relating to sentence;

(e)   to obtain a pre-sentence report (specific sentence report, standard delivery report or fast delivery report);

(f)   to obtain information to verify mitigation;

(g)   to enable the client to be represented by own solicitor (the application being made by the duty solicitor);

(h)   to obtain complete advance information (note that you are only entitled to this for an either-way offence);

(i)   the advance information is in CCTV or audio format and equipment is not available at court to view it or hear it;

(j)   it is necessary to trace and interview witnesses before advice on plea can be given;

(k)   to obtain a medical report;

(l)   to obtain a report on diversion as a disposal (including diversion of juveniles);

(m)   advance information served is too bulky to take instructions on;

(n)   a short descriptive note (SDN) shows an admission which the client denies, and there is a need to listen to the tape (if such facilities are not available at the court);

(o)   the client cannot communicate at court because the client suffers from a mental health problem or learning disability;

(p)   the client has difficulty communicating in English and an interpreter is not available;

(q)   the client is in a state of emotional turmoil (in *R. (on the application of Costello)* v. *North East Essex Magistrates* [2006] EWHC 3145 (Admin) the court decided that there was a clear risk of prejudice if the defendant was forced to defend himself and give evidence when his mind might well not have been on the issues as his son had died two days earlier);

(r)   the client is drunk or under the influence of drugs.

If you apply for an adjournment you must be realistic and specific about the reason and the desired outcome and the length of time required to achieve it.

You may have to consider whether to oppose a prosecution application for an adjournment. The court in *Crown Prosecution Service* v. *Picton* [2006] EWHC 1108 considered a familiar scenario. The court decided that the magistrates were correct in refusing an adjournment of a common assault all-day trial when the prosecution witnesses were not present. They had mistakenly been warned for 2 pm instead of 10 am. The magistrates were told that the witnesses could be at court by lunchtime at the earliest; that the trial might go part-heard then and would have to be adjourned to another date at least five months later (so the trial would take place over a year after the alleged assault); and that the court was triple listed with another all-day trial and a trial listed for the afternoon. Jack J reviewed the authorities and listed the following points for consideration:

- summary justice should be speedy justice;
- magistrates must consider both the interests of the defendant in getting the matter dealt with and the interest of the public that criminal charges should be adjudicated upon;
- the more serious the charge the greater the public interest;
- if an adjournment requested by the defence is not granted, to what degree the defendant's ability to defend himself will be compromised;
- the likely length of an adjournment and the need to decide the facts while recollections are fresh;
- if the need for an adjournment is the fault of the party requesting it, that is a factor against granting an adjournment, carrying weight in accordance with the gravity of the fault;
- account should be taken of the history of the case, whether there have been previous adjournments and if so, at whose request.

Criminal Procedure Rules 2005 and the role of the defence

You will constantly have in mind the best interests of your client. An essential element of good preparation is effective case management from the outset:

(a) taking proper control of the case;
(b) taking responsibility for the decisions that need to be made and actively planning;
(c) thinking ahead so that the defence is able at the earliest opportunity to make enquiries;
(d) raising proper issues and reacting to developments in a case.

The CPR begin with an overriding objective and principles of case management. The overriding objective is that criminal cases are dealt with justly (CPR 1.1(1)). Dealing with a case justly includes 'acquitting the innocent and convicting the guilty' (CPR 1.1(2)(a)). The objective applies very widely, to '[a]nyone involved in any way with a criminal case' (CPR 1.2(2)) and includes defence solicitors who must (CPR 1.2(1)):

(a) prepare and conduct the case in accordance with the overriding objective;
(b) comply with these Rules, practice directions and directions made by the court; and
(c) at once inform the court and all parties of any significant failure (whether or not that participant is responsible for that failure) to take any procedural step required by these Rules, any practice direction or any direction of the court. A failure is significant if it might hinder the court in furthering the overriding objective.

The CPR recognise 'the rights of a defendant, particularly those under Article 6 of the European Convention on Human Rights' (1.1(2)(c)). In the *Criminal*

Justice Reforms Handbook, one of the Appeal Court and one of the circuit judge members of the Committee write that the presence of 1.1(2)(c) confirms that the Committee could not change the rules regarding legal professional privilege or the professional duty to a client: 'if a defendant admits guilt to his legal representative but declines to plead guilty, the overriding objective does not prevent the defence from requiring the prosecution to prove its case'.

In *R. (on the application of Kelly)* v. *Warley Magistrates' Court and the Law Society* [2007] EWHC 1836 (Admin) the court noted that legal professional privilege extended to information given by potential witnesses for use in actual or prospective litigation and their identities and decided that a direction by a District Judge to disclose the names, addresses and dates of birth of all defence witnesses to be called at trial could only be in the nature of a request and not an effective order.

Under CPR 1.1(2) dealing with a case justly also includes:

(d)   respecting the interests of witnesses, victims and jurors and keeping them informed of the progress of the case;
(e)   dealing with the case efficiently and expeditiously;
(f)   ensuring that the appropriate information is available to the court when bail and sentence are considered; and
(g)   dealing with the case in ways that take into account –

    (i)   the gravity of the offence alleged,
    (ii)   the complexity of what is in issue,
    (iii)   the severity of the consequences for the defendant and others affected, and
    (iv)   the needs of other cases.

CPR 3.2(1) requires the court to manage the case actively. This includes the early identification of the real issues (3.2(2)(a)). Each party must 'actively assist the court in fulfilling its duty under rule 3.2' (3.3(a)). The client may still put the Crown to proof, though if the defence has not identified all matters in issue, the Crown may be allowed additional time to present relevant evidence (*Malcolm* v. *DPP* [2007] EWHC 363 (Admin)).

2.4   CONFIDENTIALITY AND PRIVILEGE

The solicitor's duty of client confidentiality

A solicitor is under a professional and legal obligation to keep the affairs of clients confidential and to ensure that all members of his or her staff do likewise. This duty of confidence is fundamental to the fiduciary relationship that exists between solicitor and client. It extends to all matters divulged to a solicitor by a client or (on the client's behalf) from whatever source.

Overriding confidentiality

In certain circumstances confidentiality can be overridden. For solicitors the most relevant instances will arise either when they are ordered to disclose by compulsion of law, or when there is a public duty to do so.

Compulsion of law

A court has the power to compel the disclosure of confidential information held by a solicitor. The most common examples of this are the statutory powers exercised by judges to compel production of confidential ('special procedure') material under the Police and Criminal Evidence Act 1984 (PACE), Sched.1.

A duty to the public to disclose

The circumstances in which a solicitor may make disclosure on the grounds of public interest are very limited and set out in the Solicitors' Code of Conduct 2007, 4.01 (**www.sra.org.uk**). Essentially a solicitor may reveal confidential information only to the extent necessary to prevent the client or a third party committing a criminal act that is reasonably believed to be likely to result in serious bodily harm, and in cases of continuing or anticipated child abuse if disclosure is in the public interest.

Communications in furtherance of crime

Communications by a client to a solicitor for the purpose of obtaining legal advice or assistance in the furtherance of crime are not confidential.

Confidentiality and legal professional privilege (LPP)

Certain confidential communications however can never be revealed without the consent of the client; they are privileged against disclosure. Only a client may waive privilege. This protection is called legal professional privilege (LPP).

The House of Lords has underlined the policy behind LPP, its necessity and its nature (*R. (on the application of Morgan Grenfell & Co Ltd)* v. *Special Commissioners of Income Tax* [2003] 1 AC 563):

[1]
The policy of legal professional privilege requires that the client should be secure in the knowledge that protected documents and information will not be disclosed at all.

[2]
It is necessary in our society, a society in which the restraining and controlling framework is built upon a belief in the rule of law, that communications between clients and lawyers, whereby the clients are hoping for the assistance of the lawyer's legal skills in the management of their (the clients') affairs, should be secure against the possibility of any scrutiny from others, whether the police, the executive, business competitors, inquisitive busy bodies or anyone else.

[3]
[LPP is] a fundamental human right long established in the common law. It is a necessary corollary to the right of any person to obtain skilled advice about the law. Such advice cannot be effectively obtained unless the client is able to put all the facts before the adviser without fear that they may be afterwards disclosed and used to his prejudice.

What communications are privileged?

Not everything that lawyers have a duty to keep confidential is privileged. Only those confidential communications falling under either of the two heads of privilege – 'advice privilege' or 'litigation privilege', are protected by LPP.

Who is a 'lawyer' for such purposes?

Solicitors and their employees, barristers and in-house lawyers are bound by the duties of privilege but not accountants, even if they give legal advice (subject to one very limited exception).

Advice privilege

Communications between a lawyer (acting in his capacity as a lawyer) and a client are privileged if they are confidential and for the purpose of seeking legal advice from a lawyer or providing legal advice to a client. But note:

1. Conveyancing documents are not communications (and so are not privileged).
2. A client account ledger maintained in relation to the client's monies is not a communication.
3. Appointments diaries, time records on an attendance note, time sheets or fee records relating to a client are not communications.
4. A solicitor's bill of costs and statement of account may in certain circumstances be privileged.
5. Notes of open court proceedings, or conversations, correspondence or meetings with opposing lawyers are not privileged, as the content of the communication is not confidential.

6. The mere fact that a client is speaking or writing to his or her solicitor does not make that communication privileged – it is only those communications between the solicitor and the client relating to the matter in which the solicitor has been instructed for the purpose of obtaining legal advice that will be privileged. Such communications do not need to contain advice on matters of law and construction, provided that they are directly related to the performance by the solicitor of his professional duty as legal adviser of his client.

Litigation privilege

Litigation privilege applies to *confidential* communications made, *after litigation has started*, or is *reasonably in prospect*, between:

(a) a lawyer and a client;
(b) a lawyer and an agent (whether or not that agent is a lawyer); or
(c) a lawyer or his client and a third party;

for the *sole or dominant purpose* of litigation, whether

(a) for seeking or giving advice in relation to it; or
(b) for obtaining evidence to be used in it; or
(c) for obtaining information leading to obtaining such evidence.

Pre-existing documents

An original document which is not brought into existence for either of these privileged purposes (and so is not already privileged) does not acquire privileged status merely by being given to a lawyer for advice or otherwise for a privileged purpose.

Fraud or illegality – the crime/fraud exception

It is proper for a lawyer to advise a client on how to stay within the law and avoid committing a crime or to warn a client that proposed actions could attract prosecution and such advice will be protected by privilege.

LPP does not however exist in respect of documents that form part of a criminal or fraudulent act, or communications that take place in order to obtain advice with the intention of carrying out an offence. It is irrelevant whether or not the lawyer is aware that he is being used for that purpose. If the lawyer suspects that he is unwittingly being involved by his client in a fraud, before he can consider himself released from his duty of confidentiality, the courts require there to be strong prima facie evidence before LPP can be displaced. While the lawyer may release himself if such evidence exists, he may also raise the issue with the court for an order authorising him to make disclosure to the victim.

The general 'crime fraud exception' principle is restated in PACE, s.10(2) where items held with the intention of furthering a criminal purpose are declared not to be items subject to LPP. It is important to note that the intention to further a criminal purpose need not be that of the client (or the lawyer) – it is sufficient that a third party intends the lawyer–client communication to be made with that purpose (e.g. where the innocent client is being 'used' by a third party).

Overriding privilege

By statute

LPP is a fundamental human right. Parliament can of course legislate contrary to fundamental principles of human rights; however, the House of Lords has stressed that a parliamentary intention to override rights such as LPP must be expressly stated in the statute or appear by necessary implication (see *R. (on the application of Morgan Grenfell & Co Ltd)* v. *Special Commissioners of Income Tax* above).

Public duty

Unlike the position in relation to confidential material (see above), there is no public interest exception to LPP. It is therefore prima facie unlawful for a solicitor to disclose a communication if to do so would involve a breach of LPP.

2.5   FAILURE TO DISCLOSE INFORMATION ABOUT TERRORISM – OFFENCES

How do the anti-terrorism provisions affect the duty of client confidentiality? Put in starker terms, does a solicitor risk imprisonment for failure to disclose information about terrorism?

There are three provisions of the Terrorism Act 2000 (TA 2000) that penalise, with the threat of imprisonment, persons who fail to disclose varying degrees of knowledge, belief or suspicion of the commission by others of terrorist offences:

1. **Disclosure of information: duty** – TA 2000, s.19. Under this section it is an offence for a person not to disclose to a constable as soon as reasonably practicable his belief or suspicion, and the information on which it is based, that another person has committed an offence under TA 2000, ss.15–18 when that belief or suspicion is based on information coming to him in the course of a trade, profession, business or employment.

15

2. **Failure to disclose: regulated sector** – TA 2000, s.21A. If a person knows or suspects, or has reasonable grounds for knowing or suspecting, that another person has committed an offence under ss.15–18, and the information or other matter upon which that knowledge, suspicion, reasonable belief is based came to him during the course of business in the regulated sector, he commits an offence if he does not disclose the information or other matter to a constable (or nominated officer) as soon as practicable after it comes to him.

3. **Information about acts of terrorism** – TA 2000, s.38B. If a person has information which he knows or believes might be of material assistance in preventing the commission by another person of an act of terrorism or in securing the apprehension, prosecution or conviction of another person, in the UK, for an offence involving the commission, preparation or instigation of an act of terrorism, he commits an offence if he does not disclose the information to police as soon as reasonably practicable.

Do sections 19 and 21A of the Terrorism Act 2000 override LPP?

Section 19(5) does not require disclosure by a 'professional legal adviser' of either information which he obtains 'in privileged circumstances' or a belief or suspicion based on information which he obtains in 'privileged circumstances'.

Section 21A(5) provides that a person does not commit an offence under the section if he is a 'professional legal adviser' and the information or other matter came to him in 'privileged circumstances'.

Under both provisions, 'privileged circumstances' effectively mirror LPP at common law and both are subject to the caveat that it will not cover communications in furtherance of a criminal purpose.

Guidance

A solicitor does not therefore, subject to the caveat, breach these sections of TA 2000 if he fails to disclose information which has come to him in privileged circumstances.

Does section 38B of the Terrorism Act 2000 override LPP?

In order to override LPP, the statute must do so expressly or by necessary implication. There is no provision in TA 2000, s.38B equivalent to that relating to 'professional legal advisers' in TA 2000, ss.19 and 21A. As no express words are used to override LPP, therefore only if there is a 'necessary implication' can LPP be overridden. What is meant by 'a necessary implication'?

The test has been expressed as follows:

A useful test is to write in the words 'not being privileged documents' and ask, not 'does that produce a reasonable result' or 'does it impede the statutory purpose for which production may be required?' but 'does that produce an inconsistency?' or 'does it stultify the statutory purpose?' The circumstances in which such a question would receive an affirmative answer would be rare (*per* Lord Millett in *B* v. *Auckland District Law Society* [2003] 2 AC 736).

This provides helpful assistance in the absence of specific judicial interpretation of TA 2000, s.38B. It would seem unlikely that it could be successfully argued that the statutory purpose of s.38B would be stultified if it was to read (adopting the wording in the earlier sections and adapting Lord Millett's formula), 'The person commits an offence if he does not disclose the information unless it was obtained in privileged circumstances as soon as reasonably practicable'.

Guidance

In the circumstances, therefore, the Law Society considers that LPP is not overridden by TA 2000, s.38B and that information of the kind referred to in the section, if received in privileged circumstances, cannot be disclosed without the authority of the client.

Is non-disclosure of information on the grounds that it is covered by LPP a 'reasonable excuse' under section 38B(4)?

The only defence available to an offence under TA 2000, s.38B is that the person charged has a reasonable excuse for not making a disclosure. In considering whether non-disclosure on the grounds that the information is covered by LPP provides a reasonable excuse, one must first ask in what circumstances a solicitor can disclose LPP material without his or her client's consent.

The answer is short – and to be found most helpfully expounded by Lord Lloyd in *R.* v. *Derby Magistrates' Court, ex p. B* [1996] 1 AC 487 at 509:

> Once the privilege is established, the lawyer's mouth is 'shut for ever' . . . There may be cases where the principle will work hardship on a third party seeking to assert his innocence. But in the overall interests of the administration of justice it is better that the principle should be preserved intact.

If a solicitor is prevented from disclosing information received in privileged circumstances, even in his or her own defence, it is difficult to argue that a failure to disclose information of the nature envisaged by s.38B, when received in privileged circumstances, does not amount to a reasonable excuse.

In *R. v. Robinson* [2002] EWCA Crim 2489, the Court of Appeal expressed its concern at the practice of police inducing or encouraging breaches of the right to LPP:

> The right is severely curtailed if the solicitor, or the solicitors' clerk from whom he seeks legal advice, is telling the police what passes between them. It is not only a serious breach of duty by the solicitor, or clerk, to the client but, on the face of it, and if encouraged by the police, an infringement by the police of those rights.

Guidance

The Law Society is therefore of the view that it is a reasonable excuse under TA 2000, s.38B not to disclose information received in privileged circumstances, which a solicitor knows or believes might be of material assistance in preventing the commission by another person of an act of terrorism or in securing the apprehension, prosecution or conviction of another person, in the UK, for an offence involving the commission, preparation or instigation of an act of terrorism.

It is crucial however that a solicitor when in receipt of such information should be absolutely satisfied that his client's purpose in supplying that information has been for the obtaining of legal advice and is directly related to the performance by the solicitor of his professional duty as legal adviser of his client.

If it is not, then it is not protected by LPP; it does however remain confidential.

While it remains confidential, there is a clear duty owed by the solicitor to the public to disclose confidential information to prevent the client or a third party committing a criminal act that is reasonably believed to be likely to result in serious bodily harm. It is the Law Society's view that the solicitor must disclose the information as soon as reasonably practicable.

In any event, if there is a public duty to disclose in such circumstances, it would seem to follow that confidentiality would not amount to a reasonable excuse for non-disclosure under TA 2000, s.38B and that a solicitor failing to disclose such information would risk prosecution.

2.6 AVOIDING PERVERTING THE COURSE OF JUSTICE

Perverting the course of justice is a criminal offence. Be aware that it may be committed in the following circumstances:

(a) manufacturing and helping to manufacture false evidence;[1]
(b) destroying or concealing potential evidence;

(c)   interfering with potential witnesses to persuade them not to give evidence or to give false evidence (see also the Criminal Justice and Public Order Act 1994 (CJPOA 1994), s.51);

(d)   knowingly acting for a defendant who has assumed a false name or other false details with intent to deceive the court or police (e.g. that the defendant has no previous convictions);[2]

(e)   deliberately assisting your client to evade arrest;

(f)   assisting offenders (note the Criminal Justice Act 1967 (CJA 1967), s.4);

(g)   putting forward a knowingly false defence (but the Crown can always be put to proof).

2.7   DEALING WITH POTENTIAL PROSECUTION EVIDENCE

It may happen that a client approaches you with a request that you keep an item for him or her, and you either know or suspect that the item is of an incriminating nature so far as the client is concerned. You should refuse to accept the item unless the client authorises you to hand it to the police.

You may find that an item has been left in your office by a client or friend of a client. Where it is clear that the item is of value to the prosecution, you should arrange for it to be delivered to the police. You should not offer information to the police in respect of the manner in which it came into your possession or of any other circumstances surrounding the delivering of it. Your client should be informed of your action and the question of conflict of interest with your client should be considered.

If, in the course of investigating your client's defence, you come across evidence that is clearly material to the prosecution case, you should not interfere with it in any way but should make a record of it. You are under no duty to disclose it to the police or the prosecution.

2.8   YOUR CLIENT'S INSTRUCTIONS

Refusing instructions

Generally, you are free to decide whether to accept instructions from any particular client, but it is inadvisable to refuse without good reason, such as:

(a)   refusal of public funding or failure of your client to make adequate financial provision for fees;

(b)   a conflict or potential conflict of interest between you and your client (or prospective client) or between your client (or prospective client) and another existing or former client.

Any refusal must not be based on the race, colour, ethnic or national origins, sex, religion or belief, disability, sexual orientation or age of the prospective client (Solicitors' Code of Conduct 2007, 6.01).

Change of instructions

If your client makes inconsistent statements, only where it is clear that your client is attempting to put forward false evidence to the court should you cease to act. Remember that the defendant is entitled to put the prosecution to proof of its case. The client should (except where it amounts to the offence of 'tipping-off' under the money laundering legislation) be advised of the reason for any decision not to continue to act, and that he or she is free to instruct other solicitors.

The client's identity

If, to your knowledge, your client has adopted a false name or address or date of birth with intent to deceive the court (e.g. by evading identification your client seeks to avoid being linked with his previous convictions or to impede the court's communication with him) you should advise your client of the dangers of failing to identify himself properly and if he refuses, you should withdraw. This does not apply if a change of name was without intent to deceive, or if the address given, although not your client's place of residence, is a genuine point of communication. If in doubt, decline to act (see the Solicitors' Code of Conduct 2007, Rule 11).

An innocent client pleading guilty

See **Chapter 8**.

Conflict of interest

Constantly review your client's instructions and be aware of possible conflict of interest problems. Specific guidance from the Law Society is reproduced at **Appendix 3**.

A witness for your client: advocates acting as witnesses

It is not appropriate for a solicitor to act as an advocate in a case in which he or she is to give evidence. A solicitor should not accept instructions to act as an advocate in a case if it is clear, or there is a significant risk, that he or she will be called as a witness. If, having properly accepted instructions, it becomes clear prior to trial that the solicitor will, or that there is a significant risk that the solicitor will, be called to give evidence the solicitor should cease to act as the advocate. If, having properly accepted instructions, it becomes apparent during the course of a trial that the solicitor will be called to give evidence, the solicitor advocate should normally seek a re-trial and cease to act.

It may be possible for a solicitor to accept instructions to act as an advocate, or to continue to act, if a member of the solicitor's firm is to be called to give evidence for the client, but only if the evidence is unlikely to be contested. Factors to be taken into consideration include whether the giving of evidence will create a conflict of interests between the solicitor and the client, or whether the solicitor's duty to the court is likely to be impaired. For example, evidence may be given by a member of the solicitor's firm as to the grounds for advice not to answer police questions (in circumstances where privilege has been, or is to be, waived) or as to the conduct of an identification parade, provided that the factual basis for such evidence is unlikely to be contentious. It is not appropriate for a solicitor to accept instructions, or to continue to act as an advocate, where a member of the firm is to give evidence for another party (or the prosecution).

In circumstances where it is inappropriate for a solicitor to accept instructions, or continue to act as advocate, the issue cannot be resolved by instructing an independent advocate unless the evidence to be given by the solicitor is unlikely to be contested. Having accepted instructions to act for a client, the solicitor must keep under review the question whether it is appropriate to continue to act, bearing in mind the principles set out above and other issues of conflict.

2.9 WITNESSES

Interviewing prosecution witnesses

There is no property in a prosecution witness. The Law Society advised that: 'It is permissible for a solicitor acting for any party to interview and take statements from any witness or prospective witness at any stage in the proceedings, whether or not that witness has been interviewed or called as a witness by another party.'[3]

Traditionally, English and Welsh defence solicitors have had a distinct disinclination to interview prosecution witnesses. Clearly there are risks:

1. **Rehearsing the witness for cross-examination.** There is the risk of warning the witness in advance of the defence case that will later be put to the witness, so that you inadvertently rehearse him for cross-examination at trial. If a witness is not telling the truth the jury should be able to see the witness respond to a challenging question for the first time.
2. **Legal risks.** If you interview a prosecution witness and subsequently the evidence is inconsistent with an earlier account, which the witness gave

to the police, you could find yourself accused of interfering with a witness and/or perverting the course of justice.

The Law Society advised:

> A solicitor should be aware that, in seeking to exercise the right to interview a witness who . . . is likely to be called by [the other side] . . . the solicitor may well be exposed to the suggestion that he or she has improperly tampered with the evidence. This may be so particularly where the witness subsequently changes his or her evidence.
>
> In order to avoid allegations of tampering with evidence, it is wise for a solicitor to offer to interview the witness in the presence of a representative of the other side. If this is not possible a solicitor may record the interview, ask the witness to bring a representative and ask the witness to sign an additional statement to the effect that the witness has freely attended the interview, and has not been coerced into giving the statement or changing his or her evidence.[4]

There are persuasive arguments for interviewing prosecution witnesses despite the risks. With the abolition of all oral committal proceedings ending the opportunity to cross-examine prosecution witnesses at committal and the clear research evidence of how police officers may shape witness testimony,[5] the need to interview certain types of prosecution witnesses becomes more pressing. The witness may have information that you cannot afford to leave until cross-examination at trial to obtain. It may by then be too late to follow up a lead that the witness provides.

Where appropriate, you must interview prosecution witnesses, having weighed up the factors for and against and arrived at a reasoned decision for doing so – particularly if that decision is founded upon shortcomings you, and experts, have identified in the witness's statement. You should interview the witness in a way that demonstrates best practice. You should employ appropriate procedures to ensure the treatment of the witness is beyond reproach and ensure there is a recording of this, or an independent third party or representative of the other side is present.

You should keep a full attendance note of any contact with a potential prosecution witness.[6]

In R. Ede and E. Shepherd, *Active Defence: A Lawyer's Guide to Police and Defence Investigation and Prosecution and Defence Disclosure in Criminal Cases* (Law Society Publishing, 2000) full advice is given on:

- identifying witnesses;
- weighing up factors for and against interviewing;
- shortcomings in the way in which the police interview witnesses;
- approaching a witness (including a specimen letter to a witness);
- the extent to which you should keep the prosecutor in the picture;
- who should conduct the interview;
- who else should attend;

- where the interview should be conducted;
- how the interview should be conducted;
- safeguards;
- tape recording.

Witness care

It is good practice to have regard to the needs of all witnesses. The Witness Service makes its facilities available at court for defence as well as prosecution witnesses. For more on witness care see **Chapter 4** and **Appendix 5.**

2.10   SAFEGUARDING CHILDREN'S VIDEO EVIDENCE

The Home Office and Department of Health's *Memorandum of Good Practice on Video Recorded Interviews with Child Witnesses for Criminal Proceedings* (HMSO, first edition 1992, revised edition 2002) sets out guidelines for the conduct of interviews, and the storage, custody and disposal of videotapes. It emphasises the sensitivity of such a tape which 'may well . . . contain intimate personal . . . information and images and, in the child's interests, should be held strictly in confidence . . . It is therefore essential that adequate arrangements are made to store the recording safely and securely and to ensure that access to it, and to copies which are made, is restricted to those who are authorised to view the recording'.

No one should have custody of a tape unless they are willing to safeguard it to the standard recommended in the memorandum.

Any person borrowing a tape should be made aware that the tape is the property of the police and is likely to be used in the course of a criminal trial, and that its misuse or unauthorised retention may constitute a contempt of court or other offence.

Log books should be maintained by anybody authorised to have custody of a copy, and such log books should be subject to periodic inspection by management.

Tapes are at their most vulnerable when in transit, and when passed on to third parties. CPS practice, recommended to practitioners, is to use recorded delivery post where hand delivery is impractical. When delivering tapes, do not leave them unattended in your car, because of the risk of theft. Before handing tapes to third parties, you would be wise to safeguard your position by requesting a written undertaking first.

The memorandum requires you to give a written undertaking to safeguard the recording. A form of undertaking recommended by the Law Society is set out in **Appendix 4.**

2.11 SEXUAL OFFENCES

You should be aware of your obligations under the Sexual Offences (Protected Material) Act 1997 in relation to statements by and photographs and medical assessment of the complainant of a sexual crime. If the prosecutor seeks an undertaking you must control the relevant papers and documents, not copy them to your client, or to anyone else, other than in connection with the proceedings or for the assessment or treatment of your client. Your client and any person properly given copies must be told of their responsibilities not further to distribute them.

NOTES

1. Advice on how to act in these circumstances in the investigative stage is given by the Public Defender Service, *Guidance 2/2005 Police Station Advice* issued by the Head of the Professional Service for the Public Defender Service in October 2005 (**www.legalservices.gov.uk/docs/pds**).
2. Ibid.
3. *The Guide to the Professional Conduct of Solicitors 1999*, Principle 21.10. Conduct issues occurring before 1 July 2007 are contained in *The Guide to the Professional Conduct of Solicitors 1999*, to which has been added online new conduct rules published since August 1999: the Guide Online (**www.lawsociety. org.uk**).
4. Ibid.
5. See E. Shepherd and R. Milne, 'Full and faithful: ensuring quality practice and integrity of outcome in witness interviews', in *Analysing Witness Testimony* (Blackstone Press, 1999); M. McLean, 'Quality investigation? Police interviews of witnesses' (1995) 36 *Medicine, Science and the Law* 116–22; E. Shepherd, 'Representing and analysing the interviewee's account' 35 (1995) *Medicine, Science and the Law* 122–35.
6. It is a contempt of court for the police to interfere with a defence solicitor's attempts to interview prosecution witnesses (*Connolly* v. *Dale* [1996] 1 All ER 224).

CHAPTER 3

Obtaining core information

Objectives of this chapter

- To list the information about your client that you must have on file

---

Throughout this chapter references in square brackets are to the LSC Transaction Criteria.

3.1 INTRODUCTION

In every case in which a file is opened you must obtain core information about your client. This will inform your decision making and representations and will become particularly significant in the event of a conviction or plea of guilty.

You also need to record core information on the file about the offence or group of offences, details of bail or custody and the next court hearing. You should:

1. State what each charge is in detail. Identify whether it relates to an indictable, either-way or summary–only offence. Dates are particularly significant for sentencing.
2. Summarise the allegation and establish any connection between the charges.
3. Once a decision has been made, say what your client will plead, or that he is unsure.

3.2 STATEMENT OF PERSONAL HISTORY

File reference number

This should be at the top of the statement. Print additional copies, with the appropriate reference number for each offence or group of offences to be tried together.

Date

This is the date that you took or updated the statement.

Personal details

1. Name [1.1]. Make sure that your client has identified himself correctly. Include the name at birth.
2. Address [1.2]. You will need to find out a little about the address: how long has your client been living there; does he live with anyone there; and is he a tenant/licensee/owner/guest or squatter?
3. Telephone number [1.3]. You should note if none available.
4. Date of birth and age [1.4]; place of birth.
5. Married/cohabiting/single/separated or divorced.
6. Children and other dependants, ages and relationship to your client.
7. Education:

    (a) Is your client studying for exams?
    (b) What is his attendance record?
    (c) What are his school reports like?
    (d) What are his career plans?
    (e) Has he changed schools, or left unexpectedly?
    (f) Has he attended a special school or received help with special educational needs?

8. Work, training and employment:

    (a) Find out what training schemes, apprenticeships or day release courses your client has taken part in.
    (b) Set out the different jobs your client has had in chronological order. Number them, and specify reasons for leaving and periods of unemployment between jobs.
    (c) Give the dates of starting and finishing jobs and when he was promoted.
    (d) If your client is not in permanent employment, for how much of the year does he usually work?
    (e) If your client is unemployed, what are his job prospects?

9. Income [73]. Find out the family's total weekly income[1] and source of that income, including state benefits, so that this can be compared with weekly outgoings. Does your client require welfare benefits advice?
10. Expenses. List expenses, also on a weekly[2] basis, setting them out one under the other: rent/mortgage; electricity, gas and telephone bills; travel to work and back and meals at work; hire purchase, catalogues, credit card and bank/finance house loan repayments (including how much is still outstanding and what the goods are); council tax; water rates; car running expenses (including petrol, oil, tyres, maintenance, tax and

insurance); clothes, food and other household shopping; and if currently paying fines to a court, the amount and frequency of payments and the amount outstanding.

11. Savings and debts. Take your client's instructions on what weekly[3] rate a fine could be paid at. Advise your client that the offer must be realistic and the fine should not normally take longer than 12 months to pay. What is the amount of capital owned by your client?

12. Health/disability:

    (a)   If your client has a medical condition:

        (i)   What is the nature of it? [75]

        (ii)   What is the effect of it on your client? [75.2]

        (iii)   What treatment is received or sought? [75.3]

        (iv)   Is your client partially sighted/deaf?

    (b)   Go into detail if your client has a drink, drugs or psychiatric problem. You will want to know when and in what circumstances the problem started, when it was at its worst and what it was like then, what stage it is at now, and what your client is doing to cure himself.

        (i)   Find out the relationship, if any, between your client's condition and his offending.

        (ii)   Has your client consulted his GP or a consultant about it? Has your client received any treatment? Is he receiving medication for it?

        (iii)   Note any details and obtain your client's signed authority to obtain a medical report [53.1].

        (iv)   Record the name and address of your client's doctor and/or consultant.

    (c)   Does your client have learning difficulties?

    (d)   Is your client able to read/write?

13. Interests, especially charitable work.

14. Family background. Find out anything in your client's family background that may help you understand why he committed the offence if he pleads guilty or is convicted, e.g. problems with parents, matrimonial difficulties, difficulty in forming relationships, etc.

15. Past record [50.3]. Obtain a copy of your client's past record from the prosecution. This should always be obtained as the details and dates can be significant. If the record includes Young Offenders Institution (YOI) and prison sentences you may require additional verified information on time of remand or date of release and any time lost or recalled to YOI or prison. Check for the risk of a mandatory minimum sentence being imposed on your client and for relevant convictions if your client is being prosecuted for a serious specified offence.

Check with your client:

(a) If you obtain the details from your client find out the dates he was sentenced, which courts sentenced him, the facts of the offences and the sentences and whether your client pleaded guilty or was found guilty.

(b) If your client is in breach of a court order, take instructions in some detail about the circumstances of the offence for which that order was imposed [49.2].

(c) Check whether time was spent on remand [72.1].

(d) If the present charge is similar to any of your client's previous offences you will need to have sufficient information about those offences to attempt to distinguish them.

16. Other pending charges [49.1]:

(a) Ask about other courts your client is due to appear in: when; what he is accused of; what his conditions of bail are; what stage the proceedings have reached; and who represents your client.

(b) If your client is represented by other solicitors, ask if he would prefer them to represent him in this case as well, and whether your client would like the cases consolidated if possible.

17. If your client is under 17 or has a mental disorder or handicap:

(a) What is the name and contact details of the appropriate adult? [8.2]

(b) What is the relationship of the adult to your client? [8.1]

18. If your client is involved with a social worker/probation officer. What is the name and contact details of the social worker/probation officer?

19. Ethnic origin/disability status. Use the standard classification in Figure 3.1.

White	Mixed	Asian or Asian British
☐ (a) British	☐ (a) White and Black Caribbean	☐ (a) Indian
☐ (b) Irish	☐ (b) White and Black African	☐ (b) Pakistani
☐ (c) Other	☐ (c) White and Asian	☐ (c) Bangladeshi
	☐ (d) Other	☐ (d) Other

Black or Black British	Other
☐ (a) Black Caribbean	☐ (a) Chinese
☐ (b) Black African	☐ (b) Other
☐ (c) Other	

Disability status: ☐ Able Bodied ☐ Unregistered Disabled ☐ Registered Disabled

Figure 3.1 Standard classification of ethnic origin and disability status

NOTES

1. If it is more convenient for a particular client to express this on a different time basis, e.g. monthly, this should be done, but the same period should be used consistently for the collection of all information.
2. See note 1.
3. See note 1.

CHAPTER 4

Managing the case

Objectives of this chapter

- To identify the issues that lead to excellence at peer review
- To show how to systematise your casework
- To show how to organise the case file
- To identify good client care ·
- To identify good witness care

Throughout this chapter references in square brackets are to the LSC Transaction Criteria.

4.1   PEER REVIEW STANDARDS

When examining files, peer reviewers have regard to the following matters under seven main headings. The detail is contained in *Improving your Quality: A Guide to Common Issues Identified through Peer Review* (Crime) (available at **www.legalservices.gov.uk**).

1.   The quality of file organisation

- Are files organised in chronological order and legible? This may require the typing of important memoranda.

2.   Communication with all parties

- Has the adviser demonstrated persistence and determination in obtaining instructions from clients and/or statements from witnesses? Clients are notoriously unwilling to attend appointments but need to be pressed. Peer reviewers expect to see:
   - a proof preferably signed;
   - observations on evidence;
   - personal statements.

- Are clients in custody visited or interviewed over video links to obtain instructions?
- Is there evidence of client dissatisfaction with the service they have received?
- Are clients given written advice on the strength of evidence, plea, venue and likely sentence?
- Are clients given clear and written advice regarding sentence?
- Are clients advised of the progress of their case and the next steps in a timely manner?
- Are clients sent final outcome letters explaining the effect of the disposal of the case and advice regarding appeal?
- Are letters/pro forma tailored to the client and in plain English?

3. Information and fact gathering from all necessary sources

- Are cases prepared in sufficient detail? Reviewers will expect to see detailed instructions for advocates (see **Chapter 14**).
- Are proofs and comments on the prosecution evidence taken in contested cases?
- Are statements or background detail taken in mitigation?

4. The advice and assistance given

- Does the file show detailed analysis of the evidence in the case and its use in advising on plea, place of trial and analysis for trial?
- Are clients advised of the weaknesses in the case in a timely manner?
- Are mental health issues considered when they arise?

5. The effectiveness of the work and assistance given

- Are correct pleas lodged at the right time following appropriate advice to clients?
- Are important matters relating to case preparation dealt with in a timely manner? Are you proactive in your conduct of the file?
- Is alternative disposal of the case actively pursued on behalf of clients?
- Are defence statements submitted on time and according to your client's instructions?

6. Efficiency of work on the file

- Does the fee earner have sufficient experience to deal with the case? Clear allocation criteria need to be established. Good supervision is required of delegated work.
- Are experts used appropriately?
- Are all actions/steps undertaken necessary for the case?

7. Professional ethics

- Are there adequate procedures for dealing with conflicts and other issues?

4.2 CASE MANAGEMENT SYSTEMS

It is essential to devise workable systems for the processing of criminal case work. They must be used by all fee earners. Case management systems help to:

(a) ensure all necessary work is undertaken and in good time;
(b) prevent repetition;
(c) make supervision and file review easy and enable fee earners to under-stand the state of a case quickly; and
(d) protect against error and are a defence against wasted costs applications.

Identify the person responsible for the case, having regard to the seriousness of the offence and the nature of the client. Appoint a case progression officer under the Criminal Procedure Rules 2005 and tell the other parties and the court (CPR 3.4(1)).

Each firm should aim to produce an office manual containing its procedures and standard documents.

For advice on delegation skills see **Appendix 6**.

The file

The information in the file should be kept in a uniform way so that anyone can access it easily. A quick look at a file should tell you everything of importance about a case. Key information about a client and his case should be readily available on the front cover of the flap and/or a 'state of case' pro forma in the file together with dates for specific action (see **Appendix 2, 2.1**). Examples of attendance forms used by the Public Defender Service are available on the LSC website (see **Appendix 1**).

General information

The following general information should be kept in the file:

- client's name [1.1], date of birth [1.4], address [1.2], telephone number [1.3];
- person responsible for client and conduct of case;
- police/CPS unique case reference number;
- police station/officer-in-case; CPS office;
- co-accused and representatives;
- court/next hearing date;

- charge [50.1] (and date of each arrest and each charge); this has particular importance in relation to sentencing;
- language needs;
- whether client is on bail or in custody. If on bail, conditions including sureties. If in custody, where; telephone number; custody time limits and length of time in custody;
- date advance information given (if relevant);
- date committed/sent/transferred to Crown Court;
- date intial disclosure given;
- date of service of defence statement [65.1]; hearsay and bad character notices;
- notification of guilty plea;
- stage when guilty plea entered [71.1];
- advocate instructed;
- brief delivered;
- conference held [67.1];
- agreement on taped evidence;
- prosecution witnesses required to give oral evidence at trial;
- date of conviction/sentence (for appeal); time limits for giving notice of appeal;
- all advice given and the reasons for that advice.

Public funding

The following public funding information should be kept in the file:

- unique file number;
- police station advice – whether used and detail;
- advice and assistance – whether used and detail;
- Representation Order – date lodged/date granted/details of costs estimate and date given (in private cases and in a Crown Court case where a Recovery of Defence Costs Order (RDCO) is likely) [40.1];
- details of disbursements incurred/date paid;
- public funding authorities – date sought/date granted.

Private client information

The following private client information should be kept in the file:

- fixed price;
- costs estimate (date given and by whom);
- revised estimates;
- payment arrangements: instalments;
- money on account;
- dates and amounts of interim bills;
- disbursements.

Progress sheet

Ensure each fee earner keeps a 'state of case' pro forma sheet at the front of or in a prominent position on the file (see **Appendix 2, 2.1**). This should show at a glance the present stage the case has reached, who requested any previous adjournments and the reasons for them. A form (see **Appendix 2, 2.2**) should also identify when notices are required to be served.

Check that fee earners know what will happen at the next hearing and that this has been agreed with and communicated to the court, the CPS and your client, and that it is necessary for them and their client to attend. Endeavour to adhere to agreed steps in the progress of a case, so that court hearings achieve their purpose.

4.3   CASE INFORMATION SYSTEMS

Have systems for investigating the prosecution evidence and collating, managing and analysing the information that you obtain in a case.

Active Defence advises about significant milestone stages in a case:

(a)   to analyse and take stock of the information obtained so far;
(b)   to consider the implications of this for the prosecution and defence cases;
(c)   to make decisions about the actions to be taken as a consequence, particularly defence investigation.

Milestones

1.   **Police station.** At the police station you will need to:

   (a)   seek disclosure from the police;
   (b)   ask whether they have any information they have not disclosed;
   (c)   obtain instructions from your client;
   (d)   advise on and consider disclosure to be given to the police by your client;
   (e)   consider obtaining information that was not revealed and carrying out investigations that the police did not undertake;
   (f)   record all significant events, the disclosure and instructions obtained, advice given and reasons for that advice;
   (g)   record time spent in police detention by your client (relevant as you may need to argue that sentences should be reduced because of this).

2.   **Tape recordings of police interviews.** You will need to obtain instructions from your client if you were not present at the interview. The recording is the only authentic and reliable record of the police interview. You will

wish to listen to the tape in all cases if only to establish areas of mitigation. If there is to be a trial you must listen for assertions of good character by your client and questions about your client's bad character and consider the possible implications of these under the bad character provisions. You should listen to a no-comment interview to see whether there are possible inferences from silence. See **Chapter 11** for further advice about listening to tape recordings of interviews.

3.   **Bail hearing at court.** The prosecution file can be a valuable source of information but consider what may have been omitted (such as convictions recorded against prosecution witnesses/disciplinary findings against police officers).

4.   **Advance information.**

(a)   You will generally press for witness statements.

(b)   You will need to obtain further instructions from your client.

(c)   You will consider:

- alternative disposals;
- level of charge;
- whether there is a prima facie case;
- the strength of the prosecution case;
- the merit of putting the prosecution to proof;
- the advantage of claiming a sentence discount for a plea of guilty;
- plea;
- mode of trial;
- type of committal;
- the likelihood of obtaining bail (local knowledge – if available, e.g. proclivity of this type of offence in your area/information about the likely attitude of the bench or the District Judge);
- interviewing any witnesses.

5.   **Prosecution witness statements in summary cases.** These should be available as part of Criminal Justice – Simple Speedy Summary (CJSSS) or if you make a request to the CPS following a plea of not guilty.

(a)   You will need to obtain further instructions from your client in a signed proof.

(b)   Consider:

- which witnesses need to give oral evidence;
- whether expert evidence is required;
- whether CJA 1967, s.10 admissions are appropriate to narrow issues.

6. **Committal bundle/prosecution evidence following transfer or sending.** At this stage you will:

   (a) need to obtain further instructions from your client;
   (b) need to consider:

   - missing material that you should request from the prosecutor if it is not served as initial disclosure;
   - which witnesses need to give oral evidence;
   - whether further investigations or expert evidence is required;

   (c) be able to draft the defence statement;
   (d) be able to brief the trial advocate and hold a conference with him.

7. **Prosecution initial disclosure: unused undermining material and schedule** [50.2]. At this stage you will:

   (a) establish whether there is further unused material which should have been disclosed;
   (b) request it by considering the meaning of 'material which can reasonably be considered capable of undermining the prosecution case against the accused or assisting the defence case' in the Attorney General's Guidelines on Disclosure, paras 10–14 (see **Appendix 1** for website link) and by reference to the schedule MG6C and by refining your defence statement.

8. **Prosecution further disclosure: disclosure of further material which may assist the defence cases** [50.2]. At this stage you will establish whether there is further unused material which should be disclosed to you.

Active Defence also recommends systems for managing the information obtained in your client's case:

(a) organising case files;
(b) a case chronology;
(c) an actions management sheet;
(d) collation methods.

Active Defence explains ways of analysing:

(a) statements;
(b) tape recordings of suspects;
(c) recordings of witness interviews;
(d) contemporaneous notes;
(e) records of tape-recorded interviews;
(f) the custody record;
(g) video recordings.

Time guidelines and time limits

Work out the timetable for the case. Take into account custody time limits, CPR time limits and any effective hearing date.

Some good practice points

Examples of good practice are:

- using common reference numbers;
- applying for publicly funded representation at an early stage;
- advising the CPS of changes of representation with an associated prompt exchange of case materials including advance information;
- the early notification of change of pleas.

4.4   CLIENT CARE

Client care letter

At the outset, a client care letter should be sent. Examples appear at **Appendix 2, 2.18** and **2.19**.

Professional rules as to client care appear in the Solicitors' Code of Conduct 2007 at 2.02 and as to costs at 2.03. You are required to operate a complaints handling procedure in accordance with 2.05.

SQM requires the following matters to be covered usually in a client care letter:

(a)   the effects of an order for prosecution costs, against the client;
(b)   the client's potential obligation to pay an RDCO should his case go to the Crown Court (other than on a committal for sentence or appeal against sentence) or higher court on appeal, when such an order is likely;
(c)   information about:

   (i)   the name and status of the individual responsible for case conduct;
   (ii)   the name of the individual responsible for case supervision;
   (iii)   to whom, and how, any complaints should be made.

For advice on communication skills see **Appendix 6**.

Dealing with your client: a written record

SQM and other practice management standards require firms to have written procedures for taking instructions which ensure that fee earners/advisers agree, record and confirm to the client in writing:

(a)   the requirements or instructions of the client [48];
(b)   the advice given;
(c)   the action to be taken by the firm;
(d)   key dates in the matter.

The first three items above will usually be recorded on the file on attendance notes with matching sub-headings. It may be necessary to tell the client that it is not possible to give advice until further investigations have been undertaken.

The interview

Get to know your client during the interview. For advice on communication skills, listening to and talking to your client see **Appendix 6**.

You are your client's agent, not his tool: act professionally and preserve a distance between you, otherwise your ability to give independent advice will be compromised.

1.   Be alert to any mental disability and seek medical or specialist assistance when appropriate (see page 22).
2.   Do not interview your client or take his statement in the presence of any potential witness.
3.   Explain to your client that his attitude to the conduct of his defence could have cost implications. Tell your client that you will act as his representative, within the constraints of your professional rules, but you need his constant co-operation. At the conclusion of the case, if the court is satisfied that costs have been wasted by an unnecessary or improper act or omission by your client or on his behalf, your client may be liable to pay such costs.
4.   Ensure that, to the extent practicable, all significant decisions are taken after consultation between you. Your client will need to ensure you can contact him readily.
5.   Advise your client to notify you of any change of address.
6.   Advise your client to notify you, before a trial date is fixed or a case is adjourned for any other reason, of any dates to be avoided or holiday commitments, when he cannot attend court.
7.   Confirm in writing any decisions that may have professional or cost implications.

Many clients do not appreciate that giving you proper instructions takes time. It is often helpful at the beginning of the interview to explain to your client how long it is likely to take; what you hope to achieve by the end of it; how the statement will be used and who will see it.

1.   Always write a statement for other people to use.
2.   Write your client's statement in the first person, as if he is writing it.
3.   If your client cannot give a satisfactory answer show this in the statement.

4. Do not put words into your client's mouth; use his words wherever practicable.
5. Do not coach your client – you must not suggest what your client might say or help him to invent a story.
6. Explain that everything he tells you is 'on the record'.
7. It is a matter of professional judgement how much information you should obtain from your client at any particular stage.
8. When taking the statement be positive and sympathetic.
9. Set out your client's version in chronological order.
10. The statement is essentially what your client will say in evidence but is not limited to that; it will include relevant background information which is necessary for a proper understanding of the main events. You should in addition obtain relevant personal information for the purposes of mitigation if required. It will also help anyone else who may deal with the file to know something about the client.
11. After the interview send your client a copy of the statement for checking and possible amendment.
12. Explain to the client that he should not show the statement to or discuss it with anyone who may give evidence in the case.
13. Your client should always sign and date his statement.
14. Consider putting the statement in the form of a CJA 1967, s.9 statement. Also, obtain the client's signature to the caption as well as to each page and date it.

Set out the information you obtain in a structured way, in blocks with appropriate headings. If you always follow the same pattern this will act as a checklist of the information that you need to obtain and in court the advocate will be able to find what he or she is looking for quickly. Example headings are given in **Chapters 3** and **12**.

Keeping the client informed

Clients must be kept fully advised in writing as a case proceeds. Use appropriately adapted standard letters where possible. These also assist in meeting competence standards for peer review.

SQM requires a firm to have written procedures which ensure that:

(a) information on the progress of a case (or reasons for lack of progress) is given to the client at appropriate stages. This is particularly important when new information emerges or there are changes in tactics;
(b) information about changes in the action planned to be taken in the case is given to the client;
(c) clients are informed of any change in the fee earner/adviser having conduct of the matter.

Your client will also need to know:

- how long the case is likely to take [57.1];
- what steps you are going to take on his behalf [52.2];
- what the prosecution will have to prove [54.1];
- how strong his case is;
- when he will see you next and what will happen then [57.4].

You should confirm in writing any advice given [57.3].

Keeping in contact

Keep in regular contact with your client in writing, on the telephone or in person. Further information about letters to a client on remand is given on page 90.

A solicitor's letter should not be opened and read by the prison authorities if it is sent within a double envelope. The outer envelope should be addressed as normal to the prisoner concerned; the inner unstamped envelope should be marked clearly 'Prison Rule 39' (or 'YOI Rule 14' if addressed to a young offender). The inner envelope should also be annotated with the prisoner's name and prison number, if known; address and telephone number of the solicitor's office; a reference number, if possible; and the signature of the solicitor or his clerk.

Difficulties in communication

If at any time you have difficulty in obtaining instructions you should advise the court of that fact, but your duty of confidentiality otherwise applies.

If a client fails to attend on you to give instructions, write to him saying that if the failure continues so that you would have difficulty in conducting the trial, you will have to inform the court and get the case listed for hearing. If he still fails to attend on you, write to the court informing it that you are without instructions and asking for the case to be listed without witnesses.

If your client is not fluent in English or has a hearing or speech impairment, arrangements must be made for your instructions to be taken through an interpreter: see pages 215–18 and **Appendix 7** on finding an interpreter.

Various organisations are able to provide specialist advice on the needs of clients with physical and learning disabilities. These include the Royal National Institute for the Deaf, the Council for the Advancement and Communication with Deaf People, and MENCAP. In the case of a client with a learning disability, the solicitor should consider making an application to the court to order the removal of wigs and gowns and any other measures to assist them to give evidence. The series of 'Books Beyond Words' is produced by the St George's Hospital Medical School and includes picture books that explain procedures relating to arrest, trial and going to court as a witness. Further information can be obtained from the Royal College of Psychiatrists, 17 Belgrave Square, London SW1X 8PG.

4.5 WITNESS CARE

The Witness Service

The Witness Service helps witnesses, victims, their families and friends when attending any of the criminal courts in England and Wales. It helps defence and prosecution witnesses, but not defendants in their particular case. The Witness Service works to a court code of conduct, which stipulates that no discussion of the evidence will take place. The Witness Service also offers support to and works alongside expert witnesses.

The Witness Service offers:

- a service that is free, independent of the police and courts, and adapted to individual need;
- someone to talk to in confidence (but not about the evidence);
- emotional support in dealing with the impact and experience of attending court;
- pre-court visits for witnesses, so that they are familiar with the courtroom and the roles of the various people in court before they give their evidence;
- support, in the courtroom if necessary, on the day of the trial; and during and after any sentencing hearing;
- information about court and legal processes;
- practical help, for example, with expenses forms;
- separate waiting areas for defence and prosecution where provided by the court;
- in some courts, special help and support for witnesses who are vulnerable or intimidated;
- liaison with other statutory or voluntary agencies where requested;
- referral to other agencies after the trial;
- support to witnesses in getting information about the outcome of the case.

The Witness Service also supports and works alongside other people who may accompany a witness, for example a carer, social worker, expert witness, interpreter or intermediary (see **www.victimsupport.org.uk**).

Child witnesses

Good practice for defence practitioners interviewing child witnesses includes the following:

1. Control the number (and length) of interviews with children.

41

2. Have the original interviewer go back to clarify any points with the child.
3. Do not dominate the relationship with the child.
4. Try to use open questions.
5. Interview as soon as you can after the event.
6. Be aware that children become tired and distracted more quickly than adults.
7. Proceed at the child's speed.
8. When the child pauses, do not jump in and take the talking turn too quickly.
9. Tell the child that 'I can't remember' or 'I don't know' are perfectly acceptable.
10. When asking closed questions to which the child answers 'yes' counterbalance them with questions to which the consistent answer would be 'no'.

CHAPTER 5

Shaping the case in the police station

Objectives of this chapter

- To show how to influence the decision about whether your client is charged and to identify alternative outcomes
- To show how to influence the decision about the level of charge
- To identify how to lay the foundations for a later trial

Throughout this chapter references in square brackets are to the LSC Transaction Criteria.

5.1 PREPARATION IN THE POLICE STATION

Work done in the police station plays a critical part in the later handling of criminal cases. You should regard the attendance there as the first day of trial.

Allegations of criminal conduct can result in a wide range of disposals: no further action; a fixed penalty notice (for disorder, low level theft and criminal damage); a reprimand or warning for a youth; an informal, simple or conditional caution for an adult; an offence to be taken into consideration; or a bindover or charges at different levels of seriousness.

You should be fully conversant with the codes of practice under PACE (as amended) and consider the effect of every step taken by you at the police station in the context of the eventual outcome of a case and a possible trial. A suggested checklist is at **Appendix 2, 2.4**. See also **Appendix 8** for the Solicitors Regulation Authority's Standards of Competence for the Accreditation of Solicitors and Representatives Advising at the Police Station.

Your duty is to act professionally while obtaining the best result for each client and critically, when advising, you must balance the risks involved particularly in advising whether or not your client should answer questions in interview:

1. You should make a full record of information obtained from the police and each client, advice given, reasons for the advice, decisions reached by your client, and representations made [3.2.1, 9, 9.1, 19].
2. You should take a proactive approach to obtaining information from the police, and considering the legality of the arrest and detention; and in representing your client in interview.
3. You should advise that your client does not have to provide evidence that strengthens a prosecution case.
4. However, you should take appropriate steps to avoid inferences from silence and understand the difference between CJPOA 1994, s.34 on the one hand and CJPOA 1994, ss.36 and 37 on the other [19, 20, 21, 22].
5. You should consider the need to give an early indication of matters relevant to the defence because:

    (a) they weaken or undermine the prosecution case or assist the defence case and may therefore require initial disclosure of unused material; or
    (b) they make the defence more credible; or
    (c) they provide grounds (where a case will be proved) to avoid prosecution or to mitigate its effects. The highest discount for a guilty plea is available if an indication of a guilty plea is given at the police station because that is the first reasonable opportunity and because it may enable an expression of regret. However, you should be satisfied about the strength of the prosecution evidence. In the event of an admission your client may be asked to take offences into consideration. You will need to balance the risks. Offences taken into consideration increase the seriousness of the matters charged but an admission avoids a later gate arrest, if the new offence can later be proved.

6. You should be aware that the police may ask your client in interview about any bad character evidence they may have in their possession, which they may seek to introduce at trial as to propensity to commit offences or as to untruthfulness or as relevant to other matters in issue. It is often wise to advise that no comment be made on this aspect as it is not for you to help the Crown to prove the underlying facts of those other matters.
7. Also, consider whether evidence of your client's bad character may be given at trial if your client casts imputations on another or asserts his own good character in the interview or gives a false impression. Advise appropriately and intervene to prevent this happening. Remember that a false impression may be withdrawn.

Detailed advice on these issues is contained in E. Shepherd, *Police Station Skills for Legal Advisers – Accreditation Manual* and *Practical Reference* (Law Society Publishing, 2004). See also *Active Defence*.

Evidential consequences

You should consider the evidential consequences of each step that you take or your client takes at the police station.

Privilege

When you have been at the police station you are a competent and compellable witness in relation to all that took place. You should maintain good records to assist in recollecting details (see **Appendix 2, 2.4** for a sample attendance form). However, at trial you may not answer questions about the instructions your client gave in order to obtain advice, or the advice you gave, unless your client waives or has waived privilege. Be aware that serious consequences at trial may follow the giving of reasons for advising silence when such advice was given in a privileged meeting: privilege may be waived (*R. v. Condron* [1997] Crim LR 215) and the prosecution would be able to examine your notes.

Consider ways of overcoming this by withholding the reasoning at this stage (though recording it) or by checking details of disclosure in the presence of the police and then immediately advising in their presence without reference to any privileged meeting.

Record keeping

It is essential to keep proper records: if the suspect remains silent on your recommendation, the court may still draw an adverse inference. However, where you have advised silence you must state this at the start of the interview tape so that there can be no question about the genuineness of the client's reliance upon your advice. Because the reliance must also be reasonable, it may be necessary to make sure that the court understands the circumstances that led you to advise the suspect to remain silent. This means you have to keep full, clear contemporaneous timed notes of the prevailing circumstances and of your advice so that you can:

(a) refer to these notes;
(b) produce them in court if necessary if privilege is waived.

Keep a careful note of:

(a) the physical and mental state of the suspect [7.11, 12];

45

(b)   the general conduct of the police and the 'atmosphere' in which the investigation is being conducted;
(c)   what information is made available by the police to you in a pre-interview briefing: about the offence, your client and possible outcomes;
(d)   what requests for information are made of the police by you [7.3, 7.4];
(e)   what information is given to you by the suspect [9];
(f)   the suspect's apparent understanding of the significance of the allegation, and the significance of his replies or failure to respond;
(g)   the advice given by you to the suspect, and the reasons for that advice;
(h)   the decision of the suspect;
(i)   representations made by you at all stages and the reasons for them;
(j)   as far as is practicable, what is said in the police interviews;
(k)   what was said at the time of charge/report for summons.

Confidential advice

In order properly to fulfil your role you need access to suitable facilities that recognise the need for both confidentiality and your safety. Home Office Circular 24/98 advises chief constables that 'delays in court may be avoided by ensuring that conditions are right for a solicitor to take confidential instructions from a detainee at the police station'.

Advice regarding police interviews

See the advice given in **Appendix 6** about listening to and talking to your client. Allow adequate time for obtaining instructions and giving advice.

There are three ways in which your client may handle any interview with the police. You should take sufficient time to advise your client of the evidential consequences of each:

1.   **Making no comment** [18.1]. This may have evidential consequences when an inference can be drawn under CJPOA 1994 [8.3]. When this is your advice, indicating that your client is acting 'in accordance with' that advice does not waive privilege.
2.   **Preparing a statement with your client and then making no comment.** The statement may be used at the police station, to weaken or negative any inference from silence during the investigation, or at charge, or held back to use if required at trial. It may be used should the prosecution allege a recent fabrication (in which case it is evidence of its truth under the Criminal Justice Act 2003 (CJA 2003), s.120), attack the credibility of the defendant or seek to draw an inference from silence in interview [18.2].
3.   **Answering proper and relevant questions.** Be aware that answering some relevant questions but not others may result in the whole interview being heard by the court. If your client makes some admissions but also makes

some denials then the whole statement is evidence of the truth of its contents and later will serve, for instance, to put the prosecution on notice of the need to disprove a statutory defence, or of general defences such as self-defence and duress, so that it must disprove them at trial.

5.2 REPRESENTATIONS AS TO EVIDENCE

The making of appropriate representations in the police station can play a critical part at trial. In particular they can affect:

(a) a court's decision whether to draw/allow the jury to draw appropriate inferences;
(b) a court's decision as to whether there has been oppression or whether by reason of something said or done, a confession is unreliable (PACE, s.76);
(c) the court's decision as to whether it is unfair in the proceedings to admit evidence (PACE, s.78);
(d) the court's decision whether to admit evidence of bad character.

You will need to consider representations in at least the following areas:

1. **Obligation to pursue all lines of enquiry.** Consider whether it is appropriate to ask the police to pursue any reasonable lines of inquiry, since the Code of Practice (para. 3.5) under Part II of the Criminal Procedure and Investigations Act 1996 (CPIA 1996) requires the investigator to make any such enquiries that point away from the suspect. What is reasonable in each case will depend on the particular circumstances. Some evidence, such as CCTV footage, may be lost unless it is requested immediately.
2. **Disclosure.** The prosecution must prove a prima facie case and you will need to be persuaded that there will be evidence which is admissible and will be available at trial to achieve that purpose. A lack of pre-charge disclosure of relevant information is likely to make it impossible for you to give useful advice (*R. v. Roble* [1997] Crim LR 449, CA). You should make appropriate representations about this. No one may be convicted on an inference from silence (CPIA 1996, s.38), or on evidence of propensity to commit like offences alone and this enables you to negotiate for greater disclosure
3. **Suspect's circumstances.** Be aware that in deciding whether it is reasonable for a suspect to mention facts before an inference can be drawn under CJPOA 1994, s.34 the court should have regard to the defendant's:

   - age;
   - experience of the criminal justice process;
   - mental capacity;

- state of health;
- sobriety;
- tiredness;
- personality.

The court will also consider the time of day (*R.* v. *Argent* [1997] Crim LR 346, CA) and shock (*R.* v. *Howell* [2003] Crim LR 405, CA). Be prepared to raise relevant issues even if a doctor has decided that your client is fit for interview. Have regard to the criteria set out in PACE Code C, Annex G.

4. **Police conduct before and during interview.** This will apply particularly to the legality of the arrest (which must be necessary for one of the statutory reasons) and to the legality of detention and conduct during interview. Be aware that the court will hear your representations as your client's legal representative if they are made on video or tape and they should therefore be put in a professional way.

5. **Searches and samples** [7.8.1, 7.9.1, 7.10.1]. If you do not consider that the relevant statutory criteria have been made out, be prepared to make representations accordingly and where consent is required advise your client on the arguments for and against giving that consent. Where consent is not required you are unlikely to change the view of the relevant police officer but if your representations were correct you may succeed in excluding evidence at trial.

6. **Identity procedures** [Pt III 34–38]: **PACE Code D (as modified).** In appropriate cases and with the client's agreement seek a formal procedure even if there has been a street identification (*R.* v. *Forbes* [2001] 1 AC 473, HL) as a refusal by the police to agree may exclude the street identification at trial as a breach of Code D, para.1.2. Always seek to see the first description of the suspect given by each witness. Bear in mind that a description may have been given through a police or telephone operator, which may have distorted the original description.

   Be prepared: to argue that your client is 'available' (PACE Code D, para. 2.25) if this is in issue; to test the quality of a video to be used for identification purposes (if necessary by making representations for a parade); and when appropriate to justify a parade ahead of a group identification and any procedure ahead of a confrontation. The identification officer may not be persuaded, but you may have the less good procedure excluded at trial if it produces evidence against your client.

5.3 REPRESENTATIONS AS TO BAIL

You should make appropriate representations including the offering of suitable bail conditions.

It is very common for clients to be bailed during continuing investigations as well as at charge. Conditions are available to the police at all stages, not just at charge (Police and Justice Act 2006, s.10). You have a stronger negotiating position when the police do not yet have enough evidence even to meet the Threshold Test (as defined in the Code for Crown Prosecutors). While your client may be arrested for breach of conditions this is not a criminal offence and the sanction of a charge will not yet be available. However, should a charge eventually be preferred a history of bail breaches will not assist your client at court. An application to vary pre-charge bail conditions may be made to the magistrates' court under CPR Part 19.

Despite the introduction of the Duty Prosecutor, decisions to detain or bail persons remain matters exclusively for the custody officer, who may wish to consult a duty prosecutor. Following charge, research evidence shows that a client appearing on bail has significant advantages in the later handling of the case.

5.4 REPRESENTATIONS AS TO OUTCOME

The Director of Public Prosecutions issues guidance from time to time identifying whether it is the police or the Crown Prosecution Service who are to decide whether and, if so, how a case is to proceed. Future guidance is likely to increase police discretion. There are a number of options available and you should make representations to achieve the best outcome for an individual client. Diversions from prosecution include:

(a) no further action;
(b) fixed penalty notices and notices for public disorder;
(c) for youths: reprimands and warnings;
(d) for adults: simple cautions;
(e) for adults: conditional cautions.

If a suspect is to be charged you should seek to make representations that any charge is at the appropriate level. Because in many areas it is not possible to make those representations prior to charge, you should continue to make them once proceedings have begun. Under the Code for Crown Prosecutors (see **Appendix 1** for website link) Crown Prosecutors are under a duty to keep the level of charge under continuous review and judicial review is available should they ignore relevant issues and take account of irrelevant ones.

No further action

Consider the strength of the evidence and make appropriate representations. While the Threshold Test set out in the Code for Crown Prosecutors allows cautions and outcomes that result in a criminal record, this test only requires a reasonable suspicion. You should argue that such a test is inappropriate and that no further action should be taken. The Threshold Test was held to be insufficient to justify a charge in *G* v. *Chief Constable of West Yorkshire* [2006] EWHC 3485.

Fixed penalty notices and notices for public disorder

You may be able to persuade the authorities to divert from prosecution either before or after reference to the CPS. Fixed penalty notices (FPNs) and penalty notices for disorder (PNDs) do not amount to a criminal record and where a conviction would otherwise result can represent a good outcome for your client. They are, however, kept on central records.

FPNs can be issued to anyone over 10 years old by local authority officers and in a limited capacity by police community support officers. The penalties are £50 for most offences, but £100 for noise-related offences.

Examples of offences where a FPN may be issued include:

- dropping litter;
- minor graffiti offences or fly posting;
- not clearing up dog fouling;
- where noise is causing a statutory nuisance;
- where excessive noise is coming from a private residence during the night.

Penalty notices for disorder are issued for more serious offences. PNDs can be issued by the police, and in a limited capacity by community support officers and other accredited persons. PNDs can be issued to someone over 16 years old and are for either £50 or £80 depending on the severity of the behaviour.

Examples of offences where a penalty notice for disorder may be issued include:

- behaviour likely to cause harassment, alarm or distress to others;
- drunk and disorderly behaviour in a public place;
- destroying or damaging property up to the value of £500;
- retail theft under £200;
- sale of alcohol to a person under 18 years of age;
- selling alcohol to a drunken person;
- using threatening words or behaviour;
- breach of a fireworks restriction.

Diversion for persons aged under 18: reprimands and warnings

If your client is under 18 years old, you should make representations as to whether formal action is necessary.

The first step is to decide what offence is supported by the evidence and is likely to be charged unless a reprimand or warning is given. The decision to issue a reprimand or a warning must be based on that offence, and not on any technically possible offence.

All four of the following criteria must be met before a reprimand or warning can be considered:

1. There is evidence (which you are entitled to see: *DPP* v. *Ara* [2001] 4 All ER 559, DC) against the young person to give a realistic prospect of conviction if he is prosecuted.
2. The young person admits the offence.
3. The young person has not previously been convicted of an offence (remember that a conditional or absolute discharge is not a conviction, and to keep confidential convictions of which the police are unaware).[1]
4. It is not in the public interest for the young person to be prosecuted.

Once the officer dealing with the case believes that all the above criteria are satisfied, a decision can be taken as to whether a reprimand, warning or charge is the most appropriate disposal, taking into account the following:

1. First time offenders should normally receive a reprimand for a less serious offence.
2. First time offenders should normally receive a warning for a more serious offence.
3. Second time offenders who have been reprimanded previously cannot be given a further reprimand – they should normally receive a warning.
4. Second time offenders who have received a warning should not receive a further warning and should be charged. The only exception is where the new offence is committed more than two years after the date of the previous warning and the offence is not so serious as to require a charge to be brought, having regard to the circumstances.
5. Those offending for the fourth time, or more, cannot receive a reprimand or warning in any circumstances. They must be charged.

An FPN or a PND avoids the need to proceed in these ways.

The key factors that will be relevant in deciding whether to charge, warn or reprimand a young offender for an offence are:

(a) the seriousness of the offence; and
(b) the young offender's offending history.

The seriousness of the offence relates to both the nature of the offence and the circumstances that surround it. The seriousness of an offence is crucial to decisions as to whether:

(a) a first offence warrants a warning rather than a reprimand;
(b) a second or third offence which is committed more than two years after the issue of a final warning warrants charging.

The police officer will have regard to gravity factors developed by the Association of Chief Police Officers (ACPO) to assist in assessing the seriousness of the offence.[2]

There is no precise definition of seriousness, as each case must be considered on its individual facts, taking into account the circumstances of the offender, including any aggravating or mitigating factors relating to the offence.

Mitigating/aggravating factors

The age and maturity of the offender will be of relevance in most cases, and other general factors that can affect the decision on how to proceed, may include the following.

MITIGATING FACTORS

- It was a genuine mistake or misunderstanding.
- The loss or harm is minor.
- There was provocation from the victim or the victim's group.
- There was influence by others more criminally sophisticated.
- The offender makes an expression of regret, or offer of reparation.

AGGRAVATING FACTORS

- Offender is ringleader or organiser of offence.
- There is evidence of premeditation.
- The offence was motivated by discrimination against victim's ethnic origin, religious beliefs, gender, political views or sexual orientation.
- The victim was particularly vulnerable, or suffered considerable fear, personal attack, or damage or disturbance.

Reprimands and warnings should never be used for the most serious indictable-only offences such as rape and murder, and only in exceptional circumstances for other indictable-only offences, regardless of the age or previous record of the young person. One example of such exceptional circumstances might be a child taking another's pocket-money by force (robbery in law), if the specific circumstances show that the violence was minor, that there is remorse, and that there is little likelihood of repetition. Other offences, less grave in themselves, may nevertheless be too serious for a reprimand or warning to be appropriate, even where there is no statutory bar to using one.

If a first offence is not so serious as to warrant a warning yet a police officer considers that professional help is required the young person should be referred immediately to the youth offending team (YOT) or to an appropriate local agency or scheme for advice and help.

Note the following if a reprimand or warning is given:

1. Where the young person is aged under 17, the reprimand or warning must be given in the presence of a parent or guardian or other appropriate adult, and any written information must also be issued to the adult (the term 'appropriate adult' has the same meaning here as in PACE).

2. The police officer should issue the reprimand or warning orally. This should always be supplemented with written information that explains clearly the implications of the reprimand or warning.

3. A warning leads to a referral to a YOT for assessment and participation in a rehabilitation programme if considered relevant, to rehabilitate the offender, change his behaviour and prevent him from re-offending.

4. Where a warning is given for a non-recordable offence, the young person, the police officer and, where applicable, the appropriate adult must sign a form at the point the warning is given to confirm that all parties agree that the warning was administered for the offence(s) indicated. The form will be important in any subsequent proceedings as the court will need to know of any previous warning (whether for a recordable or non-recordable offence) because of the restrictions on the availability of conditional discharge in these circumstances. If an offence is committed within two years of a warning, the court shall not order a conditional discharge unless exceptional circumstances justify its doing so.

5. For any record of an offence to be cited in court, there must be proof. In respect of warnings for recordable offences, this proof is supplied by fingerprints. In respect of warnings for non-recordable offences, the proof will be provided by the signed form.

6. The legislation provides that reprimands, warnings and failures to participate in a rehabilitation programme may be cited in court in the same circumstances as convictions (Crime and Disorder Act 1998 (CDA 1998), s.66(5)). In practice, this means that they should be made available to the court.

7. Breach of a rehabilitation programme carries no sanction. Failure to comply may be taken into account in later sentencing.

8. There is only one exception to the rule that reprimands and warnings replace cautions, and that is in respect of a prostitutes' caution. In such cases, the initial response will be the prostitutes' caution. Unlike a reprimand or final warning, this does not depend on admission of guilt. A prostitutes' caution should be accompanied by a specific warning that the prostitute will be treated as an offender if the behaviour continues.

Diversion for persons aged 18 and over: cautions

You should be familiar with:

- Home Office Circular 30/2005 on the cautioning of adult offenders (see **Appendix 1** for website link);
- Code of Practice for Conditional Cautions (see **Appendix 1** for website link).

Can you persuade the police to impose a simple or conditional caution rather than charge your client? Approach the issue with care. A caution is for many purposes the equivalent of a conviction. It can result in an entry on the Sex Offenders Register, the making of a sexual offences prevention order, and a disclosable record at the National Records Office. Cautions are never spent under the Rehabilitation of Offenders Act 1974. Home Office Circular 30/2005 gives advice to chief officers of police on simple cautions. There must be evidence of the offender's guilt sufficient to give a realistic prospect of conviction and the offender must admit the offence. By supplying information to the police about the offence and making representations to reduce its gravity, you may be able to persuade the custody officer to consider cautioning rather than charging the client.

Simple cautions

CPS National Standards for Cautioning require that the following criteria are met before a caution may be administered by the police:

1. Is there sufficient evidence of the suspect's guilt to meet the Threshold Test? If the offence is indictable only (and the available evidence meets the Threshold Test) then the disposal option may only be considered by a Crown Prosecutor. Note that you should be satisfied that there is provable evidence of guilt, not just a reasonable suspicion, before proposing this outcome. This will affect your advice about whether an admission should be made.
2. Has the suspect made a clear and reliable admission of the offence (either verbally or in writing) during the course of the police investigation? See *R. v. Commissioner of Police of the Metropolis, ex p. Thompson* [1997] 1 WLR 1519.
3. Is it in the public interest to use a simple caution as the appropriate means of disposal?
4. Is the suspect aged 18 years or over?

If all of the above requirements are met, the officer must consider whether the seriousness of the offence makes it appropriate for disposal by a simple caution.

Guide to case disposal

A gravity factor matrix has been provided to assist officers in making their decision (see note 2) to determine the seriousness of the offence and to decide whether or not a simple caution could be used as an appropriate means of disposal.

The seriousness of the offence is initially determined on a scale of one to four (with one being the least serious). Aggravating factors can increase the seriousness and mitigating factors can reduce the seriousness by one level. Aggravating and mitigating factors cancel each other out. These are then applied to disposal options.

Further considerations

1. **Does the suspect have any other cautions for similar offences?** National and local records must be checked. If 'yes' then a simple caution should not normally be considered, unless a two-year period has passed with no further convictions or cautions, or unless the offence is trivial or unrelated. If the suspect has previously received a reprimand or final warning, a period of two years should also be allowed to elapse before administering a simple caution.

2. **Has the suspect been made aware of the significance of a simple caution?** If a simple caution is being considered, then the full implications and consequences must be explained to the suspect. Under no circumstances should suspects be pressed to admit offences in order to receive a simple caution as an alternative to being charged. Be aware of additional consequences for those receiving a simple caution for sexual offences or for those who are employed in notifiable occupations.

3. **Has the suspect given informed consent to being cautioned?** If the suspect does not consent, then the police may choose to continue with a prosecution. The suspect should not be pressed to make an instant decision on whether to accept the simple caution. They should be allowed to consider the matter and, if need be, take independent advice.

National Standards for Cautioning

The Code for Crown Prosecutors states that where necessary, Crown Prosecutors should consider alternatives to prosecution and apply the principles set out in Home Office Circular 30/2005 (the cautioning guidelines – see **Appendix 1** for website link) when deciding where the public interest lies. Diverting offenders from the criminal justice system can bring positive benefits for the individual and for society as a whole if used wisely.

Whenever the prosecutor is satisfied that there is sufficient evidence to provide a realistic prospect of conviction the public interest in bringing a conviction must be considered. The Code for Crown Prosecutors explains the principles to be applied in balancing factors for and against prosecution. The public interest does not automatically require a prosecution.

The CPS cautioning guidelines reinforce Home Office guidance. The key considerations are:

(a)   whether a caution is appropriate to the circumstances of the offence and the offender;
(b)   whether the conditions for cautioning are met; and
(c)   whether the caution is likely to be effective.

Conditional cautions

A conditional caution lies between a simple caution and a charge. The effect is to impose a caution but conditional on compliance with identified conditions. If there is a failure without reasonable excuse to comply, a prosecution will be brought for the underlying offence.

Conditional cautions were introduced by the Criminal Justice Act 2003 and important amendments are contained within the Police and Justice Act 2006. Conditional cautions are only available to those of 18 or over at the time the caution is imposed.

The Director of Public Prosecutions has issued guidance on the issue of conditional cautions (see **Appendix 1** for website link).

Before a conditional caution may be imposed there are five requirements:

1.   There must be evidence that the defendant has committed the crime. It must include an admission made before there is any mention by the prosecution team of a conditional caution.
2.   There must be sufficient evidence to charge and the Crown Prosecutor must be of the view that a conditional caution is appropriate.
3.   There must be an admission to the offence with advice having been made available if required.
4.   The effect of a breach of the conditions must be explained.
5.   There must be a signed document which would be available in evidence should the case ever come to court.

The conditions imposed must be proportionate, achievable and appropriate and until the implementation of the Police and Justice Act 2006 promote either the rehabilitation of the offender or reparation of the victim. It must always be a condition not to commit further offences. Once the 2006 Act is implemented it will also be possible to impose conditional conditions as punishment with the prosecutor imposing a penalty of up to £250 or one-quarter of the statutory maximum for the offence, whichever is the less, or up to 20 hours of unpaid work. It is doubtful whether a prosecutor can be an independent party for the imposition of a penalty in this way and it will therefore be critical that the defendant gives informed consent to the outcome. Legal advice will be important in that respect and you should be aware of local practices, raising the possibility of a conditional caution with both the client and the police (for their note to the Crown Prosecutor in appropriate cases).

If conditions are imposed the onus is on the offender to show compliance with the conditions and the offender must report any failure and explain the circumstances that might amount to a reasonable excuse. The prosecution will then decide how to proceed. Judicial review is available to deal with *Wednesbury* unreasonable decisions. The conditions may be revised, instead of a prosecution being brought.

5.5   REPRESENTATIONS TO THE CUSTODY OFFICER

Under PACE Code C, Note 16 custody officers must consider the appropriateness of diversion. They must do so if the Threshold Test is passed, before referring the case to the Crown Prosecutor for charging. Where the custody officer considers that the case is suitable for a penalty notice or a simple caution (in a case which is not indictable only), he will arrange for that action to be taken. Where an indictable-only case appears suitable for a simple caution or where a conditional caution appears appropriate, the case will be referred to a prosecutor.

Only the police have the power to administer a caution. The CPS does, however, have a role to play in helping the police to ensure that the Home Office guidelines on the cautioning of offenders are applied consistently and fairly. Accordingly, the police can take early advice from the CPS at any point in an investigation as to whether a simple caution is appropriate.

5.6   REPRESENTATIONS TO THE CPS

CPS statutory charging

Statutory charging means that dedicated experienced prosecutors from the CPS work with the police on cases from start to finish. Based in police stations, they advise the police on lines of enquiry, and advise on the evidence that should be gathered. The CPS prosecutor is then responsible for deciding the correct charge in all but the most minor, routine cases.

To protect the public in cases where bail cannot be granted the custody officer will charge your client as soon as there is enough evidence, even if further evidence is anticipated in the future. The Threshold Test includes an assessment of whether in all the circumstances of the case there is at least a reasonable suspicion of the person of having committed an offence; that it is in the public interest to proceed; and a consideration of the evidence available at the time and likely to be forthcoming

The role of the defence in CPS review decisions

All cases submitted to the CPS are subject to initial and then continuous review in accordance with the Code for Crown Prosecutors. The initial review takes place before the first hearing. There will be a further review before mode of trial hearing. A full review by a lawyer takes place after the mode of trial hearing in either-way cases on receipt of the full file up to three to four weeks later. The case worker may already have begun preparation of the Crown Court case. Although information is supplied by the police, review decisions can be influenced by information from other sources. The Code states that it is the duty of the Crown Prosecutor to ensure that all relevant evidence is put before the court. It also states that Crown Prosecutors must be fair, independent and objective. Information from the defence need not be limited to the public interest test. The evidential test of the Code requires prosecutors to consider what the defence may be, and whether the evidence can be used and is reliable.

It is quite proper to request the prosecution to reconsider the decision to prosecute. In an appropriate case, much worry, time and expense may be saved. The reconsideration should be sought as early as practicable, but may be done at any stage before trial or guilty plea.

Code for Crown Prosecutors

The criteria for prosecution are set out in the Code for Crown Prosecutors, some of which is reproduced below.

You may be in possession of information personal to the defendant (illness, recent bereavement) not available to the prosecution. Similarly you may consider that a prosecution is unlikely to succeed because of the strength of the defence case.

Unless inappropriate (e.g. terminal illness not known to the client) discuss contacting the prosecution with your client first. If you propose making a detailed disclosure of the defence case, advise on the disadvantages (alerting the prosecution to weaknesses in their case which they may remedy). If your client agrees, obtain written instructions in confirmation of this. Be aware that material disclosed may be used by the prosecution at trial if the prosecution proceeds.

Consider the availability of an alternative to prosecution, e.g. administering a formal caution by the police or, in the case of those under 18 a reprimand or warning. It is an abuse of process of the court to proceed to trial if a defendant was unable to obtain informed advice on a diversion which would otherwise have been available.

The evidential test

The Code for Crown Prosecutors states that:

5.2 Crown Prosecutors must be satisfied that there is enough evidence to provide a 'realistic prospect of conviction' against each defendant on each charge. They must consider what the defence case may be, and how that is likely to affect the prosecution case.

5.3 A realistic prospect of a conviction is an objective test. It means that a jury or bench of magistrates [. . .] properly directed in accordance with the law, is more likely than not to convict the defendant of the charge alleged. [. . .]

5.4 When deciding whether there is enough evidence to prosecute, Crown Prosecutors must consider whether the evidence can be used and is reliable. There will be many cases in which the evidence does not give any cause for concern. But there will also be cases in which the evidence may not be as strong as it first appears. [. . .]

The public interest test

Some common public interest factors against prosecution are given in the Code for Crown Prosecutors:

5.10 A prosecution is less likely to be needed if:

a. the court is likely to impose a nominal penalty;

b. the defendant has already been made the subject of a sentence and any further conviction would be unlikely to result in the imposition of an additional sentence or order, unless the nature of the particular offence requires a prosecution or the defendant withdraws consent to have an offence taken into consideration during sentencing;

c. the offence was committed as a result of a genuine mistake or misunderstanding (these factors must be balanced against the seriousness of the offence);

d. the loss or harm can be described as minor and was the result of a single incident, particularly if it was caused by a misjudgement;

e. there has been a long delay between the offence taking place and the date of the trial, unless:

- the offence is serious;
- the delay has been caused in part by the defendant;
- the offence has only recently come to light; or
- the complexity of the offence has meant that there has been a long investigation;

f. a prosecution is likely to have a very bad effect on the victim's physical or mental health, always bearing in mind the seriousness of the offence;

g. the defendant is elderly or is, or was at the time of the offence, suffering from significant mental or physical ill health, unless the offence is serious or there is a real possibility that it may be repeated. The Crown Prosecution Service where necessary, applies Home Office guidelines about how to deal with mentally disordered offenders. Crown Prosecutors must balance the desirability of

59

diverting a defendant who is suffering from significant mental or physical ill health with the need to safeguard the general public;

h.   the defendant has put right the loss or harm that was caused (but defendants must not avoid prosecution solely because they pay compensation);

i.   details may be made public that could harm sources of information, international relations or national security.

5.7   REPRESENTATIONS AS TO LEVEL OF CHARGE

You may be able to persuade the police to charge your client with a lesser offence. This is particularly important both in view of the speedy process if there is an intended guilty plea and if your client is at risk of a mandatory sentence or to avoid a specified offence (see **Appendix 9** for a list of specified offences).

If you are satisfied that there is sufficient evidence to charge and convict your client, it may be worth considering giving information to the police about the offence and making representations to persuade the Crown to charge your client with a lesser offence.

It may be possible to agree with the police how the factual background to a charge will be explained. This may avoid a Newton hearing.

Charging practice and standards

The CPS and police have agreed a series of charging standards in an attempt to ensure fairness to individual defendants, consistency of charging policy and to avoid overcharging. Standards have been published on offences against the person, Theft Acts offences, public order offences, driving and drugs offences. In addition the CPS has published guidance and policy documents on prosecuting cases of domestic violence, rape and racist and religious crime. All standards and guidance are available in the legal guidance section of the CPS website (**www.cps.gov.uk**).

It will normally be in a client's interests to ensure that the charge is set at the lowest appropriate level (unless the client wants a jury trial and is prepared to take the risk of sentence). In appropriate cases you will wish to bring relevant provisions of the standards to the attention of the prosecutor who must have proper regard to them or be susceptible to judicial review. The use of the standards is particularly important when an indictable-only charge has been prepared and may justify an adjournment rather that the immediate sending of the case to the Crown Court under CDA 1998, s.51.

NOTES

1. If the police officer expressly asks your client whether he has a previous conviction, you should advise your client that if he lies in his answer you will have to withdraw from representing him and that he may be attempting to pervert the course of justice.
2. ACPO Youth Offender Case Disposal Gravity Factor System at **www. knowledgenetwork.gov.uk** and attached as Annex D to Home Office Circular 14/2006.

CHAPTER 6

Funding the case

Objectives of this chapter

- To identify clients eligible for public funding
- To enable you to work with public funding
- To give your client the best chance of obtaining a Representation Order
- To describe the requirements for privately funded clients

6.1 AVAILABILITY OF PUBLIC FUNDING

It is your professional duty to advise each client of the availability of public funding.

Your ability to undertake the work with public funding depends on a number of factors:

1. Whether your client is financially eligible. See 'Getting criminal legal aid' at the Criminal Defence Service section of the LSC website (see **Appendix 1**) for further details.
2. Whether you have the appropriate contract with the LSC to undertake the work in the relevant geographical area.[1]
3. Where the case is identified as a very high cost case, whether you are on the panel to undertake such work.[2]
4. Whether the client meets the relevant merits test and is not affected by the limitations that apply to some work.

If for any reason you cannot do the work with public funding for a client who is financially eligible, you must consider advising the client to contact a firm that can. If the client decides to proceed privately it is prudent to have their decision not to proceed with public funding confirmed by them in writing.

You should always check whether your client belongs to a trade union or membership body that might assist them financially or whether they have insurance cover available.

Public funding

The *Legal Services Commission Manual* is published by TSO. It is prepared by the LSC and Volume 4 is an essential guide for those seeking public funding. In criminal cases it contains not only the relevant legislation and General Criminal Contract but also notes for guidance issued by the LSC. The LSC's newsletter *Focus on CDS* also contains essential updating material. You should ensure that the material and newsletter are available for reference by all fee earners.

Public funding provides for:

- advice and assistance;
- advocacy assistance;
- representation.

Financial eligibility

There is no means test:

(a) at the investigation stage. All clients under arrest or volunteering to attend when a constable is present, irrespective of their means, are eligible for police station advice and assistance and for advocacy assistance for warrants of extended detention and their military equivalent;

Table 6.1 Summary of requirements as to financial eligibility

	No means test	Means test applies
Criminal investigations	Advice to those under arrest and volunteers when a constable is present	Volunteers when no constable is present
	Warrant of extended detention	Advice and assistance on criminal law prior to charge, summons or requisition
Prison law		Prison law advice and representation
Civil law (associated Community Legal Service (CLS) work)		Habeas corpus; judicial review; other associated CLS work
Criminal proceedings (including anti-social behaviour orders (ASBOs), etc.)	Duty solicitor work	
	Early cover/pre-order costs	
	Crown Courts (until a date to be announced)	Magistrates' courts
		Crown Courts (from a date to be announced)

(b) in relation to those advised and/or represented at court by the duty solicitor or when on defined conditions application for a Representation Order is made in anticipation of the grant on merits but which is eventually refused or forms are not submitted by a solicitor;

(c) at present for those being represented in the Crown Court although a scheme is under active design by the government in these cases. However, a Recovery of Defence Costs Order can be made in the Crown Court.

The following areas of work are subject to a means test:

1. Criminal investigations:

- advice and assistance to a volunteer when no constable is present;
- advice and assistance outside the police station.

The appropriate application forms (CDS1 and CDS2) should always be fully completed, dated and signed if your client is eligible, so as to cover all the work in the investigation stage. You must always seek evidence of the client's means. Your work must at all stages meet the sufficient benefit test and is initially limited to the equivalent of two hours' preparation work and, once evidence of means is available, to £300. You can obtain an extension if necessary using form CDS5. You must advise the client what is covered by the grant of advice and assistance [39.1].

2. Prison law: advice and assistance and advocacy assistance (in front of prison governors, adjudicators and the parole board).

3. Associated CLS work including habeas corpus and judicial review.

4. Criminal proceedings in the magistrates' courts. You will need to hold stocks of four CDS forms:

- CDS14: Application for a Representation Order including the merits test. This is the only form required from those who automatically meet the means test. A spouse or current partner's signature is normally required. If it cannot be obtained to this and any other form the reason should be given on this form. You should obtain your client's national insurance number where they have one and the number is known to them.

- CDS15: Application by those who must meet the test for financial eligibility. You should note the requirements for supporting documents in particular as appropriate.

- CDS16: Application for a grant on hardship grounds notwithstanding that the eligibility on financial criteria might not otherwise be made out or proved. It cannot affect the grant on merits.

- CDS17: A form to replace other forms of evidence of financial standing for completion by those who are in custody other than by the self-employed.

6.2 THE MEANS TEST

In the magistrates' court there is no capital test. Only income is relevant. There is no contribution payable: either your client qualifies or he does not. If, by the time you lodge your application in the magistrates' court, it is known that the case will be substantively dealt with in the Crown Court (offence is indictable only, or election for Crown Court trial already made, or court has already declined jurisdiction, in either-way offences) there is no means test until a Crown Court means test is introduced.

Those in receipt of three passporting benefits and those under 18 automatically meet the means test for legal aid in the magistrates' court. In calculating whether other defendants are eligible it is necessary to aggregate their gross income with that of their spouse, or partner resident with them, unless a conflict of interest arises. The actual income then has to be adjusted to allow for their personal responsibilities to a partner and children. A phased process is undertaken as illustrated by **Figure 6.1**.

Hardship

There is no closed list of circumstances when a Representation Order may be granted notwithstanding the financial position of your client. It will arise, for instance, because:

- current access to income is denied – e.g. an employee loses their job;
- there are unusual outgoings or items of expenditure not allowed for in the standard figures;
- a partner has refused to make information available;
- the estimated costs included are unusual, e.g. they may exceed £2,000 inclusive of disbursements but exclusive of VAT.

6.3 THE MERITS TEST: REPRESENTATION ORDERS

Take the first appropriate opportunity to apply for a Representation Order by completing application form CDS14.

In your application you should take particular care in identifying why it is in the interests of justice that a Representation Order should be granted. Be familiar with the relevant law and general and local policies: see the guidance on the interests of justice test at the LSC website (see **Appendix 1**).

Complete the application form carefully, tick as many criteria as are relevant and give a full explanation for each one selected. In a complex case, a supporting letter describing the difficulties in some detail may be appropriate. You may wish to send a copy of the completed form to your client, asking him to check it for accuracy. Make sure that the information you give accurately reflects the seriousness of the charges against the defendant.

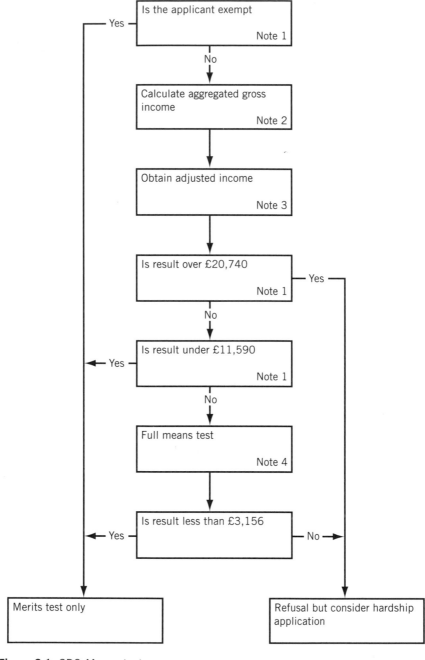

Figure 6.1 CDS Means test

Note 1: Applicants automatically qualify financially for criminal legal aid if they:

- receive income support, income-based jobseeker's allowance or a guaranteed state pension credit; or
- are under 18 years of age.

Note 2: Adjusted income = gross annual income ÷ weighting

The weighting for a single adult is 1.00 + the total weighting for any children. The weighting for a couple is 1.64 ÷ the total weighting for any children. The weighting for each child is based on their age at their next birthday:

0–1 years	0.15
2–4 years	0.30
5–7 years	0.34
8–10 years	0.38
11–12 years	0.41
13–14 years	0.44
16–18 years	0.59

Note 3: The full means test involves deducting the following from the applicant's gross annual income to obtain the disposable income:

- tax and national insurance;
- annual housing costs;
- annual childcare costs;
- annual maintenance to former partners and any children; and
- an adjusted annual living allowance (add the relevant figure for any children, as above, to 1.00 [or 1.64 for a couple] and multiply by the total).

Conflict

A Representation Order may have already been granted to another firm for a co-accused. Give details of the conflict justifying separate representation. The issue of conflict is a live one throughout the case and the service of prosecution evidence may disclose conflict or other reasons for separate representation, be prepared to act on this and inform the court of any developments that require an amendment of the Representation Order.

If defendants disagree on their presence and/or involvement, or a difference of emphasis between them may arise, consider separate representation.

Defendants with different personal backgrounds or histories of offending should be treated with care. Your duty is to act in your client's best interest. Consider whether representing one client could lead you to be critical of another or to avoid emphasising matters on his/her behalf. Consider separate representation or the use of more than one advocate. (For guidance on conflict see Appendix 3.)

Reasons for wanting representation

The following are the reasons available in CDS14.

(i) It is likely that I will lose my liberty if any matter in the proceedings is decided against me

Loss of liberty does not include non-custodial sentences but does include remands in custody and sentences of imprisonment (including hospital orders) whether immediate or suspended. If the starting point for this offence in the Magistrates' Court Sentencing Guidelines is not custody, explain why you think custody is likely in this case (e.g. relevant previous convictions, aggravating factors). Give dates of relevant convictions, if known.

Consider whether the court is likely to deprive the accused of his liberty on conviction, e.g.:

1. **Seriousness of charge(s):**

   - violent or sexual offences;
   - breach of trust;
   - extent of injuries or losses.

A court may aggregate all the offences (including TICs) for the purpose of assessing seriousness and this may have the result of taking the offender past the custody threshold.

2. **Seriousness factors:**

   - planned;
   - organised teams;
   - adult involving children;
   - committed over period;
   - casting suspicion on others;
   - sophisticated;
   - deliberately frightening others;
   - group offence;
   - soiling;
   - ransacking;
   - ram-raiding;
   - organiser or distributor;
   - stolen to order;
   - special equipment;

- gross disregard for police authority;
- vulnerable victim;
- victim public servant;
- offender in position of authority;
- weapon;
- people put in fear;
- busy public place;
- commercial production and/or cultivation.

See the 'Seriousness factors: (aggravating and mitigating factors)' in the Magistrates' Court Sentencing Guidelines and consider the 'Features relevant to individual offences' in the Mode of Trial Guidelines (see **Appendix 1**). Note also religious or racial aggravation or offence while on bail.

3. **Seriousness for defendant:**

- previous convictions;
- subject to suspended sentence;
- breach of previous court order;
- failure to respond to previous sentences.

When considering the seriousness of any offence, the court may take into account any relevant previous convictions of the offender or failure to respond to previous sentences.

4. **Committal or transfer to Crown Court likely.**

(ii) I have been given a sentence that is suspended or non-custodial. If I break this, the court may be able to deal with me for the original offence

Obtain information about outstanding sentences, if possible, from a record of your client's previous convictions as you cannot always rely upon your client to give you accurate information. He may be confused about the difference between a suspended prison sentence, conditional discharge and deferred sentence. Include details about the nature of the offence that led to the order being made and whether the order was made by a magistrates' court or the Crown Court.

(iii) It is likely that I will lose my livelihood

The loss of livelihood should be a direct consequence of conviction or sentence – provide supporting evidence where possible. This would normally refer to current livelihood, although it can apply if someone is genuinely unemployed for a short period between jobs. If your client intends to plead guilty, explain how legal representation might help avoid loss of livelihood.

Consider:

- risk of disqualification from driving when a licence is necessary to do job (and 'special reasons' if disqualification is mandatory);
- conviction for dishonesty of someone whose normal work puts them in a position of trust;
- conviction for a sexual offence of someone whose normal work is as a teacher or social worker.

(iv) It is likely that I will suffer serious damage to my reputation

Reputation refers to good character, including honesty and trustworthiness and is not related to social class or position. 'Serious' damage is judged to occur in cases where the disgrace of conviction greatly exceeds the direct effect of the penalty. If your client intends to plead guilty, explain how legal representation might help you avoid serious damage to reputation.

Consider:

- loss of good character;
- defendant may be well known or hold a position of trust in the local community.

(v) A substantial question of law may be involved (whether arising from an Act, judicial authority or other source of law)

This applies where the determination of any matter in relation to the proceedings raises a point of law that you cannot be expected to deal with unaided. Explain why the question of law is substantial and relevant to the case. Questions of fact alone are irrelevant. Where possible, specify the cases or legislation that give rise to the question of law.

Consider whether:

- interpretation of the law needs to be argued (particularly if an argument is being raised under the European Convention on Human Rights (ECHR));
- an attempt will be made to exclude evidence;
- there may be legal arguments as to proportionality and thresholds for community sentences and custody, or as to the appropriate community plea;
- a Newton hearing may be required.

(vi) I may not be able to understand the court proceedings or present my own case

There may be a number of reasons why a client may be unable to understand court proceedings or to state their own case. These may include (but are not limited to) mental or physical disability, inadequate knowledge or English, age or vulnerability. The ability to understand proceedings or to state one's own case is likely also to depend on the complexity of the case. Consider the following:

- illiteracy;
- mental disorder;
- other relevant disability;
- drink/drug problem.

(vii) Witnesses may need to be traced or interviewed on my behalf

You may require witnesses to be traced or interviewed to see whether they can assist your case (if pleading not guilty) or to help with constructing a plea in mitigation (if pleading guilty). You should explain why legal representation is needed in order to trace and/or interview witnesses. Consider the following:

- is witness for trial or mitigation?
- are photographs or plans required?
- number of witnesses;
- witnesses unwilling to co-operate;
- prosecution refuse to give witness's name and/or address, requiring application to the court;
- expert witnesses required, e.g. medical, scientific? This alone will normally justify the grant of a Representation Order.

(viii) The proceedings may involve expert cross-examination of a prosecution witness (whether an expert or not)

Careful cross-examination is likely to be required where your client is pleading not guilty and you expect the prosecution to call witnesses whose evidence you wish to probe or challenge. Your client is likely to require a lawyer to conduct skilful cross-examination on his behalf if the evidence to be given by the prosecution witnesses is complex, technical or is capable of bearing more than one shade of meaning. Factors that bear on this criterion include the complexity of the case, as well as the age or vulnerability of the defendant.

Consider:

- prosecution calling expert evidence (although it is the cross-examination which is required to be expert; not the witness);
- prosecution calling a number of professional witnesses, e.g. police officers;
- defendant not capable of conducting own case.

(ix) It is in the interests of another person (such as the person making a complaint or other witness) that I am represented

Where your client is charged with a sexual or violent offence, or where the complainant or other witness is a child, it would be inappropriate for him to cross-examine in person. This box should not be used to argue that legal representation is in the general interests of his family or of the court.

Consider:

- whether it is in the interests of someone other than the defendant that he be represented, e.g. inappropriate for defendant to cross-examine witness (personal or intimate details to be disclosed);
- relationship between defendant and complainant, e.g. family or neighbour element.

(x) Any other reasons

Provide full details of any other reasons (which you have not mentioned elsewhere on the form) why you think it would be in the interests of justice that your client is represented. For example, legal representation might be justified if your client is likely to receive a demanding community sentence if convicted or if defence witnesses require skilful examination.

Consider whether:

- committal or transfer to Crown Court for trial is likely;
- defendant will seek trial in the Crown Court;
- the facts are unusually complex (provide some detail);
- co-defendants have been granted Representation Orders;
- there are complex features (e.g. mistaken identity).

This information may need to be supplemented during the progress of the case.

Representation Order received

Check that the order is in your firm's name and covers all the offences charged. Advise your client that he is under a duty to report any changes in financial circumstances. An order granted in the magistrates' court automatically covers related substantive Crown Court proceedings – but not appeals against conviction or sentence.

Representation Order refused

Advise your client of the reasons for the refusal [4.1] and that a refusal on merits can be appealed to the court. There is no appeal on financial grounds although you should consider whether a hardship application can be made (CDS16). If the application is refused but the case proceeds to the Crown Court consider a fresh application. Advise your client that a new application can be made if circumstances change.

Extension of order

If an expert's report or other unusual expenditure is required consider applying to the LSC for prior authority on form CDS4 (see **Appendix 1**). Applications are processed by the LSC in accordance with the General Criminal Contract Specification, Part B, rule 5.2, which states:

> Where you consider it necessary for the proper conduct of Criminal Proceedings . . . for costs to be incurred under a Representation Order by taking any of the following steps:
>
> (a) obtaining a written report or opinion of one or more experts;
> (b) employing a person to provide a written report or opinion (otherwise than as an expert);
> (c) obtaining any transcripts or recordings, including police questioning of suspects;
> (d) in magistrates' courts only, where a Representation Order provides for the service of Solicitor and Counsel, instructing a Queen's Counsel alone without junior Counsel; or
> (e) performing an act which is either unusual in its nature or involves unusually large expenditure,
>
> you may apply to the Regional Director for prior authority before the expenditure is incurred.

Exception to 'no top-up' rule

If prior authority is refused you can arrange for your client to pay privately for the preparation of an expert's report. It is one of the exceptions to the restriction on private payment provided for by the General Criminal Contract Specification, Part C, rule 1.20.

The exception arises in respect of any expenses or fees incurred in:

(a) preparing, obtaining or considering any report, opinion or further evidence whether provided by an expert witness or otherwise; or
(b) obtaining or preparing transcripts of shorthand notes or tape recordings of any criminal investigation or proceedings, including police questioning

where an application under Part B, rule 5.2 for authority to incur such expenses or fees has been refused.

6.4 RECOVERY OF DEFENCE COSTS ORDERS

In the magistrates' court, whatever the outcome, a publicly funded defendant may not be ordered to pay the defence costs. This also applies in the Crown Court following a committal for sentence or an appeal against sentence. You should advise your client that in other cases in the Crown Court and higher courts a Recovery of Defence Costs Order (RDCO) may be made for all or part of the defence costs although it will only be done in exceptional circumstances if there is an acquittal [40.1]. A statement of means for the right to representation in criminal proceedings in the Crown Court will be required following the sending or committal or transfer of the case and on an appeal against conviction. It should reach the Crown Court four days before the first hearing. You must explain to your client the implications of a failure to complete and return form B [40.2] as he may then be ordered to pay all the defence costs in that court and the courts below.

Costs information must be made available to the client if an RDCO is likely to be made. This should be done following committal, transfer or sending and then updated every six months. The estimate should include advocacy fees and disbursements.

Remind the client of the need to advise the court should his means change and that he may be ordered to pay all the defence costs if he fails to do so.

6.5 PRIVATE FUNDING

If public funding is not available or has been declined by your client you are not required to advise, assist or represent a client unless and until appropriate funding is in place. In any event the person who is responsible for the client/case, and has the necessary overview, will need to:

- fix a price for the work or give a best estimate; otherwise, quote an hourly rate;
- regularly review the estimate;
- remember that factors outside their control may increase costs;
- confirm their price or estimate or hourly rate in writing in a client care letter, explaining the basis on which they charge; the factors that may affect the cost; and that they are responsible for the client/case;
- obtain money in advance;
- submit interim bills to help cash flow.

Refer to the Solicitors' Code of Conduct 2007, 2.03.

In the event of your client being acquitted, or the allegations withdrawn or discharged, you will wish to apply for any private costs for which your client is liable to be recovered from central funds. The court considering your bill will require clear evidence of the terms of business agreed with your client.

NOTES

1. At the time of writing all solicitors who hold a General Criminal Contract may undertake all publicly funded work except very high cost cases. Under the Carter proposals more restricted contracts will be introduced (see further Lord Carter's report, *Legal Aid: A Market-based Approach to Reform* at **www.legalaidprocurement review.gov.uk/publications.htm**).
2. From 2008 a new very high cost panel will be created to cover all cases likely to last over 40 days and some lasting over 25 days.

CHAPTER 7

The defendant in custody

Objectives of this chapter

- To explain the defendant's entitlement to bail under the law
- To describe the information required to prepare an application for bail
- To show how to counter objections to the grant of bail from the prosecutor or the court

---

Throughout this chapter references in square brackets are to the LSC Transaction Criteria.

7.1 BAIL APPLICATION

Restrictions on the grant of bail

Defendant already on bail

If a defendant is aged under 18 and it appears to the court that he was on bail in criminal proceedings on the date of the offence, the court must give particular weight to that fact when deciding whether it is satisfied that there are substantial grounds for believing that he would commit an offence while on bail, whether subject to conditions or not (Bail Act 1976, Sched.1, Part I, para.9AA). If the defendant is aged 18 or over he may not be granted bail in this situation unless the court is satisfied that there is no significant risk of his committing an offence while on bail, whether subject to conditions or not (Bail Act 1976, Sched.1, Part I, para.2A).

Defendant failed to surrender

If a defendant is aged under 18 and it appears to the court that, having been released on bail in or in connection with the proceedings for the offence, he failed to surrender to custody, the court shall give particular weight to that fact when deciding whether it is satisfied that there are substantial grounds for believing that if released on bail he would fail to surrender to custody, whether subject to conditions or not (Bail Act 1976, Sched.1, Part I, para.9AB). If the defendant is aged 18 or over he may not be granted bail in this situation unless the court is satisfied that there is no significant risk of his failing to surrender to custody, whether subject to conditions or not (Bail Act 1976, Sched.1, Part II, para.6).

Defendant in breach of a bail condition

If a defendant, having been released on bail in or in connection with the proceedings for the offence, has been arrested under the Bail Act 1976, s.7 (in breach of his bail conditions) he need not be granted bail if the court is satisfied that there are substantial grounds for believing that he would fail to surrender to custody, commit an offence, interfere with witnesses or obstruct the course of justice (Bail Act 1976, Sched.1, Part II, para.5).

Prosecutor objects to bail

The court must give reasons for granting bail in all cases where the prosecutor objects to bail. Always offer the court suitable reasons for the grant of bail. In cases where there are statutory restrictions on the grant of bail, be ready to assist the court in giving reasons why the restrictions should not apply.

Defendant charged with and already convicted of murder, attempted murder, rape, attempted rape or manslaughter

Bail may only be granted in exceptional circumstances if a defendant is charged with murder, attempted murder, rape, attempted rape or manslaughter and has already been convicted of any one of those offences (CJPOA 1994, s.25 (as amended)). Identify the exceptional circumstances on which you rely. These cases are excluded from the requirement to grant bail on the expiry of the custody time limits (Prosecution of Offences (Custody Time Limits) Regulations 1987, SI 1987/299, reg.6(6)).

The absence of danger to the public will normally amount to exceptional circumstances. See further the Law Commission's *Suggested Guidance for Bail Decision-takers* at **Appendix 10**, which was written to ensure compliance with the ECHR.[1]

Drug users (CJA 2003, s.19)

Where the following three conditions are satisfied, an offender aged 18 or over may not be granted bail unless the court is satisfied that there is no significant risk of his committing an offence while on bail, whether subject to conditions or not:

1.   There is drug test evidence that the person has a specified Class A drug in his body. This test will be under PACE, s.63B or CJA 2003, s.161.
2.   The court is satisfied that there are substantial grounds for believing that the misuse of a specified Class A drug caused or contributed to that offence, or (even if it did not) the offence was motivated wholly or partly by his intended misuse of such a drug, or the offence is one under the Misuse of Drugs Act 1971, s.5(2) or (3).
3.   The person does not agree to undergo an assessment as to his dependency upon or propensity to misuse specified Class A drugs, or has undergone such an assessment but does not agree to participate in any follow-up offered. When considering subsequent applications for bail the court must consider whether this condition remains satisfied.

Objections to bail

Find out if the prosecutor has any objections to bail and anticipate the concerns that may be raised by the court, then obtain adequate instructions to deal with the objections and bring these together in a single document. You should advise your client of the likely prospects of success [43]:

1.   If bail has been withheld in the present case by a court, how many applications have been made, to whom, what are the reasons for refusal [45.1] and have your client's circumstances changed since then or are there new arguments as to fact or law?
2.   Confirm with your client what bail conditions may be acceptable to him and to the court [44.1].

The following sets out information you may require, related to any objections to bail which the prosecutor raises and possible relevant bail conditions.

Unused material

The prosecutor should make disclosure to you of material that might affect a bail decision even though the prosecutor's duty has not yet arisen under CPIA 1996 (*R. v. DPP, ex p. Lee* [1999] 2 All ER 737). See the Attorney General's Guidelines on Disclosure April 2005, para.57 and the CPS *Disclosure Manual* (2006), Chapters 2 and 3 (see **Appendix 1** for website link).

Guidance for decision makers

Have regard throughout as far as appropriate to the Law Commission's *Suggested Guidance for Bail Decision-takers* (see **Appendix 10**).[2]

Client likely to abscond

Address

Obtain the following information:

(a) length of time there and proposed address on bail [57.1];
(b) whether staying with a friend/squatter/licensee/lodger/tenant or owner occupier;
(c) if not able to return there, alternative address;
(d) whether bail hostel place appropriate and available.

Sureties [42.6]

Obtain from any proposed surety details of:

(a) name, address, date of birth and employment;
(b) criminal convictions;
(c) length of time known to defendant;
(d) nature of association;
(e) frequency and means of regular contact;
(f) knowledge of current charge and antecedents of defendant;
(g) employment;
(h) financial position: income and savings;
(i) precise nature and form of monies offered to support suretyship – savings or easily realised assets of own, e.g. home owned by surety may not be acceptable to some courts.

Tell the surety of the nature of the allegations against your client and (with client's consent) of his previous convictions; of the obligations of a surety; and of the consequences of a defendant's failure to attend court, i.e. risk of forfeiture of recognisance.

Make enquiries if you suspect that the surety is not bona fide, financially worthy and willing to stand surety. Obtain evidence of assets, e.g. building society passbook. Obtain full information about recent deposits because the court will be suspicious. You must have reasonable grounds to believe that the surety can afford the recognisance into which he is entering (*R.* v. *Birmingham Crown Court, ex p. Ali* [1999] Crim LR 504).

Security

Does your client have, or have access to, money or items of value that may be deposited as a security? Items of value must normally be easily realisable. The court will make money laundering enquiries about the person providing the funds and it is unwise to be involved in the transfer of monies (Proceeds of Crime Act 2002, s.327).

Community ties [42.2]

Obtain the following information:

(a) where your client was born and brought up;
(b) whether your client is married or cohabiting – if so, for how long and whether the couple still live together;
(c) whether there are any children, how many, what ages and whether still living with your client;
(d) anyone else living with your client at the above address;
(e) address of parents/girlfriend/boyfriend/other friends or relatives;
(f) present job [42.3] – if none, length of time unemployed and job prospects.

Outcome

Consider the following:

1. If guilty or convicted, why an immediate custodial sentence is not inevitable.
2. If not guilty, what is the strength of the evidence against your client? Take into account:

   (a) location and date/time of alleged offence;
   (b) goods or weapon recovered from defendant, home or family;
   (c) witnesses referred to by police;
   (d) means and nature of apparent identification; identification parade: number of witnesses attending; number of positive identifications;
   (e) forensic evidence sought or obtained;
   (f) admissions made;
   (g) possible inferences from silence;
   (h) any co-defendants implicating defendant.

Be aware of the circumstances in which a conviction would lead to a minimum term prison sentence or to a dangerous offender categorisation.

Bail record [42.5]

Consider the following:

1. Does your client have convictions for failing to appear in court? If so, when and why did he not appear?
2. Has your client been granted bail since then?
3. Has your client answered to bail in the past when a custodial sentence was likely or imposed? If so, how long was he on bail for each time and what were the conditions?

Suggested bail conditions

Consider what bail conditions would make absconding less likely:

(a) sureties;
(b) a residence condition;
(c) a security;
(d) a condition that your client surrenders his passport and does not apply for a duplicate or travel documents;
(e) reporting to the local police station; or
(f) curfew.

See further the bail checklist at **Appendix 2, 2.12**.

Client on bail when alleged offence committed

Is your client already on bail to a court for another offence? If so, what is the offence; when was it allegedly committed; what stage has been reached in the proceedings; when is he or she next due in court; what will the plea be; and what are the conditions of bail?

Check whether the new offence is indictable-only or either-way. Remind the court of the Law Commission's *Suggested Guidance for Bail Decision-takers* (see **Appendix 10**)[3] that this fact on its own is not a sufficient reason to refuse to grant bail and invite it to look at the details of the new alleged offence.

If your client will plead not guilty to the new offence, you could argue that he/she denies committing an offence (the new offence) while on bail for another offence. However, you should assess the strength of the prosecution evidence before so arguing.

Previous bail record [42.5]

If your client has been on remand on bail before, did he commit offences while on bail? The longer the period that your client was on bail for, without committing offences, the better. Examine your client's record for clusters of offences sentenced on the same occasion. Repeated clusters may suggest a bad bail risk.

Likely to commit further offences

Previous criminal convictions [42.4]

Look at your client's previous criminal convictions:

1. How long is it since his last offence (not sentence)? It may be some time, with long gaps between his previous offences (not sentences). You may be

able to argue that the criminal record shows that your client is somebody who can stay out of trouble for long periods of time, much longer than the time that he will be on bail for in the present case.

2. Does your client have convictions for the offence he is charged with now? If not, how can the prosecution show that your client is likely to commit another offence of the present type if he is granted bail? A cluster of offences may be the prosecution's means of proof.

3. If your client's previous convictions are for a less serious type of offence, the risk must be that he will commit an offence on bail of the type that would not justify his being remanded in custody to protect the public.

4. Always check the list of previous convictions with your client. If it is factually inaccurate to his advantage you are not obliged to correct the list. If you consider it in your client's best interests to correct it, seek his consent. You should not be asked by the court to confirm the accuracy of the list. The Justices' Clerks' Society has advised its members that you should only be asked whether you have seen the list of your client's previous convictions. If you have, the court will assume that you will make representations if the list is wrong to your client's disadvantage. You must not, however, mislead the court by saying what you know to be untrue about your client's character. If he insists you do so, withdraw. If either you or the court want reports from the probation service, the true record is likely to be discovered in any event in due course.

Change of circumstances

How have your client's circumstances changed since he committed the present offence (if pleading guilty), or past offences?

If you can link the offences with something tangible, such as a family crisis or drug taking, which no longer exists, you can argue that the fact of your client's committing the present or past offences has no bearing on the likelihood of his committing offences in the future.

Suggested bail conditions

Consider what bail conditions would lessen the risk of further offending:

(a) a curfew, if the offence was allegedly committed in the evening or at night;

(b) a condition not to go to the area where the offence was allegedly committed or where offences of a similar nature often occur;

(c) if the offence is drink related, not to enter an off-licence or public house;

(d) not to contact the complainant.

Try to ensure that any condition is drafted with clarity and is no more restrictive than is necessary.

Interference with witnesses [42.7]

Which witnesses docs the prosecution allege that your client is likely to inter-fere with? Does the prosecution allege that he has actually made a threat against this witness? If so, what and when? What does your client say about this? If not, why is this case different from any other criminal case involving witnesses who are not police officers?

Has the witness made a statement in the case to the police? If so, it would be difficult for the witness to change his evidence at this late stage as a result of interference from your client. Does your client know the witness's present address? If not, interference with the witness is less likely.

How important is the evidence that this witness can give? If the case does not depend on it, it is unlikely that the defendant would risk committing a serious criminal offence by trying to persuade the witness not to give evidence or to give perjured evidence.

Suggested bail condition

A condition of bail could be imposed that your client does not approach the witness, contact him directly or through others or go within a specified distance of the witness's home address. Try to ensure that any condition is clearly drafted, is no more restrictive than necessary and can be properly monitored.

Other bail objections

Other objections to bail appear in the Bail Act 1976, Sched.1, Part I. Objections to bail in non-imprisonable cases are more restricted: see Bail Act 1976, Sched.1, Part II.

Duty psychiatric schemes/Bail information schemes

Many courts have access to duty psychiatric schemes where mental health trained doctors or community psychiatric nurses attend to see those referred to them. The schemes provide valuable information about the mental health of the defendant to the court and have led to the significant diversion of the mentally ill away from the criminal justice system.

Bail information schemes provide a valuable source of support particu-larly when the information is independently verified by them. They can locate hostel accommodation and rehabilitation programmes. Schemes exist both in courts and prisons. The prison schemes often lack critical details and you may wish to provide your client with the essential information for onward transmission. A suitable form is at Appendix 2.

Indictable-only offences

A defendant may be sent to the Crown Court on bail or in custody (CDA 1998, s.52(1)). One purpose of the preliminary hearing is to allow the magistrates to make the first decision as to bail or custody. The expectation is, therefore, that the magistrates will hear a full bail application in such cases, and they may adjourn the preliminary hearing for that purpose if the requisite information is not available.

If the magistrates have heard and refused a bail application, it is nevertheless open to them to adjourn the preliminary hearing if it appears likely that before the case would otherwise have reached the Crown Court the accused would be in a position to make a further application with a better chance of success (e.g. where a hostel place is being sought for a defendant of no fixed abode, or where there is a prospect that the defendant would be able to offer recognisances).

Although a defendant who is refused bail by the magistrates is normally entitled to make a second application to them, the effect of s.51 is that once a case has been sent to the Crown Court no further application for bail can be made to the magistrates. A defendant who is sent in custody will have the opportunity of making an application to the Crown Court. A written application should normally be lodged.

Bail conditions: interview with legal representative

The power to require a defendant, as a condition of bail, to attend an interview with a legal representative (CDA 1998, s.54, amending Bail Act 1976, s.3(6)) addresses a particular concern about the number of adjournments sought, for the purpose of seeking legal advice.

The power is to enhance the court's ability to deal with a defendant who is being obstructive in this regard. The requirement can be imposed at any relevant stage of proceedings. This power does not apply to the police.

It does not remove the defendant's right to represent himself if he so chooses. It would be inappropriate for the condition to be imposed.

The objective is to try to ensure that a defendant receives legal advice and decides on the response to the charge in advance of his next court appearance. Home Office guidance states that legal advisers will not be expected to report the non-attendance of a client in breach of such a condition which would be to disclose confidential information. However the duties under the CPR could lead to such a report being required, while breach of this condition may lead to the defendant's arrest. It does not, of itself, give grounds for a remand in custody and putting the Crown to proof does not involve obstructing the course of justice. The breach is more likely to come to light at the next hearing when, for example, the defendant requests an adjournment to seek legal advice.

If it becomes clear at the next hearing that a defendant has not sought any legal advice, needs legal advice and there is no reasonable excuse for not having complied with the condition, the court is advised to insist that he sees the duty solicitor there and then. A duty solicitor will only be able to assist if the defendant so wishes.

7.2 THE NUMBER OF BAIL APPLICATIONS

A full bail application may be made at the first hearing and at the hearing that next follows it. For these purposes hearings at which the defendant is not produced (*R.* v. *Dover and Kent Justices, ex p. Dean* (1992) 156 JP 357) and at which bail is refused for lack of information (*R.* v. *Calder Justices, ex p. Kennedy* [1992] Crim LR 496) do not count as hearings. Thereafter (even if no application was made at the first hearing) bail applications may only be made if you raise a new argument as to fact or law or the court gives leave for a further application (Bail Act 1976, Sched.1, Part II). The Law Commission's *Suggested Guidance for Bail Decision-takers* (see **Appendix 10**)[4] advises that courts should be willing, at intervals of 28 days, to consider arguments that the passage of time constitutes a change in circumstances relevant to the need to detain the defendant. If you forgo your right to make the first two bail applications, you can choose when to make an application.

Where bail is granted, advise your client of:

- the importance of answering to bail [41.1];
- any conditions, security or surety imposed [46.2];
- the consequences of breaching any bail conditions [46.3].

7.3 APPEALS IN RELATION TO BAIL

To vary conditions of bail imposed by a police officer

Police officers may grant conditional bail to persons arrested for an offence and may vary such conditions. A defendant may then seek to vary those conditions of bail by application to the magistrates' court.[5]

The application must:

(a) be in writing;
(b) contain a statement of the grounds upon which it is made;
(c) specify the reasons given by the police officer for imposing or varying conditions of bail; and
(d) specify the name and address of any surety provided by the applicant before his release on bail to secure his surrender to custody.

An example of a form of application is provided in **Appendix 2, 2.5**. A copy of the application must be sent to the custody officer for the relevant police station. The clerk to the justices will then fix the time of the hearing, not later than 72 hours after receipt of the application, no account being taken of Christmas Day, Good Friday, any Bank Holiday or any Sunday.

When the court considers the matter it has powers to vary the conditions to grant unconditional bail or, in relation to post-charge conditions, to refuse bail altogether.

While a police officer may vary the bail conditions he cannot withhold bail.

Against a refusal of bail by a magistrates' court

If bail is refused, keep an accurate note of the reasons given [45.1]. Advise your client of the possibility of an appeal or future application and its prospects of success [47.1, 47.2].

If the case has not been committed/transferred/sent to the Crown Court, you must obtain a certificate of full argument. Complete a notice of application (for an example see **Appendix 2, 2.6**) and lodge it with the certificate of full argument and copy record of convictions 24 hours before the hearing with the Crown Court and the prosecution.

Applications should specify:

- details of defendant;
- solicitor;
- charges;
- history of bail applications;
- proposed bail conditions;
- proposed sureties (who should attend).

Consider the effect of too early an application. Consider whether the length of time the client has spent in custody will amount to a new argument justifying a further application.

A solicitor can make the application and will be covered by his pre-committal/transfer Representation Order. The defendant will not be produced at court for the application. Tell your client when the application will be made and what the result is.

If the magistrates grant your client conditional bail, but he cannot meet the conditions, you can apply to the Crown Court before committal to vary the following conditions:

(a)   that the person resides away from a particular place or area;
(b)   that the person concerned resides at a particular place other than a bail hostel;
(c)   for the provision of a surety or sureties or the giving of a security;
(d)   that the person concerned remains indoors between certain hours;

(e)   requirements with respect to electronic monitoring;

(f)   that the person concerned makes no contact with another person.

Otherwise an application for judicial review should be made.

Against the grant of bail

The Bail (Amendment) Act 1993 gives the prosecution a right of appeal against the decision to grant bail in certain cases.

The right of appeal against bail granted by the magistrates' court is limited to an offence punishable by imprisonment (or where, in the case of a child or young person, the offence is so punishable in the case of an adult).

Where it wishes to appeal, the prosecution must give oral notice immediately the bail hearing finishes and before the defendant leaves court, and serve a written notice on the court and the defendant confirming the intention to appeal, within two hours.

The appeal is to a Crown Court judge and the Crown Court hearing must begin within 48 hours from midnight on the day that oral notice was given (not including weekends or public holidays). The hearing will usually be in chambers without the defendant present.

7.4   CUSTODY TIME LIMITS

You must make careful records of the custody time limit that applies in a particular case. You must not warn the prosecution if they fail to notice that a limit is about to expire.

Magistrates' court

For either-way offences the time limit is 70 days unless the court has accepted jurisdiction within 56 days, when the limit is 56 days.

For indictable-only offences the time limit is 70 days.

For summary-only offences the time limit is 56 days.

In the Youth Court, if the court accepts jurisdiction within 56 days in respect of an offence which for an adult would be an indictable-only offence, the time limit is 56 days (*R. v. Stratford Youth Court, ex p. S.* [1999] Crim LR 146).

Crown Court

The time limit following transfer or committal is 112 days. Where a case is sent under CDA 1998, s.51 the time limit is 182 days less any time the defendant spent in custody during the magistrates' court stage.

Expiry

The time limit ceases to apply at the start of committal proceedings, plea or trial. A plea and case management hearing (PCMH) is not such a hearing.

Extension

To obtain an extension the Crown must apply within the time limit and the court shall not grant the application unless it is satisfied that:

(a)   the need for the extension is due to:

- the illness or absence of the accused, a necessary witness, a judge or a magistrate;
- a postponement which is occasioned by the ordering by the court of separate trials in the case of two or more accused or two or more offences; or
- some other good and sufficient cause;

and

(b)   the prosecution has acted with all due diligence and expedition.

You should seldom concede that an extension is appropriate (*R.* v. *Manchester Crown Court, ex p. McDonald* [1999] Crim LR 736). Applications for extensions of time limits should not be regarded as routine but should be challenged whenever possible. A routine listing problem in a routine case cannot amount to a good and sufficient cause for an extension (*R. (on the application of Miah)* v. *Snaresbrook Crown Court* [2006] EWHC 2873 (Admin)).

Appeals

Both the defence and the prosecution have rights of appeal from the magistrates' court to the Crown Court against the grant and refusal of an extension of the custody time. Appeals from decisions made during Crown Court proceedings are by way of judicial review. Such hearings require funding from the Community Legal Service but can be undertaken by firms holding a General Criminal Contract.

Bail

If a time limit has expired, bail shall be granted, without application of the exceptions referred to in the Bail Act 1976, s.4. Bail conditions may be imposed, but the court cannot require sureties, security, or conditions to be met before release (Prosecution of Offences (Custody Time Limits) Regulations 1987, SI 1987/299, reg.8). In cases covered by CJPOA 1994, s.25 the custody time limits are of relevance and the section may be read down to allow bail to be granted (*R. (on the application of O)* v. *Harrow Crown Court* [2007] Crim LR 63).

7.5 COMMUNICATING WITH A DEFENDANT IN CUSTODY

TV links

CDA 1998 allows many hearings in a magistrates' court or Crown Court, to take place where a defendant in custody sees the court, and is seen by the court, over a video link rather than being physically present in court.

A court may direct that the accused be treated as present if:

(a) the court has heard representations;
(b) the accused is in custody;
(c) the accused is able to see and hear and be seen and heard;
(d) the Home Office has notified availability;
(e) it is before the start of the trial[6] or it is a sentencing hearing.

The Act creates a presumption that video links will be used.

At the first hearing in the magistrates' court, when the case is adjourned, magistrates will hear any representations from the defence about why subsequent hearings – a further bail application, plea before venue, mode of trial, the taking of a plea, a committal for trial or sentencing – should not take place over the video link.

There are no statutory criteria to form the basis of the decision but it is in cases where the defendant is vulnerable that the magistrates are most likely, having given reasons, not to make a video link direction. When the provision was before Parliament, the government indicated that 'good' reasons for requiring the defendant to come to court might include where:

(a) the need for an interpreter arises;
(b) the defendant is nervous and unable to communicate through that medium;
(c) the defendant has a psychiatric history;
(d) the defendant has a fear about the use of technology.

Other reasons that might form the basis of an application for the defendant to be brought to court include:

1. It is a multi-handed or very complex case.
2. The defendant has poor literacy skills and documents need to be considered.
3. The defendant suffers from a mental health problem or visual or hearing or learning difficulties.
4. It is not possible to take instructions from the defendant on material to be served by the prosecutor at the hearing.

5. The defendant has been unable to see his legal adviser in person at the prison.
6. The defendant needs to be interviewed by a bail information officer at the court.

You will wish to make representations if your client might be prejudiced by an unwillingness (because of his perception of a lack of confidentiality) to provide critical information to you over a video link or if there will otherwise be unnecessary visits to the prison at public or private expense.

Consultation booths with video link equipment are available at the court and the prison to allow a conference to be held before or after the video link hearing. The absence of the defendant may result in an adjournment if you require a signed authority from your client as to your handling of the case and there is insufficient confidentiality in the use of fax connections.

You should keep under review the need for your client to attend the court in person.

Many solicitors have now established video suites or use court facilities close to their offices to avoid unremunerated travel to prisons.

Communication – correspondence

It is important that any legally privileged correspondence from solicitors to prisoners does not contain cash. A solicitor needing to send a prisoner money should send it to the prison governor instead, with an explanation of what the payment is for, and the money will be credited to this prisoner accordingly.

Mail clearly marked 'Prison Rule 39' (or 'YOI Rule 14' if addressed to a young offender) will be treated as legally privileged and passed to the prisoner unopened, unless a governor has reason to suspect that it is not actually privileged.

Governors have power to order suspected letters to be opened: by observing these guidelines, you can ensure your correspondence reaches your client unopened in all but a bare minimum of cases.

NOTES

1. The Guidance is Part XIII of Law Commission Report No.269 *Bail and the Human Rights Act 1998* (see **Appendix 10**).
2. Ibid.
3. Ibid.
4. Ibid.
5. The procedure is set out in CPR Part 19.
6. In the Crown Court the start of trial is defined as the swearing in of the jury.

CHAPTER 8

Determining if there is a case and advising your client to plead guilty or not guilty

---

Objectives of this chapter

- To show how to establish whether there is a case to answer
- To list the information that should be available as a basis for this decision
- To list the information that you need before you can advise your client about plea
- To show the range of alternatives open to your client
- To emphasise the importance of engaging with your client and discussing the advice and his initial decision with him

---

Throughout this chapter references in square brackets are to the LSC Transaction Criteria.

8.1 ADVICE ON PLEA

Advise your client about plea [54.3] and record that you have done so. The decision is crucial and should not be rushed. For further guidance see the Solicitors Regulation Authority's *Standards of Competence for Accreditation of Solicitors Representing Clients in the Magistrates' Court* in **Appendix 11**.

Action to be taken with your client

Your client will need to know:

(a) how long the case is likely to take [57.1];
(b) what steps you are going to take on his behalf [52.2];
(c) what the prosecution will have to prove [54.1];
(d) what the evidence in the case is [54.2];
(e) how strong the prosecution case is;
(f) how strong the defence case is;
(g) when he will see you next and what will happen then [57.4].

You should confirm in writing any advice given [57.3]. This also assists on peer review.

Your client must take the decision; you must assist him to reach it by advice. Be aware that failure to make adequate investigation of the proposed plea can result in a serious miscarriage of justice. Special care must be taken if your client is mentally disordered or of poor understanding.

8.2 PROCEDURAL BARS

The following is only a summary. If relevant issues arise, you should refer to detailed sources.[1]

Invalidity

Examine the written charge, summons or requisition for possible invalidity:

1. Does it fail to describe accurately an offence known to law? It must contain a brief description of the offence using non-technical language and identify the statute and section contravened, or identify the offence correctly as being against common law.
2. Is it out of time? The general rule is that there are no time limits in criminal cases, but there are important exceptions: if the offence is summary only, a court may not try an information unless it was laid at the magistrates' court within six months of the offence (Magistrates' Courts Act 1980 (MCA 1980), s.127). There are exceptions to this rule including taking motor vehicles without consent and vehicle excise offences. A list of examples of these appears in *Stone's Justices' Manual* (Butterworths), para.1–62.
3. Is a summons not properly signed? The signature on the summons must be that of a JP or the justices' clerk or delegated officer. In practice ordinary court clerks check summonses and use signature stamps to sign the documents.
4. Does it fail accurately to describe the informant and give his address?
5. Has a necessary consent been overlooked? Note that this may be corrected at any time provided that there is no prejudice to the defence.

   - Some statutes require the consent of the Attorney General or the Director of Public Prosecutions (DPP) to the bringing of the prosecution, e.g. bribery, terrorism, official secrets. A Crown Prosecutor is empowered to provide the consent of the DPP.
   - Note: Prosecution of Offences Act 1985 (POA 1985), ss.1(7), 25 and 26.

6. Is it duplicitous?

- Each charge or summons may allege only one offence unless several offences arise out of a single activity (but note the amendment to this rule effected by CPR Part 17).
- Alternative allegations of what is essentially a single offence are permitted.
- Alternative allegations of different offences are not permitted (even if created by the same statutory provision).
- Note: two or more defendants may be jointly charged with having committed an offence jointly.

7. Is it vexatious?
8. Are these 'defences' relevant: *res judicata*, estoppel, *autrefois acquit* or *autrefois convict*?

Abuse of process

In the exercise of the court's discretion, a case may be dismissed for:

(a) prosecution misconduct that deprives the defendant of a protection provided by the law, or enables the prosecution to take advantage of a technicality, or allows a trial to proceed when it would not otherwise have done so;

(b) unjustifiable delay by the prosecution (*R*. v. *Norwich Crown Court, ex p. Belsham* [1992] 1 WLR 54, QBD); serious prejudice to the defendant is required to stay for abuse based on delay and the problems created for the defence must be incapable of resolution by judicial management at trial (*Chief Constable of Merseyside* v. *Harrison* [2007] QB 79, DC). Arguments based on delay should be raised at the earliest opportunity.

However, you should be aware that decisions following the implementation of the CPR hold that technical, rather than jurisdictional, grounds will not be allowed to impede the 'overriding objective' (*R*. v. *Ashton* [2006] Crim LR 1004, CA). However, the issue of summary proceedings out of time (*Sainsbury's Supermarkets Ltd* v. *Plymouth City Council* [2006] EWHC 1749 (Admin)) or against the wrong party goes to jurisdiction.

8.3 INVESTIGATING THE EVIDENCE

Before you can advise a client how to proceed you must be able to judge whether the prosecution has admissible evidence that will be available at trial to make out any, and if so which, charges. Identify all the points to prove for each offence and the evidence relevant to each issue.

You must investigate the evidence available, which may come from a number of sources:

- the police station;
- police files;
- evidence served;
- unused material.

You must then be satisfied that there are no procedural bars to the prosecution proceeding.

You will have investigated the police case and assessed its strength:

(a) what evidence has been disclosed;
(b) how strong is that evidence;
(c) whether it is admissible;
(d) whether it will be available at trial;
(e) whether there are any admissions already made (in a signed pocket book entry or an earlier interview);
(f) which defences have been raised.

If you did not attend the police station or the information obtained there is insufficient or unreliable, you will have to consider other sources. Whether you attend the police station or not, you will wish to investigate the custody record [50.4].

Material available – police files

The amount of information available from the CPS is dependent upon the type of police file prepared. The police case is submitted to the prosecution in a file, which is prepared in accordance with the national *Prosecution Team Manual of Guidance*. The Manual sets out the standard content of police files (see **Appendix 1** for website link).

If the case is to be bailed to an initial hearing, the prosecutor will determine whether it is appropriate for an early first hearing (EFH) court or an early administrative hearing (EAH) court and indicate that on form MG3.

Following the charging of the defendant for an either-way offence, the prosecution will make advance information (AI) available to the defence as soon as possible or on the morning of a court hearing. The AI file will contain the evidence on which the charging decision was made and any CPIA 1996 material. With the introduction of Criminal Justice – Simple Speedy Summary (CJSSS), the defendant can expect to receive AI at the point of charge and in summary cases as well. A copy will also be available for the legal adviser and justices or District Judge to read on the first day of hearing. The defendant is then expected to indicate a plea at that first hearing.

File content for an EFH: expedited file

Straightforward guilty plea cases are listed for an EFH. An expedited file will normally be prepared (see Appendix B to the Adult Criminal Case Management Framework for file contents and **Appendix 1** below for website link).

File content for an EAH: evidential file

The category of cases listed for an EAH includes CDA 1998, s.51 hearings, anticipated not guilty plea cases, plea not known cases and guilty plea cases that are not straightforward. The police will not have a full file, which will take three to four weeks to prepare. An evidential file will be submitted for the first hearing (see Appendix B to the Adult Criminal Case Management Framework for file contents and **Appendix 1** below for website link). Following CJSSS, defendants who indicate a plea of not guilty at the police station are likely to be bailed to return to the police station some days later, to enable the police and CPS to build a file of the evidence for service on the defendant on charge and on the court at the first hearing so that the court can exercise its case management powers and fix a trial date there and then, without adjourning to a pre-trial review.

File content for indictable-only cases

A remand file is used, which has the same content as the file for an EAH. Where the court is considering sending a related either-way or summary case to the Crown Court, defence practitioners will need to ensure that they obtain sufficient information from the prosecution to enable them to dispute the relationship, if appropriate, on an equally informed basis.

Advance information (AI)

In an either-way case, if insufficient evidence has been made available, take steps immediately to obtain AI. This includes a copy of any document on which the prosecution intends to rely (CPR 21.3(3)). Do not delay doing this until you have had the time to take your client's instructions at a formal appointment/interview.

AI must be served by the CPS on the defence promptly to avoid unnecessary adjournments. The court 'shall adjourn' the proceedings if there has been a failure to disclose 'unless the court is satisfied that the conduct of the case for the accused will not be substantially prejudiced by non-compliance' (CPR 21.6). You will wish to advise your client whether the prosecution can make out a prima facie case (*R. (on the application of Donahue)* v. *Calderdale Magistrates' Court* [2001] Crim LR 141, DC).

In summary-only cases, the CPS should provide to the defence all evidence upon which the Crown proposes to rely in a summary trial (Attorney General's Guidelines on Disclosure April 2005, para.57; see **Appendix 1** for website link)[2] as otherwise the defence cannot be satisfied about the quality of the prosecution evidence. The prosecution is required to serve written versions of evidence it proposes to call in sufficient time before the hearing to allow the defendant to deal with it, rather than the court allow short adjournments during the trial to consider how to deal with the evidence as it emerges (*R. on the application of Cleary*) v. *Highbury Corner Magistrates' Court* [2006] EWHC 1869 (Admin), DC). Recommended practice is for the CPS to serve copies of all the prosecution witness statements on the defence if requested to do so, following a plea of not guilty.

Unused material

Consider whether the prosecution or a third party may possess information which would materially affect the outcome of the prosecution or assist you in the early preparation of the defence case. If so, you may wish to consider that information before deciding whether there is a case to answer. A guilty plea in the magistrates' court deprives your client of the statutory rights to any unused material (CPIA 1996, s.1(1)) but at that stage the common law right to enforce fair disclosure remains (*R.* v. *DPP, ex p. Lee* [1999] 2 All ER 737, QBD).

Your client should be given the right to comment on all these documents [51.1].

8.4   CONSIDERATIONS BEFORE ENTERING A GUILTY PLEA

Each case has to be considered on its own merits but there are strong arguments for care before rushing to enter a guilty plea, and your client should be advised about these [57.2].

The following will be relevant considerations.

1.   Has there been a sufficient CPS review as to whether it is in the public interest for the matter to proceed?
2.   Is the level of charge correct?
3.   Is there sufficient evidence to satisfy the defence lawyer that a plea of guilty is proper?
4.   Is there sufficient material then available on which properly to mitigate on the defendant's behalf?
5.   Is there a need for unused material that could only be obtained by representations under the Attorney General's Guidelines on Disclosure, para.58 and the CPS *Disclosure Manual*, Chapter 2 (material relevant to

sentence, e.g. information that might mitigate the seriousness of the offence or assist the accused to lay blame in part upon a co-accused or another person), or unused material that could be obtained by a not guilty plea or a committal for trial?

8.5 INVESTIGATING THE DEFENCE CASE

Researching the law

Before giving advice you must clearly identify, by reference to an appropriate legal text, each point to prove in relation to each allegation and all possible defences, both special and general.

Interviewing the defendant

Just as a criminal prosecution relies upon a complete and reliable investigation of the prosecution witnesses by the police officer, a well-prepared defence requires a similarly professional approach to the defendant and the defence witnesses by you. You need to be aware of what experts can teach you about how these interviews should be conducted.[3]

The aims should be:

(a) to help the witness to give the fullest possible report of his experience;
(b) to enable the interviewer to create a mental representation as well as a full and faithful written representation of the witness's disclosure;
(c) that the account should give sufficient detail to enable the interviewer to re-create mentally the sequence of events and descriptions reported by the witness and to follow the witness's line of reasoning or logic. There should be no missing steps in a narrative sequence.

For information on communication skills and interviewing a witness, see **Appendix 6**.

Your client admits the offence

Do not necessarily accept your client's admissions at face value: enquire as to his reasons. Challenge the basis of a suspect plea: it may be based on anxiety, poor understanding, outside pressure, the desire to protect another or a mistake as to the law. Give clear advice.

If appropriate, explain that you cannot go behind the plea and mitigate on the basis that your client 'didn't really do it'.

Your client properly admits the offence but insists on entering a not guilty plea

You are entitled to put the prosecution to proof but explain carefully to your client the professional limitations on your conduct, including your duty not to mislead the court.

You may:

(a) challenge the court's competence;
(b) challenge the form of the charge;
(c) object to inadmissible, irrelevant or prejudicial evidence;
(d) cross-examine prosecution witnesses to test their credibility or reliability;
(e) make a submission of no case to answer;
(f) if that fails, address the court solely on the failure of the prosecution to prove its case.

You may not:

(a) by your questions put forward any defence that involves an assertion of your client's innocence;
(b) suggest that a third party may be responsible;
(c) allow the defendant to give evidence or call a witness to mislead the court, i.e. mount a positive defence.

If your client does not accept these limitations, you must withdraw.

Exceptionally your client may tell you that he is 'innocent' but insist on pleading guilty and ask you to represent him. It is not improper to continue to act, but unwise. Discuss carefully and, if appropriate, try to persuade your client to plead not guilty; but if you fail, advise your client fully and, in particular, that, in mitigation, he cannot assert his innocence. If that is accepted, you may continue, but confirm your advice in writing. If in doubt withdraw. Appeals against conviction are not normally possible once a guilty plea has been entered.

Your client admits the offence but disputes the evidence

Explain the procedure for a Newton hearing and discuss the evidence. The court will normally sentence on the prosecution's opening or evidence.[4] If, after discussion with the prosecution, this is not accepted by the defence, formal notice should be given and then the court must sentence on the defence version save to the extent that the Crown proves by admissible evidence to the criminal standard that the prosecution version is correct. If a basis of plea is agreed between prosecution and defence it should be set out in writing, signed by the parties and a copy placed in the court file.

Your client denies the offence

Do not necessarily accept your client's denial at face value: enquire as to his reasons. If the prosecution evidence appears strong, challenge your client with it, while making it clear that you are not prompting him or her to concoct or strengthen a false defence. Cross-examine him as robustly as appropriate, taking care to explain why you are doing so ('only a foretaste of things to come'). Do not let your client think you are hostile or no longer on his side. Give clear advice as to the risks and consequences of losing a trial, i.e. if your client's evidence is disbelieved he risks possible destruction of any mitigation. If the case is in the Crown Court, ask your client if they would be assisted by asking the court for a *Goodyear* indication (*R.* v. *Goodyear* [2005] EWCA Crim 888). If your client's real concern is the possible sentence, he may be assisted by knowing the sentence the judge actually has in mind. This procedure can only be followed with your client's consent. Give clear time to reflect. If a denial is maintained, carry on to consider mode of trial.

If you remain doubtful, strive to avoid prejudgement and to remain detached. If you think your client is guilty, that does not prevent you from fully defending him. Your opinion may be erroneous and, in any event, it is not your function to judge your client. However, the relationship of solicitor and client is based on mutual trust: if quite exceptionally your belief that your client is guilty is so strong that it prevents you properly representing your client, you should withdraw.

Your client, while denying the offence, may give inconsistent accounts to you. Challenge your client with these and seek his explanation. If your client's explanation is acceptable you may continue to act.

Your client does not know how to plead

If your client does not know how to plead, you will have to face the difficult question, 'what would you do?'. Stress that the decision is the client's but give clear advice. Weigh up the strengths and weaknesses of the prosecution and defence cases and the factors your client considers important. If in real doubt, advise that he puts the prosecution to proof.

Confirmation

Unless your client is in custody (when there may be concerns about how to keep documents confidential) you should write confirming your client's instructions. When the instructions are against your firm advice, you should:

(a) set out the reasons for your advice and, if appropriate, invite your client to reconsider;

(b) put your client's instructions in writing and have him sign them.

Your client has mistakenly pleaded guilty

Before instructing you, your client may have entered a plea of guilty and you may decide that this was an incorrect plea. It was decided (*Revitt, Borg and Barnes* v. *DPP* [2006] EWHC 2266, QBD) that magistrates had correctly refused to allow three defendants to change their pleas to riding motor cycles dangerously where, before entering their guilty pleas, they:

- were informed of the nature and cause of the accusation against them:
    - promptly;
    - in a language which they understood; and
    - in detail;
- were given every opportunity to obtain further information by advance information;
- were offered the opportunity of an adjournment of the case for the preparation of their defence;
- were told of their right to be legally represented, and were advised:
    - that it was in their interests to be represented; and
    - that they could receive a custodial sentence if convicted.

8.6 ADVICE ON SENTENCE

Before seeking a client's final instructions on plea you should give realistic advice as to the likely sentence as appropriate and prosecution costs that may be ordered against your client in the event of:

- a plea;
- an adverse Newton hearing;
- a conviction in the magistrates' court;
- conviction in the Crown Court.

You must be familiar with the Magistrates' Court Sentencing Guidelines,[5] any local variations and the Sentencing Guidelines Council guidelines as follows:

1. *Reduction in Sentence for a Guilty Plea.* If your client has decided to enter a guilty plea, this should be indicated at the earliest proper opportunity to earn the maximum available credit under CJA 2003, s.144. That provision requires the court to confirm when passing sentence the extent to which it has taken into account the stage at which and the circumstances in which the defendant indicated an intention to plead guilty.

    The Sentencing Guidelines Council[6] issued a revised guideline in 2007, *Reduction in Sentence for a Guilty Plea.* In para.4.2 it recommends that the normal level of reduction should be on a sliding scale ranging from a recommended one-third (where 'willingness to admit guilt' was entered at the first reasonable opportunity in relation to the offence for which the sentence is being imposed), reducing to a recommended one-quarter (where a trial date has been set) and to a recommended one-tenth (for a guilty plea entered at the 'door of the court' or after the trial has begun). Reasons must be given for ordering different percentage reductions. This guideline is available at **www.sentencing-guidelines.gov.uk**. Courts are recommended in para.3.1, when pronouncing sentence, to state what the sentence would have been if there had been no reduction as a result of the guilty plea.

The first reasonable opportunity may be when the person was interviewed by the police or the first time that the defendant appeared before the court, if appropriate disclosure was given. The fact that an offender's version of the circumstances of the offence is rejected after a Newton hearing should be taken into account.

There is no reason why credit should be witheld but it may be reduced to a recommended 20 per cent because the offender was caught red handed.

A court, instead of committing for sentence to the Crown Court, when a sentence of nine months' imprisonment is indicated, may impose a sentence of six months' imprisonment instead, giving the full sentence discount.

2. *Overarching Principles: Seriousness* guideline.
3. *New Sentences: Criminal Justice Act 2003* guideline, including specific offences.
4. The Sentencing Guidelines Council's *Guideline Judgments Case Compendium* containing guideline decisions of the Court of Appeal.
5. The circumstances in which obligatory sentences must be imposed and the limited exceptions available in relation to:

- serious offences (for offences before 5 April 2005);
- drug trafficking;
- domestic burglary;
- firearms offences (see **Appendix 12**);
- serious specified offences listed in CJA 2003, Sched.15 and committed after 4 April 2005 (see **Appendix 9**);
- specified offences, other than serious offences, listed in CJA 2003, Sched.15 (see **Appendix 9**).

You should adjust this advice to take account of mitigating factors known to you. A table of sentences available to the court can be found in **Appendices 12** and **13**.

Such advice may encourage clients whose guilt is likely to be proved but sentence will be below their expectation, to enter a proper guilty plea. Such advice may encourage clients who are not guilty to avoid a guilty plea.

NOTES

1. For example *Wilkinson's Road Traffic Offences* (Sweet & Maxwell), Chapter 2, contains a useful summary of jurisdictional and procedural points.
2. See also *R. v. Stratford Justices, ex p. Imbert* (1999) *The Times*, 25 February; *R. v. Kingston upon Hull Justices, ex p. McCann* (1991) 155 JP 569.
3. E. Shepherd and R. Milne, 'Full and faithful: ensuring quality practice and integrity of outcome in witness interviews', in *Analysing Witness Testimony* (Blackstone Press, 1999).
4. *R. v. Newton* (1983) 77 Cr App R 13; *R. v. Tolera* [1998] Crim LR 425. Although the court is not bound to do so and may itself direct a Newton hearing. In this situation the defendant cannot change his plea (*R. v. Beswick* [1996] 1 Cr App R (S) 343).
5. The Magistrates' Court Sentencing Guidelines will be replaced in 2008 by revised guidelines issued by the Sentencing Guidelines Council and available on **www.sentencing-guidelines.gov.uk**.
6. The Sentencing Advisory Panel (SAP) and the Sentencing Guidelines Council (SGC) are two closely related independent bodies. The SGC receives advice from the SAP on a particular topic and uses this to formulate guidelines on the subject. These draft guidelines are published, consulted on and then revised. Final sentencing guidelines are then issued.

CHAPTER 9

Choosing a place of trial

Objectives of this chapter

- To explain the plea before venue procedure and the consequences of entering a guilty plea at that stage
- To explain the different powers of magistrates to commit to the Crown Court
- To list the advantages of summary and of Crown Court trial

If your client is charged with an either-way offence, you will have to advise him about plea before venue and if appropriate mode of trial. The Criminal Justice Act 2003 proposes a different procedure but the relevant part has not been brought into force.

9.1 PLEA BEFORE VENUE

If your client is pleading guilty it will usually be advantageous to enter the plea in the magistrates' court at the plea before venue hearing. In the Crown Court greater sentences are generally imposed.

If the magistrates have sufficient sentencing powers, after allowing for guilty plea discount, they should retain the case. Be aware of the Magistrates' Court Sentencing Guidelines.

If the contents of a pre-sentence report or a Newton hearing may result in the magistrates having sufficient sentencing powers they should order a report or hold a Newton hearing before deciding whether to commit for sentence (*R.* v. *Warley Magistrates' Court, ex p. DPP* [1998] 2 Cr App R 307, DC).

If a defendant is on bail prior to the plea before venue hearing, bail should continue (*R.* v. *Rafferty* [1998] Crim LR 433, CA). You should, however, consider with a client in custody the impact of the conviction on his prison status, and balance this against any possible loss of discount for a later entry of a guilty plea. The level of discount that should be given for a guilty plea depends on the stage of the proceedings at which it is entered: see the

Magistrates' Court Sentencing Guidelines, 'Reduction in sentence for guilty pleas' (**www.sentencing-guidelines.gov.uk**).

The procedure

The procedure applies to those facing either-way charges who are aged 18 and over at the date the procedure begins. If a defendant is willing to indicate that he will plead guilty, there will not be any representations by either party as to the place of trial and the magistrates are not able to decline jurisdiction. The case will proceed to sentence. However, within their jurisdiction, the magistrates have power to commit the defendant to the Crown Court for sentence under the provisions of the Powers of Criminal Courts (Sentencing) Act 2000 (PCC(S)A 2000), s.3. The primary advantage to the defence of this procedure is that magistrates are not limited at the early stages to hearing the Crown's version of events; indeed the reverse is true as *R.* v. *Newton* (1983) 77 Cr App R 13 applies in full force. Thus the court has to sentence on the basis of the version of the facts indicated by the defence unless the Crown has proved another version to the criminal standard. Furthermore, the defence is able to place before the court all personal mitigating circumstances. Be aware of the relevance of the Mode of Trial Guidelines (see **Appendix 1** for website link) when arguing for sentence in the magistrates' court. The discount for a plea of guilty may mean that the magistrates can and will retain sentence (*R.* v. *Warley Magistrates' Court, ex p. DPP* [1998] 2 Cr App R 307, DC). This enables some thousands of cases to be concluded within the magistrates' court jurisdiction rather than be committed for sentence.

If a defendant wishes to indicate a not guilty plea or to indicate no plea at all, then there is a mode of trial hearing. The prosecution makes representations as to the place of trial and the defence has the same opportunity. The court may decline jurisdiction if it considers that on the prosecution's version of its facts, the court's sentencing powers may be insufficient. If the court accepts jurisdiction the defendant retains the right to elect jury trial.

The consequences of using the procedure

However, it is necessary to advise defendants of the practical consequences of using the procedure [56.1]. The following questions are critical:

1. Will the court be willing to order a pre-sentence report within its own jurisdiction rather than by immediately committing for sentence, allowing the report to be obtained at the Crown Court stage?
2. In custody cases will the defendant be content to lose privileges as occurs immediately upon conviction?

A defendant who pleads guilty before the justices to an offence triable either way and is committed to the Crown Court for sentence should normally be entitled to a greater credit on sentence than a defendant who delays making such a plea until appearing on indictment in the Crown Court. Such a guilty plea does not normally alter the position as to the defendant's bail or remand in custody. In the usual case, when a person who had been on bail enters a guilty plea at that stage, the practice should be to continue his bail, even if it is anticipated that a custodial sentence will be imposed by the Crown Court, unless there is good reason for remanding him in custody (*R.* v. *Rafferty* [1998] Crim LR 433, CA).

If the defendant is in custody, then after entering such a plea at that stage, it would be unusual, if the reasons for remand in custody remained unchanged, to alter the position. The defendant would, however, have the benefit of a greater discount than if he had delayed his plea until the Crown Court.

Committals for sentence are regarded as incidental to the proceedings for the purposes of a Representation Order and an extension is not required (Criminal Defence Service (General) (No.2) Regulations 2001, SI 2001/1437, reg.3(3)(a)). An RDCO can not be made against a defendant who is committed for sentence to the Crown Court: Criminal Defence Service (Recovery of Defence Costs Orders) Regulations 2001, SI 2001/856, reg.4(2)(b)).

Where the defendant pleads guilty to some either-way offences but elects trial in relation to other related offences (i.e. offences that could have been placed on the same indictment) PCC(S)A 2000, s.4 requires that the court shall adjourn the cases where the guilty plea is entered until the committal of the other matters. At that stage the court has a discretion to commit for sentence even if its own powers would have been sufficient to deal with the matter. The Crown Court can then deal with all sentencing at the same time.

File standards

Table 9.1 The Crown Court's sentencing powers

Committals under	Court powers
PCC(S)A 2000, s.3	Full powers of the Crown Court
PCC(S)A 2000, s.4	Full powers of the Crown Court unless acquittals in all matters on indictment in which case magistrates' powers
PCC(S)A 2000, s.6	Magistrates' court powers
Criminal Justice Act 1988, s.40	Magistrates' court powers
Criminal Justice Act 1988, s.41	Magistrates' court powers

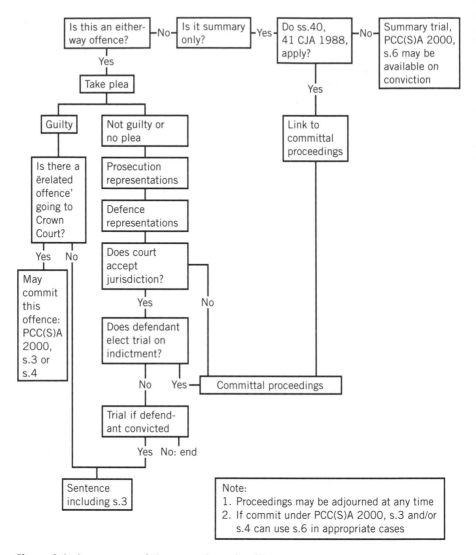

Figure 9.1 A summary of the procedures in either-way cases

9.2 MODE OF TRIAL

If your client is pleading not guilty, be aware that, whatever the immediate pressures on your client, with hindsight your client would, in most cases, choose the tribunal most likely to acquit him. Bring to bear your experience of the local courts. Perhaps there is a greater likelihood of acquittal in the Crown Court, but not for every type of case.

If you consider the Crown Court most appropriate, but your client favours trial in the magistrates' court, ask your client his reasons and discuss them in detail. Your client may be worried about the delay before trial; try to put it in context and remove exaggerated concerns.

Summary trial advantages

1. There is usually less delay before trial.
2. The prosecution case may be less well prepared.
3. Your client will not be liable to pay towards his defence costs (Criminal Defence Service (Recovery of Defence Costs Orders) Regulations 2001, reg.4(2)(a)) and prosecution costs will be lower.
4. No duty to have a defence statement (when secondary disclosure not required).
5. Lesser sentencing powers and lesser sentence likely.
6. Less intimidating surroundings.
7. Reasons, although limited, are given for the verdict.

Crown Court advantages

1. The greater and timely disclosure of the evidence.
2. More time to prepare the defence case.
3. The pace of the trial is slower, for the benefit of the jury, providing the opportunity for a more thorough examination of the evidence.
4. Perhaps a greater prospect of acquittal by the jury, e.g. where the prosecution case depends entirely on police evidence.
5. The judge is a qualified lawyer who will readily understand any legal issues raised by the defence and be able to deal with them in the absence of the jury, e.g. a disputed confession or a disputed inference from silence in the police station is dealt with by a *voir dire*.
6. Better forum for dealing with expert evidence and complex issues.
7. There is currently no means test for public funding, though this is planned and an RDCO may be made.

Arguments

If you wish to argue for summary trial be aware of the relevant provisions of the Mode of Trial Guidelines (see **Appendix 1** for website link). They recommend that all either-way cases should be tried summarily unless there are specific arguments to the contrary. The absence of an aggravating factor is a powerful, if not decisive argument in favour of summary trial. Your client should be advised about the procedure [56.2].

9.3 YOUTHS

Those under 18 do not normally have a right to elect jury trial but issues can arise as to the preferred place of trial for them.

You should be aware of your client's age at all stages. See **Chapter 15** for information about the place of trial for youths.

CHAPTER 10

Preparing for sentence: plea of guilty or conviction

Objectives of this chapter

- To describe the process of calculating a sentence
- To identify the material relevant to mitigation and how to ensure that it covers all the relevant issues
- To enable you to argue for the optimum sentence

Throughout this chapter references in square brackets are to the LSC Transaction Criteria.

Whether your client is pleading guilty or not guilty it will be essential to prepare, at the earliest opportunity, as much as possible of a statement, for use on entry of the plea or in the event of a conviction. This information should be added to the core information about your client (see **Chapter 3**).

10.1 STATEMENT: FOR GUILTY PLEA OR CONVICTION

Remember that for sentencing there can be no specimen charges.[1] The court may only sentence matters that are charged or taken into consideration (TIC).[2] Careful consideration should therefore be given to the evidence in support of a TIC before advising a client to accept it in court. If a TIC is offered and refused, the defendant will be charged with the offence at a later date should the evidence become available, and this may affect their decision.

A plea in mitigation will normally be structured in four parts:

(a) offence mitigation;
(b) offender mitigation;
(c) discount for guilty plea;
(d) recommendation as to outcome(s).

This approach is adopted by the Magistrates' Court Sentencing Guidelines (**www.sentencing-guidelines.gov.uk**).

Courts are now required to take the approach set out in the Sentencing Guidelines Council's guideline, *Overarching Principles: Seriousness*, which applies to defendants aged 18 and over. This incorporates eight stages.

10.2 THE DECISION-MAKING PROCESS

The process set out below is intended to show that the sentencing approach is fluid and requires the structured exercise of discretion.

1. **Identify dangerous offenders.** Many offences are specified offences for the purposes of the public protection provisions in CJA 2003. The court must determine whether there is a significant risk of serious harm by the commission of a further specified offence. The starting points in the guidelines are (a) for offenders who do not meet the dangerous offender criteria; and (b) as the basis for the setting of a minimum term within an indeterminate sentence for those who do meet the criteria.
2. **Identify the appropriate starting point.** Because many acts can be charged as more than one offence, consideration will have to be given to the appropriate guideline once findings of fact have been made. The sentence should reflect the facts found to exist and not just the title of the offence of which the offender is convicted.
3. **Consider relevant aggravating factors, both general and those specific to the type of offence.** This may result in a sentence level being identified that is higher than the suggested starting point – sometimes substantially so.
4. **Consider mitigating factors and personal mitigation.** There may be general or offence-specific mitigating factors and matters of personal mitigation which could result in a sentence that is lower than the suggested starting point (possibly substantially so), or a sentence of a different type.
5. **Reduction for guilty plea.** The court will then apply any reduction for a guilty plea following the approach set out in the Sentencing Guidelines Council's guideline, *Reduction in Sentence for a Guilty Plea*.
6. **Consider ancillary orders.** The court should consider whether ancillary orders are appropriate or necessary.
7. **The totality principle.** The court should review the total sentence to ensure that it is proportionate to the offending behaviour and properly balanced.
8. **Reasons.** When a court moves from the suggested starting points and sentencing ranges identified in the guidelines, it should explain its reasons for doing so.

When determining seriousness, the court is required to consider the culpability of the offender and any harm that the offence caused, was intended to cause or might foreseeably have caused, and assess relevant aggravating and mitigating factors. General aggravating and mitigating factors set out in the Sentencing Guidelines Council's guideline, *Overarching Principles: Seriousness* are referred to below.

Culpability may be:

- intention to cause harm;
- reckless as to whether harm was caused;
- knowledge of the risks although not intending to cause harm;
- negligent.

Harm may be:

- to individual victims;
- to the community;
- other types of harm, e.g. cruelty to animals.

Aggravating factors indicate:

- a higher than usual level of culpability;
- a greater than usual degree of harm caused by the offence; or
- both of the above.

Next the sentencer considers:

- mitigating factors, such as youth or that the person played a minor role;
- offender mitigation, such as remorse;
- reduction for a guilty plea.

Table 10.1 includes some factors (such as the vulnerability of victims or abuse of trust) which are integral features of certain offences; in such cases, the presence of the aggravating factor is already reflected in the penalty for the offence and cannot be used as justification for increasing the sentence further.

Factors indicating a more than usually serious degree of harm include:

- multiple victims;
- an especially serious physical or psychological effect on the victim, even if unintended;
- a sustained assault or repeated assaults on the same victim;
- victim is particularly vulnerable;
- location of the offence (for example, in an isolated place);
- offence is committed against those working in the public sector or providing a service to the public;
- presence of others, e.g. relatives, especially children or partner of the victim;
- additional degradation of the victim (e.g. taking photographs of a victim as part of a sexual offence);

- in property offences, high value (including sentimental value of property to the victim), or substantial consequential loss (e.g. where the theft of equipment causes serious disruption to a victim's life or business).

Table 10.1 Aggravating and mitigating factors (Sentencing Guidelines Council)

Aggravation	Mitigation
Factors indicating higher culpability	*Factors indicating lower culpability*
Offence committed while on bail for other offences	A greater degree of provocation than normally expected
Failure to respond to previous sentences	Mental illness or disability
Offence was racially or religiously aggravated	Youth or age, where it affects the responsibility of the individual defendant
Offence motivated by or demonstrated hostility to victim based on his sexual orientation or disability	The fact that the offender only played a minor role
Previous convictions, particularly when pattern of offending	
Planning of an offence	
Intention to commit more serious harm	
Offender operating in groups or gangs	
Professional offending	
Commission for financial gain when not inherent in the offence itself	
High level of profit	
Attempt to conceal or dispose of evidence	
Failure to respond to warnings or concerns expressed about the offender's behaviour	
Offence committed while on licence	
Offence motivated by hostility towards minority group	
Deliberate targeting of vulnerable victims	
Commission of an offence while under influence of drink/drugs	
Use of weapon to frighten or injure victim	
Deliberate and gratuitous damage to property	
Abuse of power	
Abuse of trust	

You should also be aware of the aggravating and mitigating factors listed in individual offence guidelines. The Attorney General's Guidelines on Disclosure (see **Appendix 1** for website link) provide in para.58 that in all cases the prosecutor must consider disclosing in the interests of justice any material that is relevant to sentence (e.g. information that might mitigate the seriousness of the offence or assist the accused to lay blame in whole or in part upon a co-accused or another person). See also the CPS *Disclosure Manual*, Chapter 2 and for a sample mitigation checklist see **Appendix 2, 2.14**. In preparing a mitigation the following are among the relevant issues.

10.3   MITIGATING FACTORS: THE OFFENCE

Reasons for the offence/the offence itself

1.   Try to find a cause for why your client committed the offence.

 (a)   If the crime was opportunistic, why was he tempted?
 (b)   If this was your client's first offence, why did your client do it when he has managed to resist the temptation before?

2.   What does your client think about the offence, and himself, now? Remorse is a powerful mitigating factor. Consider how evidence of remorse is to be presented, e.g. by your client's statement in the police interview.
3.   You will need to relate the information above to the instructions you already have about any drink, drugs, psychiatric or gambling problems. If you know, from what your client has told you, that he has such a problem, find out what this means for him on a daily basis.
4.   Were there financial problems? If so, how did they begin and why could they not be brought under control? Explain why your client committed the crime in a way that puts the act in the context of his life generally.
5.   Was your client related to the victim and acting out of revenge or in retaliation? At best you can establish a chain of events, each apparently outside his control at the time, ending with a situation where the crime was irresistible.
6.   Was your client influenced by others? The court will want to try to understand your client and why he committed the offence.
7.   Be receptive to all the signals about your client that he is giving out, consciously and unconsciously.
8.   Think about the sort of information the advocate will want by reference to recommendations on sentencing[3] – the factors that make the offence more serious and those that help the mitigation [70.1, 70.2]. See the factors indicating higher culpability (page 12 above) and factors indicating a more than usually serious degree of harm in the Sentencing Guidelines Council's guideline, *Overarching Principles: Seriousness*.
9.   Check whether the offence is shown on CCTV or other video recording. It may make nonsense of the client's instructions. Make sure that the client sees the video in such circumstances.

10. Consider the 'Features relevant to the individual offences' in the Mode of Trial Guidelines (see **Appendix 1**).
11. Pay particular regard to any aggravating factors so that you can minimise them as far as possible and put them in context.
12. Where others were involved, consider how your client was influenced by them and the extent of your client's role [69.1].

Attitude to offence

1. Did your client admit the offence to the police?
2. Did your client plead guilty or was he convicted?
3. Did your client tell the police about offences which they could not otherwise have proved against him?
4. Did your client help the police recover stolen property or provide other information of value?
5. Did your client show distress, regret or remorse?

Consequences of offence

Think of ways in which your client has been punished already.

1. How has the offence affected his personal relationships?
2. Has your client waited a long time to be sentenced? [72.2]
3. Has he spent time in custody, on remand? [72.1]
4. Was this your client's first time in custody? What was it like? If you can use his own words it is more likely to get the court's attention.
5. Has your client lost his job? [74] How difficult will it be to find another one?
6. It may be your client's first conviction – losing his good name.

Positive steps awaiting sentence

1. How has your client spent his time waiting to be sentenced? Has your client kept out of trouble?
2. Has your client taken positive steps to tackle the problems that led him to commit the crime?
3. How have your client's circumstances changed for the better?
4. If appropriate, advise him to save up money to pay a fine or compensation.
5. Make sure that the advocate knows the history of the case and whether your client pleaded guilty (and at what stage [71.1]) or was convicted.
6. What is your client's income and its source at the time of sentencing? [73]

Consequences of sentence

What are the detrimental effects of the likely sentence:

(a)   on your client?
(b)   on others?

10.4   MITIGATING FACTORS: PERSONAL

You will also need to consider personal mitigating factors such as:

(a)   age;
(b)   character;
(c)   mental disability or illness;
(d)   physical disability or illness;
(e)   family relationships;
(f)   employment history.

Your statement of core information should contain most of the details.

Be aware of your client's criminal history or whether this is your client's first offence [73]. What is your client's record of discharging previous sentences imposed [73.1]? The existence of previous convictions or a failure to comply with previous sentences may have the effect of removing personal mitigation that would otherwise have been available.

Welfare

You should be aware of any problems (such as drink, drugs, debts, family, housing, employment) from which your client suffers and refer to the relevant agency. It may assist in a guilty plea to show that constructive efforts are being made to deal with the problem. You should then actively liaise with the agency.

Credit for guilty plea

Be aware that the courts should give credit for a guilty plea related to the stage of the proceedings at which a guilty plea was entered (see the Sentencing Guidelines Council guideline, *Reduction in Sentence for a Guilty Plea* and PCC(S)A 2000, s.152). They are required to indicate the extent to which they have done so when announcing their decision. Be prepared to challenge the court's refusal to give a full discount when the defendant was caught 'red-handed'. Guilty plea discounts can also move a case down through a threshold.

10.5 MITIGATION AS TO PENALTY

Be aware of the primary sentences and ancillary sentences which are available to the court which will sentence your client. A schedule of the availability of primary sentences appears at **Appendix 13**.

You should normally keep your recommendations close to, but below, the likely penalty and should consider how a primary penalty may be lessened if an ancillary penalty is attached. You should always seek your client's instructions before advocating a particular ancillary penalty.

Dangerous offenders

You should identify every case involving an allegation of a specified or serious specified offence as special preparation is required. Obligatory sentences have to be imposed in the event of conviction (even of a first offence) if the court is satisfied that there is a significant risk that:

(a) the defendant will commit a further specified offence; and
(b) that offence will cause serious harm to a member of the public.

If the defendant is an adult with a previous conviction for a specified offence, there is a presumption that such risks exist unless the defence can show otherwise. However, the court may consider all previous convictions. You should therefore:

- carefully examine any previous record of convictions;
- consider the facts of the case to identify factors tending against a finding of dangerousness;
- consider the need for expert evidence that the defendant does not represent a significant risk;
- require the court to consider an assessment contained in a pre-sentence report;
- warn your client of the need for careful answers to any questions put by the probation service.

A lack of appreciation by a defendant of the seriousness of their own behaviour is identified as a high risk factor. Consider particularly the judgments in *R.* v. *Lang* [2006] All ER 410 and *R.* v. *Johnson* [2007] Crim LR 177 and the guidance on dangerous offenders issued by the Sentencing Guidelines Council.

Threshold for community sentence

CJA 2003, s.148(1) states that the threshold is reached when: 'the offence, or the combination of the offence and one or more offences associated with it, was serious enough to warrant such a sentence'.

CJA 2003, s.148(2)(b) states that where a court passes a community sentence consisting of or including a community order, 'the restrictions on liberty imposed by the order must be [. . .] commensurate with the seriousness of the offence, or the combination of the offence and one or more offences associated with it'.

CJA 2003, s.149 states that '[i]n determining the restrictions on liberty [. . .] the court may have regard to any period for which the offender has been remanded in custody'.

Requirements should be demanding enough, but not setting up the offender to fail.

Having reached the view that a community sentence is the most appropriate disposal, the sentencer should:

(a)   request a pre-sentence report;
(b)   indicate which of the three sentencing ranges is relevant: low, medium or high;
(c)   state the purpose of the sentence.

There may be no need for any type of report if the sentencer just intends to impose a sentence that does not involve the probation service, e.g.:

• an exclusion requirement;
• an electronically monitored curfew.

Sentence indication

When a court states that sentence is being postponed so that a report can be obtained to examine alternatives to imprisonment and the offender is justifiably led to believe that if those alternatives are found to be satisfactory in all respects then the court will adopt them, the court is bound by its promise of a non-custodial sentence (*R.* v. *Gillam* (1980) 2 Cr App R (S) 267). The expectation created by a decision of the magistrates cannot be treated as unqualified. In *R. (on the application of White)* v. *Barking Magistrates' Court* [2004] EWHC 417 (Admin) magistrates had adjourned for a pre-sentence report with 'all options open including custody' but with no express reference to the possibility of committing for sentence. The applicant was to be sentenced for the production of cannabis on a commercial scale. He had previously been sentenced to two years' imprisonment for possession of a controlled drug with intent to supply. Burnton J said that if the magistrates wished to retain the option to commit to the Crown Court it was essential that they expressly state that. But he decided that the offences were so serious that no reasonable bench of magistrates could have come to the conclusion that it was appropriate to retain jurisdiction over sentencing and refused to quash the magistrates' subsequent decision to commit.

Deferred sentences

The Sentencing Guidelines Council's guideline, *New Sentences: Criminal Justice Act 2003* provides that deferred sentences should predominantly be for a small group of cases where the sentencer feels that there would be a particular value in giving the offender the opportunities listed:

(a) not to re-offend;
(b) to do something where progress can be shown within a short period;
(c) to behave/refrain from behaving in a particular way that is relevant to sentence.

If the offender complies with the requirements a different sentence will be justified at the end of the deferment period, i.e.:

• community sentence instead of custodial sentence;
• fine/discharge instead of community sentence.

Custody threshold

The court must not impose a custodial sentence unless it is of the opinion that the offence or a combination of the offence and one or more other offences associated with it was so serious that neither a fine alone nor community sentence can be justified (CJA 2003, s.152).

New Sentences: Criminal Justice Act 2003 states that in cases approaching the custody threshold courts will have particular regard to:

• admissions and genuine remorse;
• youth and immaturity;
• attempts to overcome addiction;
• physical or mental disability;
• character;
• family responsibilities;
• the fact (if such is the case) that it could amount to a first prison sentence (*R. v. Howells* [1998] Crim LR 836).

Sentencing for breach

Although a court is prohibited from passing a custodial sentence unless it is of the opinion that the offence was so serious that a community sentence cannot be justified for the offence, exceptions permit the imposition of a custody sentence for breach of a community order even for a non-imprisonable offence (CJA 2003, s.152(2); PCC(S)A 2000, Sched.3, para.4; CJA 2003, Sched.8, para.9).

New Sentences: Criminal Justice Act 2003 provides that:

Custody should be the last resort – reserved for those cases of deliberate and repeated breach where all reasonable efforts to ensure that the offender complies have failed. . . .

Before increasing the onerousness of requirements, sentences . . . should avoid precipitating further breaches by overloading the offender with too many or conflicting requirements.

There may be cases where the court will need to consider re-sentencing to a differently constructed community sentence.

Relevance of previous convictions

By CJA 2003, s.143 when considering the seriousness of an offence committed by an offender who has one or more previous convictions, the court must treat each previous conviction as an aggravating factor, having regard to:

(a)   the nature of the offence and its relevance to the current offence; and
(b)   the time that has elapsed since the conviction.

Suspended custodial sentence

Courts can suspend for up to two years (the operational period) a custodial sentence of imprisonment or detention in a YOI which is of up to six months' total length[4] (magistrates' court) or 12 months' total length (Crown Court). The offender must be set one or more requirements (*R. v. Lees-Wolfenden* [2006] EWCA Crim 3068) to be complied with during a supervision period (which cannot be longer than the operational period). If an unlawful suspended sentence without requirements was passed by a magistrates' court, the court should rescind the unlawful sentence under MCA 1980, s.142 and re-sentence for the original offence. Courts have imposed a residence (at home) requirement (where the offender was already living at home) where no requirement was recommended in a pre-sentence report, just so that they could suspend sentence. By CJA 2003, s.206(3) before making a suspended sentence order containing a residence requirement, the court must consider the home surroundings of the offender.

A magistrates' court dealing with two or more either-way offences, which wished to suspend a custodial sentence that totalled between 6 and 12 months, would need to commit the offender to the Crown Court to be sentenced. The court should first decide if a custodial sentence is inevitable. If it is, the court should decide on the appropriate length of the sentence. Only then should the court consider whether the sentence can be suspended.

When considering whether to recommend this disposal, bear in mind that if it is breached, the court that deals with the breach must activate the sentence (for the same or for a lesser term) unless the court is of the opinion that it would be unjust to do so, in view of, for example, the offender completing the requirements imposed or the nature and circumstances of the new offence. Then the court must extend the operational period or impose more stringent requirements and give reasons for adopting that course.

The Sentencing Guidelines Council's guideline, *New Sentences: Criminal Justice Act 2003*, states that the operational period for a suspended sentence should reflect the length of the sentence:

Magistrates' court	Suspended sentence 6 months	Operational period 12 months
Crown Court	Suspended sentence 12 months	Operational period 18 months

Time on remand

New Sentences: Criminal Justice Act 2003 states that the court should seek to give credit for time spent on remand in custody in all permitted cases. When announcing sentence, it should be made clear whether or not credit for time on remand has been given. The credit must be given unless the matter was first raised with you or would be unlawful.

Secondary penalties

These include:

(a) compensation (which can be a sentence in its own right);

(b) disqualification (from driving or company directorship or working with children). Always discuss attendance at a drink drive rehabilitation course. It reduces the disqualification and can lead to a reduced insurance premium on regaining the licence;

(c) exclusion/banning (banning orders in relation to association football/ exclusion from public houses);

(d) deprivation;

(e) forfeiture;

(f) restitution;

(g) confiscation;

(h) costs;

(i) deportation recommendation;

(j) restraining order;

(k) reparation order;

(l) ASBO on conviction;

(m) sexual offences prevention order;

(n) travel restrictions.

10.6   PREPARATION

Consider with your client, as appropriate, the obtaining of references, medical or pre-sentence reports; if it is an endorsable offence, inform your client that both parts of his driving licence will be required at court.

Pre-sentence reports

Advise your client of the seriousness of the meetings with probation officers or members of the youth offending team. Comments made to them, such as a lack of remorse or understanding of the seriousness of his actions, or admissions to uncharged offences, may be used in evidence and can be critical in supporting a finding of dangerousness or the need for ancillary orders.

Witness to character

Consider obtaining a letter of reference from your client's school, youth club, work or elsewhere. For a character witness whom you may call to give evidence at court obtain details as follows:

(a)   name and address;
(b)   occupation, employment, positions of responsibility, qualifications;
(c)   relationship to client: personal, employment, other, and how long/how well known;
(d)   opinion of client's character and trustworthiness;
(e)   opinion as to effect on client of offence, court hearings and potential penalty;
(f)   practical offer of help or employment.

Before calling a character witness, ensure he is aware of the precise charges; the defendant's previous convictions; the nature of the prosecution case; the nature of the defendant's account; and the potential sentence.

An unrealistic or overprotective character witness will not be persuasive.

Make a note of the availability of a character witness on the file [73.2].

Experts

Consider obtaining medical or other experts' reports you need for your mitigation with such authorisation to incur the expenditure as you consider appropriate. This may avoid causing unnecessary adjournments for the court to order a report and you will retain control of the report.

Tapes of interviews

It may not be necessary to listen to the tape in the case of an unequivocal guilty plea in a straightforward case where the short descriptive note of interview accords with the client's instructions. In all other cases it may prove beneficial to listen to a tape to check the accuracy of the prosecution's records and to identify further mitigating factors. If your client is mentally disordered or of poor understanding, you should routinely listen before considering the plea.

See **Chapter 11** for further advice about listening to tape recordings of police interviews with defendants.

NOTES

1. *R.* v. *Kidd, Canavan and Shaw* [1997] Crim LR 766. While the Domestic Violence, Crime and Victims Act 2004, s.17 allows for some charges to be tried in the Crown Court by judge alone, following conviction on specimen charges by a jury, the law on sentencing is unchanged.
2. However, other 'information' may be used by the court to assess dangerousness upon conviction of a specified or serious specified offence (see *R.* v. *Considine*; *R.* v. *Davis* [2007] Crim LR 824).
3. The Sentencing Guidelines Council guidelines, *Reduction in Sentence for a Guilty Plea*; *Overarching Principles: Seriousness* and *New Sentences: Criminal Justice Act 2003*; and the Sentencing Guidelines Council's *Guideline Judgments Case Compendium* containing guideline decisions of the Court of Appeal.
4. Criminal Justice Act 2003 (Sentencing) (Transitory Provisions) Order 2005, SI 2005/643.

CHAPTER 11

Preparing for trial: investigating the prosecution case

Objectives of this chapter

- To emphasise the importance of the defence proactively investigating the prosecution case
- To describe the different types of information that should be obtained
- To list the unused material that may be available to help prepare the defence case

---

Throughout this chapter references in square brackets are to the LSC Transaction Criteria.

11.1 THE NEED FOR TIMELY PREPARATION

Preparation of a criminal case should begin in the police station and proceed without undue delay. You should obtain material from the prosecution, or defence evidence, without waiting for the mode of trial hearing or entry of a not guilty plea.

In particular:

1. Obtain, listen to (and in video areas, watch) tapes of interview.
2. Obtain and consider custody records.
3. Consider the need for a defence statement and begin work on it.
4. Consider the need for supporting evidence such as videos, which may be 'wiped' if not obtained early. You may need, with your client's authority, to bring such material to the attention of the police.
5. Consider the need to trace and interview witnesses.
6. Consider the need to consult experts.

11.2 TESTING THE PROSECUTION CASE

Testing the evidence

The first stage of preparation for trial is to test the prosecution case thoroughly.

To do so, you will first wish to ensure that there has been full and sufficient disclosure – information about unused material is given by the police to the prosecution on the MG6 series of forms. If you are seeking to cast doubt upon the prosecution's case and/or build an alternative case theory, you will need:

(a)   all evidence on which the prosecution relies;[1]
(b)   all tape recordings of interviews with the defendant, co-defendant and other witnesses (some of these may be unused material);
(c)   all relevant custody records;
(d)   all relevant charge sheets;
(e)   disclosure schedules and appropriate disclosure.

The police investigation

Do not assume that the police investigation is thorough or complete. *Active Defence* gives advice on:

- the manner of the police investigation;
- what prevents effective and ethical investigation by the police;
- forensic investigation on behalf of the police: theory and practice;
- how the police investigation is recorded.

Investigating material that has been disclosed to you

Active Defence gives advice on:

- identifying problematic evidence;
- spotting missing evidence;
- analysing prosecution witness statements;
- analysing antecedents to prosecution witness statements;
- analysing tape recordings of PACE interviews;
- analysing video recordings of witness interviews;
- analysing contemporaneous notes;
- analysing written records of tape-recorded interviews.

Tape recordings

The Law Society has issued guidance on listening to tape recordings of police interviews with defendants.

It is guidance only, however, and your decision whether it is reasonable to listen to a tape recording of an interview calls in each case for the exercise of professional judgement based on the facts known to you at the time that decision is made. You should listen to the tape recording if, after considering the guidance and any other relevant factors, you remain in doubt about whether or not to do so, but it will usually be advisable to record in writing why it was necessary to listen to the tape recording in those particular circumstances.

Applications to the police for tapes of interviews should be made expeditiously to avoid delay (they should be provided as part of advance disclosure).

If there is a delay in a record of interview being made available enquiries should be made as to when the record will be received by the solicitor. If, as a result of those enquiries or in the absence of a meaningful reply, the solicitor believes that the record will not be received in time to prepare the case properly and the solicitor has a tape of the interview, the solicitor will have to listen to the tape instead.

A solicitor attending a police station should take as full a note as possible of a tape-recorded interview. However, these interviews often take place at a speed which makes it difficult for a solicitor to take a comprehensive note. There may be facilities available for providing copies of tapes on the spot following charge. In stations where these do not exist, police are encouraged to make 'every effort' to ensure that a copy of the tape is forwarded to the defendant's solicitor as soon as possible. Home Office Circular 24/98 confirms that there is nothing to prevent a solicitor from making his own audio recording of the interview with the suspect. The request to do this may only be refused if there are individual circumstances specific to the case that may prejudice the course of the investigation.

A solicitor's main aim should be to ensure that the interview is conducted fairly. But the solicitor should also be able to note at the time, or if necessary, immediately after the interview:

- whether the client exercised his right of silence and, if so, whether the client remained entirely silent or not;
- whether there were any problems of 'tone', timing, phrasing, intonation or other matters that might affect the interpretation of the interview; and
- whether there were any points of mitigation.

If a solicitor was present during the interview, when deciding whether it is necessary to listen to all or part of a tape recording of the interview the solicitor should first (so far as practicable) consider any notes of the interview that are available and the extent to which they accord with the formal record of interview.

The police written record of taped interview (ROTI) is a summary intended to be a balanced account of the interview including points in mitigation and/or defence made by the suspect. Research published in 1992 and 1995[2] showed that little reliance could then be placed on these written records. Solicitors should use their present experience of written records (ROTIs and SDNs) in deciding to what extent to rely on them.

If the solicitor doubts the reliability of these types of written record it will be necessary to listen to the tape recording in the following circumstances.

1. When the client:

   (a) instructed the solicitor to do so; or
   (b) is unable to confirm the accuracy of the contents of the summary; or
   (c) is a juvenile or a mentally disordered or mentally handicapped person.

2. If the client is uncertain about how to plead or intends to plead not guilty:

   (a) where the written record is materially disputed and resolution of the dispute is relevant to the conduct of the case;
   (b) where the client complains of oppression or circumstances tending to create unreliability in the confessions made by the client;
   (c) where the solicitor is informed by the client, or the solicitor present at the interview, that the 'tone', timing, phrasing or intonation in the interview, as would be disclosed by the tape recording, is relevant to the conduct of the defence and is not apparent from the written record;
   (d) where the Crown Prosecution Service and/or prosecuting counsel has listened to the tape in the course of preparing the prosecution case.

3. In the case of a guilty plea where the solicitor has reason to believe that there may be mitigating factors that are not revealed in the written record of the interview or to identify the degree of assurance given by the defendant to the police.

The Lord Chancellor's Department (as it then was) was consulted about this guidance and was content with it.

Note that a written record is not intended to be a complete record of what was said in the interview and it will at times be necessary for the solicitor to prepare a transcript of part or all of the interview.

Some police stations have facilities for videotaping of interviews under caution; if it is necessary to listen to such a tape (an audio record will be kept) you should also consider the need to watch it.

Custody records

You have the right to receive you own client's custody record and an early request should be made to the relevant Criminal Justice Unit [64.3]. Other connected custody records should appear on the schedule of unused material.

The custody record will show:

- whether your client attended the police station voluntarily or under arrest;
- whether your client requested and received legal advice and who the former adviser was;
- whether your client was interviewed or questioned.

Close scrutiny of the custody record may reveal points of significance both in what is recorded and in what is omitted. It should, therefore, be a golden rule of defence preparation that your client's custody record is obtained as soon as possible after you have been instructed.

The custody record will reflect the state of the investigation shortly after your client's arrival at the police station. Check the information recorded therein against the facts alleged by the police witnesses, paying particular attention to the following:

1. **Reason for arrest.** Does the reason for arrest bear a proper relation to the offence charged at the conclusion of your client's detention?
2. **Request for legal advice.** Is this section completed in accordance with your client's instructions? If the suspect requested legal advice and then changed his mind, is the inspector's agreement to the interview proceeding in these circumstances recorded in the custody record together with an indication of the reasons for the change of mind?
3. **Notification to named person.** Was this requested? If so, what genuine efforts were made to comply with it? Are there entries showing attempts by the officer to get in touch?
4. **Time of arrest and arrival at station.** Check that these agree with the times given in the officers' statements.
5. Check that **reviews and detention periods** comply with PACE and reasons for detention.
6. **Property.** This may help or hinder you, and needs careful scrutiny:

   (a) Did your client appreciate what he was signing?
   (b) The apparent absence of certain items may help your client.
   (c) The presence of some items might assist.

7. **The log.** The subsequent page(s) constitutes the 'diary' of a prisoner and should be looked at word for word. Compare the chronology of events in the log with that stated by the officers.
8. **Consider the 'logic' of the enquiry.** What would you have expected the officer to have done; when would they have done it? Then ask yourself which entries in the record do not ring true or show up the statements to

be unreliable. Pay particular attention to the times and chronology recorded.

9. **Make sure that you obtain a copy of the original record rather than typed highlights or a duplicate.** Ask for a copy of the original handwritten record and a copy of any computer generated version.

Charge sheet

You should obtain from your own client his charge sheet; other connected charge sheets should appear on the schedule of unused material.

11.3 DISCLOSURE

Early disclosure

An evidential report to a prosecutor for a charging decision must contain any unused material which satisfies the disclosure test. An expedited report must include a consideration of whether there is unused material which affects the strength of the prosecution case. These duties arise outside CPIA 1996 (see CPS *Disclosure Manual*, Chapters 2 and 3).

The CPS must consider from the early stages of a case whether any unused material should be disclosed to the defence outside the CPIA 1996 scheme. In *R. v. DPP, ex p. Lee* [1999] 2 All ER 737, QBD, Kennedy LJ stated:

The prosecutor must always be alive to the need to make advance disclosure of material of which he is aware (either from his own consideration of the papers or because his attention has been drawn to it by the defence) and which he, as a responsible prosecutor, recognises should be disclosed at an earlier stage. Examples canvassed before us were:

(a)   previous convictions of a complainant or deceased if that information could reasonably be expected to assist the defence when applying for bail;

(b)   material which might enable a defendant to make a pre-committal application to stay the proceedings as an abuse of process;

(c)   material which will enable the defendant to submit that he should only be committed for trial on a lesser charge, or perhaps that he should not be committed for trial at all;

(d)   material which will enable the defendant and his legal advisers to make preparations for trial which may be significantly less effective if disclosure is delayed (e.g. names of eye witnesses who the prosecution do not intend to use);

(e)   material that is relevant to sentence.

Even before committal a responsible prosecutor should be asking himself what, if any, immediate disclosure justice and fairness requires him to make in the particular circumstances of the case. Very often the answer will be none, and rarely if at all should the prosecutor's answer to that continuing piece of self-examination be the subject matter of dispute in this court.

The examples above are reproduced in the CPS *Disclosure Manual*, Chapter 2, para.7.

Initial disclosure

Under CPIA 1996, on the defendant pleading not guilty in the magistrates' court or being committed to the Crown Court for trial, the prosecutor is required to disclose to the accused previously undisclosed material, which satisfies the disclosure test. CPIA 1996, s.3(1) (as amended) provides:

(1) The prosecutor must –

(a) disclose to the accused any prosecution material which has not previously been disclosed to the accused and which might reasonably be considered capable of undermining the case for the prosecution against the accused or of assisting the case for the accused.

The test is an objective one. The CPS *Disclosure Manual*, Chapter 11, para.4 provides:

Prosecution material is defined in the Act [CPIA 1996] in section 3(2) and is material which is in the prosecutor's possession, and came into his possession in connection with the case for the prosecution against the accused, or which the prosecutor has inspected under the provisions of the Code in connection with the case against the accused.

If the accused discloses a defence to the police during the investigation, the prosecutor should clearly respond by giving any material that assists that defence when applying the disclosure test. The prosecution case may be undermined as a result of a particular defence which the defendant may or may not run and the mere fact that material is in the possession of the prosecution which raises a new issue in the case that may assist the defence is sufficient to fulfil the test 'might undermine' (Attorney General's Guidelines on Disclosure April 2005; see **Appendix 1** for website link).

The CPS *Disclosure Manual*, Chapter 12, para.11 states: 'if the material satisfies the disclosure test, it should be disclosed even though it suggests a defence inconsistent with or alternative to one already advanced by the accused.'

In addition, the Attorney General's Guidelines on Disclosure, paras 10–14 (see **Appendix 1** for website link) define material for primary disclosure as follows:

10. Generally, material which can reasonably be considered capable of undermining the case against the accused or asssisting the defence case will include anything that tends to show a fact inconsistent with the elements of the case that must be proved by the prosecution. Material can fulfil the disclosure test:

a. by the use made of it in cross-examination; or

129

    b.   by its capacity to suggest any potential submissions that could lead to:

        i.   the exclusion of evidence; or

        ii.   a stay of proceedings; or

        iii. a court or tribunal finding that any public authority had acted incompatibly with the defendant's rights under the ECHR, or

    c.   by its capacity to suggest an explanation or partial explanation of the accused's actions.

11.   In deciding what material may fall to be disclosed under paragraph 10, especially (b)(ii), prosecutors must consider whether disclosure is required in order for a proper application to be made. The purpose of this paragraph is not to allow enquiries to support speculative arguments or for the manufacture of defences.

12.   Examples of material that might reasonably be considered capable of undermining the prosecution case or of assisting the case for the accused are:

        i.   Any material casting doubt upon the accuracy of any prosecution evidence.

        ii.   Any material which may point to another person, whether charged or not (including a co-accused) having involvement in the commission of the offence.

        iii. Any material which may cast doubt upon the reliability of a confession.

        iv. Any material that might go to the credibility of a prosecution witness.

        v.   Any material that might support a defence that is either raised by the defence or apparent from the prosecution papers.

        vi. Any material which may have a bearing on the admissibility of any prosecution evidence.

The CPS *Disclosure Manual*, Chapter 12, para.11 adds the following to the list:

* any material that might assist the accused to cross-examine prosecution witnesses as to credit and/or to substance;
* any material that might enable the accused to call evidence or advance a line of enquiry or argument;
* any material that might explain or mitigate the accused's actions.

The CPS *Disclosure Manual*, Chapter 12, para.14 lists material which 'experience suggests has the potential to satisfy the disclosure test'. This list includes the following items that were included in an earlier edition of the Attorney General's Guidelines on Disclosure but removed from the revised Guidelines:

* those recorded scientific or scenes of crime findings retained by the investigator which relate to the accused, and are linked to the point at issue, and have not been previously disclosed;
* where identification is or may be in issue, all previous descriptions of suspects, however recorded, together with all records of identification procedures in respect of the offence(s) and photographs of the accused taken by the investigator around the time of his arrest;

- information that any prosecution witness has received, has been promised or has requested any payment or reward in connection with the case;
- plans of crime scenes or video recordings made by investigators of crime scenes;
- names, within the knowledge of investigators, of individuals who may have relevant information and whom investigators do not intend to interview;
- records which the investigator has made of information which may be relevant, provided by any individual (such information would include, but not be limited to, records of conversation and interviews with any such person).

Paragraph 14 adds:

- Disclosure of video recordings or scientific findings by means of supplying copies may well involve delay or otherwise not be practicable or desirable, in which case the investigator should make reasonable arrangements for the video recordings or scientific findings to be viewed by the defence.
- Experience suggests that any material which relates to the accused's mental or physical health, intellectual capacity, or to any ill treatment which the accused may have suffered when in the investigator's custody is likely to have the potential for casting doubt on the reliability of an accused's purported confession, and prosecutors should pay particular attention to any such material in the possession of the prosecution.
- It is not necessary, prior to the receipt of a defence statement, to speculate about every possible defence or submission that may be raised. Nevertheless, where a distinct explanation has been put forward by the accused, or is apparent from the circumstances of the case, it must be considered in the context of assessing whether there is any material requiring disclosure. This consideration should take place at the earliest opportunity, and does not need to await the receipt of a defence statement.
- In deciding what material should be disclosed (at any stage in the proceedings) prosecutors must determine whether the material satisfies the disclosure test. Prosecutors should resolve any doubt they may have in favour of disclosure, unless the material is sensitive and to be placed before the court in a PII application.
- If material subsequently undermines the prosecution case, assists the accused or raises a fundamental question about the prosecution, the prosecutor will need to reassess the case in accordance with the Code for Crown Prosecutors, and decide after consulting with the police whether the case should continue.

In most cases it should be possible for the prosecutor to disclose all necessary material in the initial disclosure. The defence is usually known, and material that might assist a different defence from that falls to be disclosed then anyway. The case must be constantly reviewed by the prosecutor, so that any undermining material, or material that assists the defence that comes to light after the initial disclosure either as a result of following further reasonable lines of enquiry or reviewing the defence statement, is disclosed. As a consequence, defence practitioners must carefully consider initial disclosure as is made by the Crown. They must critically examine any statement that there is no initial disclosure to be made. They may wish to bring further lines of enquiry to the attention of the prosecution (for example the existence of undisclosed medical evidence at the police station).

A Fair Balance,[3] an evaluation of the operation of disclosure found that more than one-third of CPS respondents said that their area routinely disclosed crime reports, logs of messages and police officers' notebooks to the defence as initial disclosure.

The CPS *Disclosure Manual*, Chapter 12, para.11 states:

> . . . all previous convictions and/or cautions, regardless of age or type offence (except minor traffic type offences), recorded against a prosecution witness should be regarded as material that satisfies the disclosure test.

The schedule of non-sensitive material

This will be provided to the accused at the same time as initial disclosure.

Examine the schedule with care: consider which other items should appear on the list and be prepared to challenge their absence. Examples of matters that lawyers reported were not listed[4] include:

(a) telephone calls to the police from members of the public reporting the crime and messages between the police control room and individual officers describing the offence and the offender;
(b) statements made by witnesses whom the prosecution were not calling;
(c) previous drafts of witnesses' statements and notes of interviews with witnesses.

Identify the true nature of each item listed and consider how it might assist the defence. Be ready to give reasons for its disclosure in a specific request to the prosecution and ensure that the reasons are supported by the defence statement. Examples of matters that lawyers reported were not adequately described include:

(a) the contents of police officers' notebooks;
(b) the contents of statements of witnesses who were not being called by the prosecution;
(c) the contents of crime reports;
(d) the contents of incident report books.

Preparation of schedules generally

Unless otherwise stated, the following extracts are from the CPS *Disclosure Manual*.

Chapter 6 states:

1.   The disclosure officer is responsible for preparing the schedules and submitting them to the prosecutor. The schedules, signed and dated by the disclosure officer, should be submitted to the prosecutor with a full file.
2.   Where the disclosure officer is unsure whether an item is relevant to the investigation and should therefore be described on a schedule, the prosecutor should be consulted as soon as practicable.
3.   In some cases there may be advantages in starting the schedule(s) at an early stage. [. . .]
4.   [. . .] the items [will be listed] into two schedules for the prosecutor describing:

     • any non-sensitive unused material (MG6C)
     • any sensitive unused material (MG6D)

5.   [. . .]
6.   Any comments, observations or explanations regarding the contents of the schedules should be made on the MG6, which should accompany the submission of the MG6C and MG6D.
7.   The disclosure officer must also indicate on the MG6 whether the investigation started on or after 4 April 2005. This will tell the prosecutor which [CJA 2003] provisions to apply in disclosing material to the accused [. . .]. It will also inform the prosecutor of what obligations will apply to the accused.
8.   All items of material relevant to the investigation must be described on one of the above schedules for the prosecutor.

Non-sensitive material

Chapter 7 covers non-sensitive material as follows:

1.   Non-sensitive unused material should be described on the MG6C. This form will be disclosed to the defence.
2.   In the description column of every schedule, each item should be individually described and consecutively numbered. Where continuation sheets are used or additional schedules sent in later submissions, item numbering must be consecutive to all items on earlier schedules.
3.   Every description in non-sensitive schedules should be detailed, clear and accurate. Each should include a summary of the item's contents to allow the prosecutor to make an informed decision on whether it could satisfy the disclosure test. For example, it is not sufficient merely to refer to a document by way of a form number or function which may be meaningless outside the Police Service.
4.   In cases where there are many items of a similar or repetitive nature (messages for example) it is permissible to describe them by quantity and generic title. However, inappropriate use of generic listing is likely to lead to requests from the prosecutor and the defence to see the items. [. . .]

5. When items are described by generic titles or quantities, the disclosure officer must ensure that items which might meet the disclosure test are also described individually.

6. The disclosure officer should keep a copy of the schedules that are sent to the prosecutor, in case there are any queries that need to be resolved. A copy will also assist the disclosure officer to keep track of the items listed, should the schedules need to be updated.

7. Sometimes documents that fall to be disclosed under the Act [CPIA 1996] because they contain material that satisfies the disclosure test may contain a mixture of sensitive and non-sensitive material. For example, a prosecution witness's address or personal telephone number may appear on an item that is otherwise entirely non-sensitive.

8. In these cases there may be no objection to the sensitive part being permanently blocked out on the copy document which is to be sent to the prosecutor. The original should not be marked in any way. The document should be described on the MG6C. (The unedited version should not be described on the MG6D, but made available to the prosecutor for inspection if required.) The prosecutor should be informed of the nature of the edited material, if not obvious, on the MG6. The disclosure officer should edit out issues of sensitivity whenever material is routinely revealed.

9. The responsibility to edit rests with the police but the prosecutor should be consulted where editing or separating is other than straightforward.

The contents of the MG6E

Chapter 10 provides as follows:

1. The disclosure officer should use the MG6E to bring to the prosecutor's attention any material that could reasonably be considered capable of undermining the prosecution case against the accused or of assisting the case for the accused. This also applies to sensitive material. Examples include:

   • records of previous convictions and cautions for prosecution witnesses
   • any other information which casts doubt on the reliability of a prosecution witness or on the accuracy of any prosecution evidence
   • any motives for the making of false allegations by a prosecution witness
   • any material which may have a bearing on the admissibility of any prosecution evidence
   • the fact that a witness has sought, been offered or received a reward
   • any material that might go to the credibility of a prosecution witness
   • any information which may cast doubt on the reliability of a confession. Any item which relates to the accused's mental or physical health, his intellectual capacity, or to any ill-treatment which the accused may have suffered when in the investigators custody is likely to have the potential for casting doubt on the reliability of a purported confession
   • information that a person other than the accused was or might have been responsible or which points to another person whether charged or not (including a co-accused) having involvement in the commission of the offence.

2. The disclosure officer should also explain on form MG6E (by referring to the relevant item's number on the schedule) why he or she has come to that view.

The MG6C itself should not be marked or highlighted in any way, as it will be provided to the defence.

3. This will include anything that may weaken an essential part of the prosecution case. Any material that supports or is consistent with a defence put forward in interview or before charge or which is apparent from the prosecution papers should be supplied to the prosecutor. It also includes anything that points away from the accused, such as information about a possible alibi. [. . .] Items of material viewed in isolation may not satisfy the test, however several items together can have that effect.

4. Such material should be brought to the prosecutor's attention regardless of any views about the accuracy or truth of the information, although where appropriate the disclosure officer may express a reasoned opinion on whether in fact the prosecutor should disclose it.

5. A wide interpretation should be given when identifying material that might satisfy the disclosure test. [. . .] The disclosure officer should consult with the prosecutor where necessary to help identify material that may require disclosure, and must specifically draw material to the attention of the prosecutor where the disclosure officer has any doubt as to whether it might satisfy the disclosure test.

[. . .]

8. [C]opies of the crime report and the log of messages should be routinely copied to the prosecutor in every case in which a full file is provided. (These documents are known in different police forces by different names, for example the incident record report or CAD for the log of messages).

9. Copies of the crime report and log of messages should be edited (if necessary) by the police before they are sent to the prosecutor. If it is impossible to edit any sensitive parts of the material, then it should be listed on the MG6D and be sent to the prosecutor with that schedule.

10. This requirement routinely to reveal the crime report and the log of messages does not prejudice any other locally agreed arrangements between the police and the CPS that allow for the similar treatment of other additional categories or types of document.

[. . .]

18. Disclosure officers must deal expeditiously with requests by the prosecutor for further information on material which may lead to it being disclosed.

19. A prosecutor may ask to inspect material, or request a copy of material where one has not been sent. The disclosure officer is responsible for arranging this. Material should be copied to the prosecutor on request unless it is too sensitive or too bulky, or can only be inspected. This applies to disclosure throughout the life of the case.

20. After considering the schedule(s), the prosecutor will endorse them with the decisions as to whether each item described will be disclosed to the defence. A copy of the endorsed schedule(s) should be sent to the disclosure officer.

Sensitive schedules

Chapter 8 provides as follows:

Assessment of sensitivity and schedule preparation

1. This schedule should be used to reveal to the prosecutor the existence of unused material which the disclosure officer believes should be withheld from

135

the defence because it is not in the public interest to disclose it. However, such material must be revealed to the prosecutor.

2. The disclosure officer must describe on the MG6D any material the disclosure of which he or she believes would give rise to **a real risk of serious prejudice to an important public interest** and the reason for that belief. This form will not be disclosed to the defence.

3. In those cases where there is no sensitive unused material, the disclosure officer should endorse and sign an MG6D to this effect and should submit this together with the MG6C and MG6E.

4. To assist the officer in considering the examples given in the Code paragraph 6.12, reference should be made to the following associated public interests:

    - the ability of the security and intelligence agencies to protect the safety of the UK
    - the willingness of foreign sources to continue to co-operate with UK security and intelligence agencies, and law enforcement agencies
    - the willingness of citizens, agencies, commercial institutions, communications service providers etc to give information to the authorities in circumstances where there may be some legitimate expectation of confidentiality (e.g. Crimestoppers material)
    - the public confidence that proper measures will be taken to protect witnesses from intimidation, harassment and being suborned
    - the safety of those who comply with their statutory obligation to report suspicious financial activity (whilst they are under a statutory obligation and therefore do not give suspicious activity reports in confidence, their safety is a consideration to be taken into account in disclosure decisions)
    - national (not individual or company) economic interests
    - the ability of the law enforcement agencies to fight crime by the use of covert human intelligence sources, undercover operations, covert surveillance, etc
    - the protection of secret methods of detecting and fighting crime
    - the freedom of investigators and prosecutors to exchange views frankly about casework.

5. These lists are not check-lists. Other items not listed there may be sensitive and not in the public interest to disclose, but equally, items listed there may not cause any harm to the public interest if disclosed. The examples are not 'classes' of material. Each item must be considered independently before it is included in the sensitive schedule and before any claim for public interest immunity from disclosure is made.

6. Some items by their very nature will reveal why disclosure should be withheld. Others require more explanation. [. . .] Both the '*Description of item*' and the '*Reasons for sensitivity*' sections must contain sufficient information to enable the prosecutor to make an informed decision as to whether or not the material itself should be viewed. Schedules containing insufficient information will be returned by the prosecutor. If there is any doubt about the sensitivity of the material, the prosecutor should be consulted.

7. In order to make a proper assessment of the material which is said to be sensitive, the prosecutor will need to be fully informed of its contents or see the material or part of it. In cases where it is not possible to describe the nature of the material in sufficient detail to enable the prosecutor to determine whether or not it should be viewed, it will be for the disclosure officer to make arrangements with the prosecutor to view the material with an appropriate level of physical and personal security.

Amending the schedules

Chapter 10 provides as follows:

21. On occasions it may be necessary to amend the schedules. When the schedules are first submitted with a full file, the disclosure officer may not know exactly what material the prosecutor intends to use as part of the prosecution case. The prosecutor may create unused material by extracting statements or documents from the evidence bundle, in which case the prosecutor may disclose material that satisfies the disclosure test directly to the defence without waiting for the disclosure officer to amend the schedule. However where this is done, the prosecutor should advise the officer accordingly. Police officers should ensure that obviously non-evidential material is not included in the evidence bundle.
22. The prosecutor is required to advise the disclosure officer of

    • items described on the MG6C that should properly be on the MG6D and vice versa
    • any apparent omissions or amendments required
    • insufficient or unclear descriptions of items
    • a failure to provide schedules at all.

    The disclosure officer must forthwith take all necessary remedial action and provide properly completed schedules to the prosecutor. Failure to do so may result in the matter being raised with a senior officer.
23. The Code places the responsibility for creating the schedules and keeping them accurate and up to date on the disclosure officer. Consequently, the prosecutor should not amend schedules. In these circumstances the prosecutor should inform the disclosure officer of the changes required, and return the schedules for amendment where appropriate.
24. The disclosure officer should effect the amendments promptly and return the amended or fresh schedules to the prosecutor as soon as possible with a further MG6E as appropriate.

Forensic science index

Chapter 23 provides as follows:

FSP actions: preparation of the index

23. The FSP [forensic science provider] should provide to the police an index of all material in their possession. When the index is prepared, it will not necessarily be known what material is to be used as part of the prosecution case, and which will remain unused. Therefore the index should take the form of a list describing the material held by the FSP.
24. The scientific reporting officer should prepare the index and submit this to the police investigator when the report or statement is supplied in all cases except where an analyst's certificate is supplied in drink-drive cases.
25. All material should be individually listed on the index and described clearly and accurately so as to allow an informed decision on disclosure. (Where there are many documents or items of a similar type or repetitive nature, these may be described by quantity and a generic title. But, inappropriate use

of generic listing may result in requests from the CPS or defence to see the items, with consequent delay and wasting of resources).

26. Any single item which is known to be of particular significance should be separately listed.

27. If not mentioned in the report or statement, the reporting officer should indicate on the index any material that satisfies the disclosure test, so far as this can [be] assessed or is known. Wherever practicable, copies of material that satisfies the test should be sent to the police with the index.

28. The disclosure officer's duty of revelation to the prosecutor and the prosecutor's duty of disclosure to the defence are continuing obligations. Therefore the index must be kept up to date by the FSP. Where new material comes to light or is generated or received after the initial preparation and submission of the index, a supplementary index should be supplied to the police.

Police actions: dealing with the forensic index

29. Where a police officer receives an index from the FSP, this must be retained, together with any other report, statement or document supplied. Any relevant oral information received by the investigator, or by the disclosure officer relating to material held by the FSP should be recorded and retained in accordance with the Code.

30. Upon submission of a full file, the disclosure officer should check the material listed on the forensic index. The index should list all material retained in the possession of the FSP. The disclosure officer should list the index itself on the MG6C. The index may be described generically; for example: 'Forensic Science Service Index – compiled 21 January 05 – list of all material in possession of FSS'.

31. Where the disclosure officer believes that any of the material appearing on the index, satisfies the disclosure test the item should be listed on form MG6E. The disclosure officer should consult the reporting officer where he or she is in any doubt.

32. The schedules, the index and any undermining or assisting material should be sent to the CPS with the full file in the usual way in accordance with the instructions in this manual.

33. Where the prosecutor indicates that unused material in the possession of FSP requires disclosure, the disclosure officer should send a copy of the index endorsed with the prosecutor's decision to the FSP.

11.4 PROSECUTOR REVIEWS SCHEDULES

Receipt of schedules and review

Chapter 11, para.2 provides as follows:

In order to carry out the duties set out in the Act [CPIA 1996], the prosecutor will need to consider the schedules of unused material and copies of any items supplied by the police to see if the disclosure test is satisfied. [. . .]

If the schedule of unused material fails to describe the contents of documents adequately, they should be closely examined (by the CPS) and appropriate action taken. But *A Fair Balance* (see note 3) found that 66 per cent of CPS respondents said that their lawyers could not review schedules accurately in the time available.

The Code of Practice issued under CPIA 1996, Part II requires (para.6.9) that: 'The description of each item should make clear the nature of the item and should contain sufficient detail to enable the prosecutor to decide whether he needs to inspect the material before deciding whether or not it should be disclosed.' *A Fair Balance* found that the descriptions of items on schedules were 'poor' in 78 per cent of volume crime cases studied and 73 per cent of all cases studied.

The CPS *Disclosure Manual*, Chapter 11, continues:

7. [. . .] The prosecutor should carry out a review of the schedules and the material received in accordance with the procedures set out below.
8. The prosecutor should examine the schedules carefully to check for possible omissions from them. If there are any omissions, the prosecutor should ask the disclosure officer to provide a continuation schedule, but should not delay disclosure. Where there are apparent errors on the schedules, the prosecutor should seek further details from the disclosure officer, and return the schedules for correction. If, following this, the prosecutor remains dissatisfied with the quality or content of the schedules, the matter must be raised with a senior officer and persisted with if necessary.
9. The date of receipt of the schedules and any accompanying material must be recorded on the disclosure record sheet.

Chapter 12 adds:

2. Where the prosecutor has reason to believe that the disclosure officer has not inspected, viewed or listened to material, a request that this be done should be made.
3. Additionally, where the prosecutor believes there are further reasonable and relevant lines of inquiry to pursue, the officer in charge of the investigation should be told as soon as possible.

Chapter 11 continues:

12. Where the prosecutor considers that material that has been described on the form MG6D is not in fact sensitive and should be described on the form MG6C, the disclosure officer must be consulted to ensure that the matter is resolved.
13. The prosecutor should always inspect the material, whether sensitive or non-sensitive where:
    • it satisfies the disclosure test
    • the description (or the reasons given as to its sensitivity) remain inadequate despite requests for clarification
    • the prosecutor is unsure if the material satisfies the disclosure test.

14. A record should be made of all decisions, enquiries or requests and the date upon which they are made, relating to:
    - the disclosure of material to the defence
    - withholding material from the defence
    - the inspection of material
    - the transcribing or recording of information into a suitable form.

This information should be noted on the disclosure record sheet. In addition, the disclosure record sheet should be used to record all actions and events that occur in the discharge of prosecution disclosure responsibilities.

[. . .]

Reviewing sensitive material

17. Where the prosecutor considers that the sensitive material should be disclosed to the defence because it satisfies the disclosure test, the police (or any person having an interest in the material) should be consulted before any final conclusions are reached.
18. Where the prosecutor determines that an application to the court is necessary, consultation with the police must take place to establish the proper basis for the application [. . .].
19. Material may be edited, summarised or formally admitted without compromising its sensitivity. Police and prosecutors should consider at an early stage whether this is possible.
20. However, if the prosecutor in editing, summarising or formally admitting, holds back any material that satisfies the test, an application to the court should be made and the approval of the court obtained for any such partial disclosure.
21. If any third party, such as social services or the prison service, has an interest in the sensitive material, the prosecutor must ensure that the third party is consulted by the police before a final decision is made.
22. [. . .]
23. There should be consultation between the prosecutor and the prosecution advocate where there is any question of an application being made to the court to withhold unused material. A record of that consultation should be made, and a note of its location cross-referenced on the disclosure record sheet. [. . .]
24. There will always be a need to consult regarding sensitive material unless the prosecutor is satisfied on the basis of the information provided on the schedule that the material clearly could not satisfy the test for disclosure. Special considerations will apply to the handling of highly sensitive material [. . .].
25. [. . .] Notes of decisions and reasons should be endorsed on the MG6D, or if necessary, on a continuation sheet. Notes of discussions about sensitive material or of PII applications should be kept with the MG6D and the material itself [. . .].

The prosecutor must obtain the court's permission to withhold relevant but sensitive material. This will take place by a procedure set out in CPR Part 25. The decision to allow non-disclosure must be kept under review. Be ready to bring to the court's attention any change of circumstance.

The CPS *Disclosure Manual* continues, at Chapter 15:

9. Where an accused's solicitor purports to give a defence statement on behalf of the accused, the statement shall, unless the contrary is proved, be deemed to be given with the authority of the accused.

Review of defence statements

10. Prosecutors should be open, alert and responsive to requests for disclosure of material where the request is supported by a comprehensive defence statement. [. . .]
11. Prosecutors should also be proactive in identifying inadequate defence statements. [. . .]
12. Where there is no defence statement, or it is considered inadequate, the prosecutor should write to the defence [. . .] indicating that further disclosure may not take place or will be limited (as appropriate) and inviting them to specify or clarify the defence case. Where the defence fails to respond, or refuses to clarify the defence case, the prosecutor should consider raising the issue at a pre-trial hearing to invite the court to give a statutory warning under section 6E(2) of the Act.
13. However, section 6A does not mean that the defence is required to strengthen the prosecution case by providing evidence to fill any gaps. Where further details are provided late, and substantial additional costs are incurred (for example, where a trial has been adjourned or witnesses inconvenienced) an application for a wasted costs order against the accused should be considered in appropriate cases.

11.5   INVESTIGATING UNUSED MATERIAL

Active Defence gives advice about the unused material which is obtained as part of the police investigation, the information in that material which may be of assistance to the defence and how to formulate the request for secondary disclosure, linking it to the defence statement.

Examples of unused material which lawyers report (see note 4) has not been disclosed under CPIA 1996 include:

- police messages showing an account of the offence or description of the offender which contradicts that given by prosecution witnesses;
- police notebooks showing an initial complaint by a victim which is inconsistent with his later statement;
- crime report showing names and addresses of potential witnesses who were not interviewed by the police and that the victim initially gave a different description of the offender;
- a statement from a witness which is inconsistent with the victim's account;
- a statement from a witness which is inconsistent with that witness's later statement;
- previous convictions of the victim or a witness;

- a forensic report showing the detection of fingerprints which were not the defendant's.

A Fair Balance (see note 3) found that results of criminal record checks on prosecution witnesses were disclosed to the defence at the primary stage in 4 per cent of study cases; and that most forces relied on the integrity of officers with disciplinary findings to communicate this to the CPS either directly or through the complaints and discipline department.

Table 11.1 is a checklist of types of unused material that you may wish to request from the prosecution. Tick any item that is likely to support the defence set out in the defence statement. Find out if the prosecutor has inspected the item concerned.

Table 11.1 Checklist of unused material you may request from the prosecution

Checklist of types of unused material	✓	MG6(c) no. if referred to in police schedule	Has the prosecutor inspected it?
Operational information			
Request for a police response			
Deployment of police officers			
Requests and reports from deploying and deployed officers			
Circulation of reports and descriptions by officers			
Tasking of officers			
Crime report information			
Offence: finally recorded, legal description			
Complaint details: time, date, whether discovered by police, reporting officer, investigating officer			
Complainant details			
Details of the offence: time, date, location			
Description of suspect			
Vehicles seen			
Modus operandi			
Property – stolen and damaged			
Details of offenders			
Details of enquiries: enquiries at the scene: in the vicinity; actions: details of action, including all persons involved			
Details of all people spoken to by the police, including those who did not make a witness statement			

Table 11.1 *Continued*

Checklist of types of unused material	✓	MG6(c) no. if referred to in police schedule	Has the prosecutor inspected it?
House to house enquiries			
Pro forma questionnaires			
Key documentary material generated by police officers/civilian support staff			
Police officers' notebooks/incident report book			
Verbal exchanges with complainant/other witnesses			
Actions taken			
Suspect description			
Sketches made			
Custody records			
Witness statements			
Notes made/drafts/final versions			
CCTV film			
Forensic scientist/scene of crime officer			
Crime scene examination form			
List of items and contact trace material (CTM) collected/removed			
List of items and CTM submitted for testing (pro forma); not submitted for testing			
Fingerprints lifted/identified			
Photographs/video recordings/sketches			
Reports of work carried out by forensic scientists			
Medical examiner/police officer			
Samples taken			
Samples submitted for testing (pro forma); not submitted for testing			

11.6 ONGOING DUTY OF DISCLOSURE

Because of the single test, the majority of what should be disclosed should have been dealt with under the initial disclosure. The prosecutor is under a continuing duty to review what amounts to disclosable material. In theory, the continuing duty never ends. Look back at the wording of your defence statement and ensure that it supports your request for any of this material which has not been previously disclosed and which might reasonably be considered capable of undermining the case for the prosecution against the accused, or of assisting the case for the accused. Note, however, that *A Fair Balance* found that 78 per cent of prosecution barristers questioned said that they would allow the defence access to non-sensitive material, even if it fell outside the statutory criteria.

Examine the disclosure made and compare it with your initial request. Keep the matter under review. Be prepared to make an application to the court for further prosecution disclosure (CPIA 1996, s.8).

CPR 25.6 requires that an application under CPIA 1996, s.8(2) is made by notice in writing to the court officer with a copy to the prosecutor and must specify:

(a) the material to which the application relates;
(b) that the material has not already been dislosed to the accused;
(c) the reason why the material might be expected to assist the applicant's defence as disclosed by the defence statement given under CPIA 1996, ss.5 or 6.

The prosecutor shall give notice in writing to the court officer within 14 days of service of the notice that:

(a) he wishes to make representations to the court concerning the material to which the application relates and specifying the substance of those representations; or
(b) that he is willing to disclose that material.

The fact that a defence statement is late or inadequate should not preclude a s.8 application and a disclosure being made by the court (*DPP* v. *Wood and McGillicuddy* [2005] EWHC 2986, QBD).

11.7 THIRD PARTY DISCLOSURE

Consider what further evidence may be in the hands of people other than the investigators. Be prepared to approach them to see if they will consent to the inspection and/or disclosure of the relevant material.

In the event of refusal, you should consider other ways to obtain the evidence:

1. Consider inviting public authorities (such as local authorities) to consider their obligations to ensure a fair trial under ECHR, Art.6.
2. Consider inviting the police to carry out further investigations under the CPIA 1996 Code of Practice.[5]

   • There is a duty under the Code for an investigator to pursue all reasonable lines of enquiry, whether these point towards or away from a

144

suspect. What is reasonable will depend upon the circumstances of a particular case. Reasonable lines of enquiry may include enquiries as to the existence of relevant material in the possession of a third party. The investigator need not make speculative enquiries but frequently the existence of the material can be deduced from the circumstances.

- Once the investigator has examined the material, it must appear on a schedule of unused material provided that it is relevant. However, this will give notice of the issues to the prosecutor.

3. Consider the issue of a summons for the production of the material or evidence. In the magistrates' court the application is made under MCA 1980, s.97. In the Crown Court, it is made under the Criminal Procedure (Attendance of Witnesses) Act 1965, s.2 (as amended). The procedure for making such applications is set out in CPR 28.3. Such applications must be made as soon as possible. It is necessary in both cases to identify why the evidence or documents are likely to be material to the issues in the case. For this purpose clarify what are the issues in the case. The application must be in the stipulated form. Consider whether you wish documents to be produced at a time and place ahead of trial.

The principles relevant to the test of materiality are (*R.* v. *Reading Justices, ex p. Berkshire CC* [1996] 1 Cr App R 239, DC):

(a) the documents must be relevant to the issues arising in the criminal proceedings;
(b) the documents must be admissible as such in evidence;
(c) documents that are desired merely for the purpose of possible cross-examination are not admissible in evidence and, thus, are not material for the purpose of MCA 1980, s.97;
(d) whoever seeks production of documents must satisfy the court with some material that the documents are 'likely to be material' in the sense indicated, likelihood involving a real possibility, although not necessarily a probability;
(e) it is not sufficient if the applicant merely wants to find out whether or not the third party has such material documents.

The disclosure test under CPIA 1996, s.8 is broader than the specific admissibility of evidence test under MCA 1980, s.97.

Court proceedings can be adjourned so that the court's decision to issue a witness summons can be judicially reviewed (*R. (on the application of Cunliffe)* v. *West London Magistrates' Court* [2006] EWHC 2081).

Where the defence seeks disclosure of a complainant's medical records by witness summons, the complainant should be given notice of the application and have the right to make representations. It is not sufficient to delegate that to the NHS (*R. (on the application of B)* v. *Stafford Combined Court* [2006] EWHC 1645).

NOTES

1. In cases of ABH or common assault where the injury is minor, uncomplicated and temporary and has been described by the victim in a statement, illustrated by a photograph and supported, where possible, by a police officer's statement, the prosecution may not be required to obtain a medical report to prove injury. In cases of murder, manslaughter, infanticide and death by dangerous driving consider the need for a second post mortem.
2. J. Baldwin, *Preparing the Record of Taped Interviews*, RCCJ Research Study No.2 (HMSO, 1992). A. Hooke and J. Knox, *Preparing Records of Taped Interviews*, Research Findings No.22, Home Office Research and Statistics Department (HMSO, 1995).
3. J. Plotnikoff and R. Woolfson, *A Fair Balance*, Research Development and Statistics Department Occasional Paper No.76 (Home Office, 2001).
4. Surveys of solicitors' and barristers' experiences of how CPIA 1996 is working in practice were conducted by the Criminal Bar Association and the Law Society in 1999.
5. CPIA 1996 and its Code of Practice require the police, in conducting an investigation to pursue all reasonable lines of enquiry, whether they point towards or away from the suspect. What is reasonable in each case will depend upon the particular circumstances (CPIA 1996, s.23(1)(a) and Code of Practice, para.3.5).

CHAPTER 12

Preparing for trial: investigating the defence case

Objectives of this chapter

- To describe the different investigations that should be carried out by the defence (such as an inspection of the crime scene)
- To explain how expert evidence should be treated and used by the defence
- To describe the range of information that should be gathered from the defendant and the defence witnesses

---

Throughout this chapter references in square brackets are to the LSC Transaction Criteria.

12.1 INTERVIEWING YOUR CLIENT

State of case

Keep a 'state of case' pro forma in the file with a brief note of the advice that your client has been given about what to plead, where to be tried and the type of committal (see **Appendix 2, 2.1**). This will keep anyone looking at the file up to date about the stage that the instructions have reached. The advocate will also know what is expected to happen at the next hearing.

Make sure that the advocate also knows enough about the case at a remand hearing to supply details of the number of witnesses to be called, give a best estimate of the likely length of the trial and consider whether issues in the case can be identified and evidence agreed.

Not guilty statement

Allow enough time to take full instructions from your client for the trial. Do not take the statement in the presence of any potential witnesses.

Co-defendants

Take details of whether your client has co-defendants. If he has, record who they are, what they are pleading (if you know), and which firm of solicitors represents each of them. Ask what your client knew of them and their criminal records (if anything), and what their role was (if any) [35.2].

Taking the instructions

Relate the events in chronological order. Make sure that you start right at the beginning and set the scene before you deal with the incident itself.

Even if you are taking a statement for a trial, you will need to include full details of the defendant's personal history for use if he is convicted.

Detail

Try and get down what happened in plenty of detail. You should be able to follow the events, picturing them in your mind's eye. Take it step by step – one action at a time.

Structuring material

Topics should be grouped together, with separate sub-headings. Each different action or thought merits a separate paragraph in the statement. A separate chronology is often useful.

Ask why

Do not take what your client says at face value – probe until you are satisfied. If he cannot give you a satisfactory answer then show this in the statement. When you can, use the actual words that he and other people said.

Identify people referred to

Ask your client to describe the person. Then if that person is one of a group (of police officers, for example), give that person a reference (Officer 1) to save you having to repeat the description every time you refer to him.

Arrest and interrogation

It is proper to delay taking instructions on the arrest and interrogation until advance information, custody record and tapes are available and the client has had access to these.

If the circumstances of his arrest or interview may be relevant you will need to include the following.

1. **Arrest**

   (a) Give the circumstances, place, time.
   (b) Cover all conversations between your client and the police officers.
   (c) Identify the officers individually: 'Officer 1', 'Officer 2'; plain clothes, uniformed; car marked, unmarked.
   (d) Words of arrest: were they used, what were they?
   (e) Reason for arrest: was any given?
   (f) Caution: was one given, when?
   (g) Details of questioning or admissions at the time of arrest or in the police car.
   (h) Time of arrival at the police station.
   (i) Custody officer: what was said to your client by the arresting officer?
   (j) Right to contact a friend/relative: was client told?
   (k) Right to contact a solicitor, was client told?
   (l) Was solicitor asked for; if so when?
   (m) Did any solicitor attend? If so, who and when?
   (n) What instructions did your client give the solicitor?
   (o) What advice did he receive?
   (p) Did he act on that advice?
   (q) Did any discussions take place with officers investigating the case in the absence of the solicitor? If so, obtain details.

2. **Interview**

   (a) Deal separately with each interview and its content.
   (b) Note times (approximately).
   (c) How many interviews?
   (d) Did your client answer some/all/no questions in each interview?
   (e) Did he give a written statement or prepared oral statement?
   (f) Was he medically fit to be interviewed? If not, why not? Were any representations made about this?
   (g) Did your client understand the caution?
   (h) If he remained silent, did the solicitor explain the reasons for this on tape? And that it was as a result of the solicitor's advice?
   (i) Was a special warning given during this interview? If so, did it relate to an object/mark/substance or suspect's presence and how did he account for himself?
   (j) Obtain details of the object/mark/substance or facts of the suspect's presence at a particular time.
   (k) Was your client cautioned appropriately at each stage?
   (l) How was the interview recorded?

(m) Was your client asked to sign notes at any stage? Did he? Examine content of notes and client's endorsement.

(n) Who was present?

(o) Was access to legal advice before the interview formally denied?[1]

(p) Was your client asked to confirm a significant statement or silence on tape at the beginning of the interview? If so, did he do so? What was the content of the significant statement?

(q) What questions were put?

(r) Did the officer introduce evidence of bad character into the interview?

(s) What answers did your client make; were they the truth; if not, why not?

3. **Other**

(a) Were there any breaches of PACE, Code C during your client's time in custody – breaks, meals, etc.?

(b) Was your client injured [13]?

(c) Were any photographs taken of the injury; if so, by whom?

(d) Was a police surgeon/forensic medical examiner called; if so, why?

(e) Were non-intimate or intimate samples taken [7.9, 7.10]? If so, by whom, when?

(f) Did your client consent?

(g) When was he charged?

(h) What time was he released?

(i) Were bail conditions attached to his release [47.2]? If so, obtain details.

(j) Did he make any complaint [27]? Was he advised to make a complaint?

(k) Find out date and time and venue of court hearing [59.1].

Be aware of the fundamental importance attached by the courts to the right of access to a solicitor (PACE, s.58) and that breach of that right and significant and substantial breaches of Code C relating to detention, treatment and questioning may result in the court exercising its discretion to exclude a confession (PACE, s.78).

Be aware too of the court's duty to exclude a confession obtained as a result of oppression or in circumstances tending to render the confession unreliable (PACE, s.76).

Be aware of the special care necessary when considering the position of those who are mentally ill or have learning difficulties.

Alibi

Evidence in support of an alibi is evidence tending to show that by reason of the presence of the accused at a particular place or a particular area at a particular time he was not, or was unlikely to have been, at the place where the offence is alleged to have been committed at the time of its alleged commission (CPIA 1996, s.5(8)).

You need to consider whether the charge allows a defence of alibi to be raised: the time and place of the offence must be specifically defined.

The details which you must obtain, and which must be included in a defence statement, include the name and address of any witness the accused believes is able to give evidence in support of the alibi. If the accused does not know the name and address of the witness, the particulars must include any information in the accused's possession that might be of material assistance in finding any such witness (CPIA 1996, s.5(7)).

You should normally:

(a)   take a statement from an alibi witness;
(b)   tell the alibi witness that:

- the police may seek to interview him;
- the police should not interview him without notifying you and enabling you to be present;
- you will contact him if the police notify you that they wish to interview him;
- he should refuse to allow the police to interview him until the police have contacted you and allowed you to be present.

Taking your client's comments

Your client's comments should be taken on the prosecution statements, any unused material disclosed to you and any documentary exhibits. The comments should be in a document separate from his statement to you.

The comments serve two functions:

1.   The advocate needs to know in great detail which parts, if any, of a witness's statement your client does not agree with so that he can challenge these in cross-examination.
2.   The comments enable you, through your client, to raise any evidential matters, contradictions, inconsistencies or other cross-examination points that occur to you in respect of that witness and in respect of that witness's evidence in relation to the others.

Go through each witness's statement line by line with your client. Was something said or not? Did something happen or not? What has the witness left out? Number each comment in the text, against the item it refers to. Keep the comments short and to the point.

Remind your client that he must not discuss the case, or arrange for anyone else to discuss it, with a prosecution witness.

12.2 GATHERING EVIDENCE TO SUPPORT THE DEFENCE CASE

Investigating the crime scene

Active Defence and *Forensic Practice in Criminal Cases*[2] give detailed advice on looking for and reviewing the evidence of the offender having entered or left or been at the crime scene and whether the offender was your client, including:

(a) evidence of the offender's presence at the crime scene;
(b) entry/exit routes;
(c) CCTV;
(d) potential witnesses and house-to-house questioning;
(e) vehicles;
(g) contact trace material;
(h) police surveillance;
(i) objects.

Remember Dr Edmond Locard's exchange principle,[3] that 'whenever two objects meet (such as the offender and the crime scene, the victim and the crime scene or the offender and the victim), there is an exchange of material from each to the other'.

Active Defence also advises on assessing the credibility of:

(a) eye witness evidence;
(b) ear witness evidence.

Inspection, photographs and plans

Obtain photographs of your client's relevant injuries urgently. The earlier they are taken the more helpful they will be.

It is particularly useful to visit the locus yourself as part of your investigation and preparation of the case. Consider the need for photographs and a plan of the scene of an incident. In appropriate cases seek prior authority for photographs and/or plans on CDS4 from the Legal Services Commission for the magistrates' court and for the Crown Court by way of extension of the Representation Order. *Forensic Practice in Criminal Cases* gives advice on photographing and documenting a crime scene.

Obtain a CJA 1967, s.9 witness statement from the person who takes, makes or prints any photographs and plans to confirm the date and time of preparation and what they disclose.

Serve the statement and exhibits, if uncontroversial, upon the prosecution in good time before trial (at least seven days) and request their acceptance. You may prefer the element of surprise, but will need to be able to prove the exhibits at court (by oral evidence or by acceptance of s.9 statements).

Witnesses

Note whether any witnesses may exist to assist the defence. Can they be traced, are they available or willing? Consider whether the prosecution has disclosed details of possible witnesses. Advise your client as to reasonable steps that may be taken, in view of the financial implications and resources available. An enquiry agent may need to be instructed. Leave no room for doubt who is to try to contact the witness. An important witness should be interviewed at an early date.

Bear in mind the provisions of the Youth Justice and Criminal Evidence Act 1999 in case you or the prosecution want a special measures direction.

Obtain a statement [52.1], dated and signed by the witness. Do not interview a witness in the presence of another witness. The statement should include:

(a) name, address and telephone number;
(b) occupation and employment;
(c) date of birth;
(d) age and marital status;
(e) previous convictions: in particular any of dishonesty or of a similar nature to the current charge against the client; any occurring with the client; any custodial sentences;
(f) relationship to client; frequency of contact;
(g) account of incident;
(h) comments on prosecution evidence (including exhibits) where relevant;
(i) whether interviewed by police; account given to them; consistent or inconsistent with above; explanation for inconsistencies;
(j) first knowledge of case against client;
(k) extent of knowledge of case; discussion with client (if any);
(l) whether willing witness in court; if not, reasons;
(m) dates when witness available to give evidence;
(n) any disabilities suffered by the witness.

Beware of calling at court a witness who has previous convictions.

Send a typed copy of the statement to the witness and explain that he should not show it to or discuss it with anyone who may give evidence in the case. Ask the witness to check its accuracy and correct any errors. He should then return it to you for you to amend it and return it to him for signature. Within four working days of being informed of a trial date or the appearance of the case in a warned list, warn the witness of the date, time and place of any court hearing when attendance is required [66.1] and of the relevant court procedure [66.2]. Explain to an unwilling witness the position regarding a witness summons and 'conduct money'. Advise upon court procedures and practice.

Consider obtaining a s.9 witness statement for the purpose of impressing on the witness the need for honesty and clarity. If it is uncontroversial, consider serving it on the prosecution (see **Appendix 2, 2.7** for an example of a s.9 witness statement).

If you have a child witness, see the witness in the presence, where appropriate, of a parent or social worker; consider whether in court special facilities may be required to protect the child; unless inappropriate, provide a copy of the statement to parents; advise with particular care.

Obtain a witness summons from the court for any witness whom you intend to call and think will not attend court voluntarily. Consider how to serve the summons and whether it is possible to take a statement at the same time, if the witness will allow this and has not made a statement to you already. Consider whether a reluctant witness is worth calling.

A summons can now be obtained whenever it is in the interests of justice.

Guidance on preparing young witnesses for court

Arrangements for the preparation of young witnesses, including pre-trial court visits, should be made available on request to young witnesses called by the defence.

A handbook *Preparing Young Witnesses for Court: A Handbook for Child Witness Supporters* is published by the NSPCC and Childline to prepare young witnesses for court. It has been produced to accompany the Young Witness Pack.[4]

Items in the Young Witness Pack series include: *Let's Get Ready for Court*, an activity book for child witnesses aged 5–9; *Tell Me More About Court*, a book for young witnesses aged 10–15; *Inside a Court Room*, a card model of a courtroom with slot-in characters for use with witnesses aged 13–17; *Young Witnesses at the Magistrates' Court and Youth Court*, for witnesses aged 9–17; *Screens in Court*, an information sheet for witnesses aged 9–17; and *Your Child is a Witness* for parents and carers. There is also a video available called *Giving Evidence – What's it Really Like?*

Preparing Young Witnesses for Court is aimed at child witness supporters. They liaise with the criminal justice agencies to ensure that they are aware of the child's needs and that those needs are met. They also ensure that the agencies are committed to expediting the case.

Child witness supporters are independent of the prosecution and defence. The police will arrange a child witness supporter for a prosecution witness. They have only basic information about why a child is going to court and there will be no discussion of the child's evidence or expression of belief in the child witness. Preparation work is not confidential and if a prosecution child witness begins to talk about the evidence, the supporter must notify the police and ask the child to speak to the person who conducted the interrogative interviews.

Child witness supporters should have undertaken training accredited by all the agencies involved and conduct the preparation according to a written programme agreed on an inter-agency basis. The independent supporter is accountable to the court and must be prepared to give evidence about the work undertaken with young witnesses and produce written records if requested to do so.

Local initiatives for child witness preparation have developed under the auspices of the NSPCC, the Crown Court Witness Service, Social Services Departments and Area Child Protection Committees. A defence solicitor can contact any of these organisations to arrange a child witness supporter for a young defence witness. Be familiar with *A Case for Balance*: the good practice video on court proceedings involving child witnesses produced by the NSPCC. Further guidance on child witnesses is given in **Appendix 5**.

Additional evidence

If you are served with additional evidence, ensure that the statement and comments are updated. Make sure you notify the prosecution within the time limits whether any witness or witnesses whose statements have been served by way of additional evidence are required to attend court to give evidence in person. If in doubt about whether their attendance is required, notify the prosecution that they should attend (for sample notification see **Appendix 2, 2.8**). You should cancel this requirement if they no longer need to attend.

Sensitive statements

Ensure that your client is aware of all prosecution and defence evidence. You should, however, use your discretion in providing copies of 'sensitive' statements and exhibits relating to a defendant's case, subject to your client's right to have access to material forming part of the case against him. In providing any such material, you should remind your client that the use of papers must be limited to use in connection with the purposes of litigation, and that any misuse of the papers by your client may amount to contempt of court.

Enquiry agent

If you are unable to do all the work yourself, you may need to instruct an enquiry agent on your behalf to take photographs, prepare plans, trace witnesses, visit any witnesses who will not co-operate and take statements from them, and make other particular enquiries of an urgent, delicate or unusual nature or at unusual times or great distances or when you cannot guarantee the security of a member of your staff.

Consider seeking prior authority for this work under your Representation Order; otherwise be prepared to justify the time and costs on audit or determination.

Ensure such enquiries are relevant and that the agent is properly briefed on your behalf.

Other evidence

Note whether your client has any documents, receipts, letters or photographs. Advise him to deliver them to you speedily for safekeeping.

12.3   EXPERTS

In the course of preparing for a trial, consider the need for expert evidence, e.g. to explain or rebut prosecution evidence; to support a laced drinks argument or post-driving consumption defence; to establish nature, extent and causation of injuries; to support an application to exclude evidence (see 'Ways of finding an expert and types of expert' below).

It will not always be obvious from the prosecution forensic scientist's written statement what the strengths and weaknesses of the evidence are. There is a danger that if the prosecution forensic scientist gives oral evidence he will strengthen the evidence contained in his witness statement by commenting on the significance of the findings. Scientists in the Home Office laboratories will have looked at thousands of scenes of crimes and exhibits and acquired a 'feel' for what they would expect to see following any given crime.

A forensic scientist instructed by you should be able to warn you of any such risk, in advance. The area in which a defence forensic scientist is likely to make most ground is the interpretation of the evidence in the context of the facts of the case rather than faulting the identification of the sample or its comparison with another exhibit.

Seek appropriate prior authority on CDS4 from the Legal Services Commission for the magistrates' court and for the Crown Court by way of extension of the Representation Order. You will have to obtain an estimate of the expert's fees. An example of how you can do this is set out in **Appendix 14**.

Provide your expert with the following (as appropriate):

(a)   the charge sheet or indictment;
(b)   relevant prosecution witness statements including the victim's statement;
(c)   prosecution photographs (not colour photocopies) and other exhibits that the expert may need to examine;
(d)   prosecution expert's statement or report;
(e)   defendant's proof of evidence;
(f)   relevant defence witness statements;
(g)   client's letter of authority for medical report.

If authority is granted, you can then instruct the expert in the knowledge that the expert's fees will be publicly funded providing that the terms of the authority are not exceeded. Your expert may have to examine an exhibit held by the prosecution. The prosecution will not (normally) release exhibits to the expert:

1. The expert must go to them at whichever laboratory dealt with the case.
2. Instructing solicitors must obtain CPS approval for the proposed examination and then, having obtained some documentary proof of that, write to the police and the laboratory concerned. Once all have signalled that they consent, but not until then, there is normally no objection to the expert contacting the scientist direct to work out the details.

Forensic Practice in Criminal Cases (note 2) gives advice on:

- forensic evidence: its nature, uses, types and importance;
- forensic investigation: the people involved in the investigation of the scene;
- forensic investigation: police organisation, training and awareness and the process of identifications;
- the process of examining the crime scene;
- documentation of examination, removal and submission of contact trace material and other material and objects;
- the collection, removal and submission of forensic material for examination;
- the forensic scientist working for the prosecution;
- the forensic scientist working for the defence;
- finding a forensic scientist;
- defence investigation of the crime scene;
- forensic evidence pre-trial;
- forensic evidence in court.

Advance notice of expert evidence

In the Crown Court and the magistrates' court, expert evidence (except in relation to sentence) may not be given unless advance notice of the evidence is provided to the other parties (CPR 24.1). The party seeking to admit the evidence must provide other parties with a written statement of the findings or opinions to be relied upon. On request, the party must provide an opportunity for the other party to examine the material on which the finding or opinion is based.

A party who fails to disclose expert evidence must obtain leave of the court to adduce it. The court will balance the interests of both parties in reaching a decision. The purpose of the rule is to give the other party the opportunity to evaluate any evidence before trial.

Privileged information

If the defence instructs a forensic practitioner but decides not to call the expert to give evidence, the information obtained by the defence from the expert is privileged. The expert's opinion, which is based on that privileged information, is also privileged and the defendant is entitled to assume that any communication the defendant has with the expert is protected in the same way as any communication the defendant has with his solicitor (*R. v. Davies* [2002] EWCA Crim 85).

The Criminal Justice Act 2003 has provisions not yet in force that require the defence to notify the court and the prosecutor of the name and address of any person whom the defence instructs with a view to that person providing an expert opinion for possible use as evidence at the trial. This could range from a scientist whom the defence solicitor telephones to sound him/her out and obtain some advice, but who never provides an opinion, to an expert who provides a report to the defence which the defence decides not to use. There is not a similar duty on the prosecutor.

Although this would allow the prosecution to interview an unused expert, the expert would consider himself/herself bound to keep confidential any information relating to or following from the defence instructions and if required to appear in court could rely upon legal professional privilege.

The prosecution would be able to comment at trial on the fact that the scientist was instructed but was not called to give evidence – the implication being that the unused expert would not have given evidence favourable to the defence. In fact the reason for not using the expert may be something quite different: the expert's opinion was unhelpful in peripheral matters; the report was poorly prepared or formulated on a wrong basis; or a report was subsequently obtained from a scientist who would carry much more weight in court.

During the Second Reading debate in the House of Lords on 16 June 2003, Lord Woolf referred to a document which he had placed in the Lords' Library setting out what the judiciary regarded as the problem areas in the Criminal Justice Bill. In an article in the *New Law Journal*, 8 August 2003, Professor Michael Zander gave extracts from the document. Referring to the requirement on the defence to disclose the identity of any witness who had been instructed, it said:

> It is not clear what legitimate use can be made of the information about 'unused' experts . . . this procedure must not be used as a backdoor way of obtaining privileged information . . . The question arises as to what use is to be made of the names of experts instructed by the defendants. Is it intended that they should be interviewed by the police? If so, this could be highly undesirable because in order to instruct an expert, it is often the case that privileged information has to be given to the expert. Are questions to be asked at the hearing by the prosecution about experts instructed by the defence who are not called? If so, should not the defence be in the position to ask similar questions about the prosecution's experts . . .

Contamination

Be aware of how forensic evidence can be contaminated. Some examples of possible contaminants are:

(a) the placing of a hand or finger inside an exhibit bag;

(b) blood or semen is inadvertently transferred to other surfaces of an item, e.g. by folding items without separating the surfaces, so that the surfaces contact each other;

(c) a suspect being placed in a cell used by another suspect and sharing the cell blanket;

(d) shaking or disturbing an item of clothing;

(e) poking a finger through a stab or bullet hole in a given item or surface;

(f) scraping of a body part, clothing or item across a blood stain;

(g) removing debris;

(h) more than one item being placed in one bag;

(i) the first officer attending (FOA) coming into contact with both the victim and the suspect cross-contaminating the two, e.g. attending to the victim then arresting the suspect; arresting the suspect and then attending to the victim;

(j) the FOA failing to ensure that the same vehicle does not transport the victim and the suspect at different times;

(k) the same forensic examiner inspecting items from the suspect and the victim without decontamination in between;

(l) the same room in a laboratory being used to inspect items from the suspect and the victim without cleaning in between. Where possible, laboratories will keep separate rooms for suspect and victim material inspections;

(m) the same tools, such as a fibre collection kit, being used to collect trace evidence from the suspect and the victim.

Forensic Practice in Criminal Cases gives fuller information about how evidence can become contaminated.

Ways of finding an expert and types of expert

Be aware that there has been no form of regulation of the forensic science profession and you will need to satisfy yourself about the competence and ability of a particular 'expert' to undertake work in an individual case. To remedy this, the Council for the Registration of Forensic Practitioners has been established with support from the Home Office.

You should find out on what basis the person feels qualified to advise in that particular case, including what recognised scientific qualifications the 'expert' has, what practical experience he has of investigating that sort of case and applying scientific techniques to the evidence at issue. For assistance in finding an expert see **Appendix 15**.

NOTES

1. See PACE, s.58; inferences from silence may not be drawn in these circumstances (CJPOA 1994, ss.34, 36, 37 as amended by the Youth Justice and Criminal Evidence Act 1999).
2. R. Ede and E. Shepherd, *Active Defence: A Lawyer's Guide to Police and Defence Investigation and Prosecution and Defence Disclosure in Criminal Cases* (2nd edn, Law Society Publishing, 2000); L. Townley and R. Ede, *Forensic Practice in Criminal Cases* (Law Society Publishing, 2003).
3. In 1910 Dr Edmond Locard, the director of the first crime laboratory, working at the University of Lyons, formulated his exchange principle.
4. *Preparing Young Witnesses for Court, A Handbook for Child Witness Supporters* (NSPCC/Childline 1998); the Young Witness Pack and the video *Giving Evidence – What's it Really Like?* are available from NSPCC Publications, tel: 020 7825 7422; e-mail: publications@nspcc.org.uk.

CHAPTER 13

Directions for trial

Objectives of this chapter

- To explain what directions may be given before trial
- To explain how these directions may impact upon the case
- To describe what needs to be in a defence statement

13.1   CASE MANAGEMENT DIRECTIONS

When a plea of not guilty is entered, 'case management' directions automatically apply. A form containing standard directions for cases to be tried in magistrates' courts is set out in Annex E to the Consolidated Criminal Practice Direction (see **Appendix 1** for website link) and is available on the Ministry of Justice website. Some of these standard directions may be altered; others are laid down in the CPR. The standard directions deal with:

- defence statement;
- bad character evidence;
- hearsay evidence;
- witness statements;
- written admissions under CJA 1967, s.10;
- special measures;
- prosecution case and disclosure;
- further disclosure;
- expert evidence;
- points of law;
- trial readiness and further case management hearings.

Additional case management directions may also be given where appropriate.

Timetable for trial

Table 13.1 Preparation by defence

	Insert date	How to calculate and relevant rules
Defence statement		14 days from initial disclosure: Criminal Procedure and Investigations Act 1996 (Defence Disclosure Time Limits) Regulations 1997, SI 1997/684
Character notice for prosecution witness		14 days from initial disclosure or the information first becoming available if later: CPR 35.2
Counter-notice against defendant's character		14 days from service of prosecution notice: CPR 35.6
Hearsay notice		14 days from initial disclosure: CPR 34.4
Objection to hearsay		14 days from receipt: CPR 34.5
Expert evidence		As soon as practicable: CPR 24.1(1)
Special Measures Notice		28 days from lst appearance in Youth Court
		14 days from not guilty plea in magistrates' court
		28 dates from committal/service of s.51 case evidence in Crown Court: CPR 29.1

The requirements for magistrates' court trials, committals for trial and sendings can be illustrated by **Figures 13.1**, **13.2** and **13.3**.

13.2 DEFENCE STATEMENT

If the case is to be tried summarily and the accused pleads not guilty:

1. The prosecutor must make disclosure under CPIA 1996, s.3.
2. The accused may give a defence statement to the prosecutor and the court which must satisfy the conditions set out in CPIA 1996, s.6A.

If the case is to be tried in the Crown Court, when the case has been committed, or a serious and complex fraud or a case involving a sexual or violent offence against a child has been transferred, or a voluntary bill of indictment has been preferred and the prosecutor has made disclosure, the defence must give a defence statement within 14 days from initial disclosure or risk an adverse inference being drawn at trial.

A CPS letter that there is no disclosable material, without service of the unused material schedule, starts time running for the issue of the defence statement (*DPP* v. *Wood and McGillicuddy* [2006] EWHC 32, QBD).

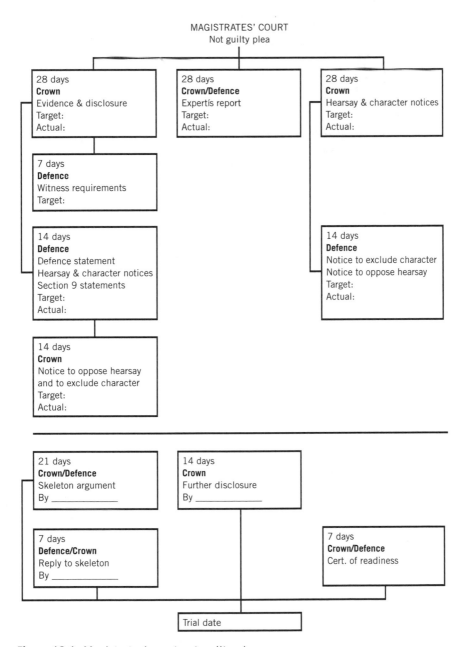

Figure 13.1 Magistrates' court not guilty plea

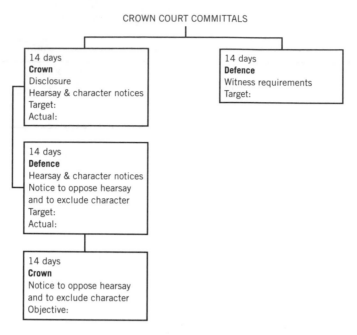

Figure 13.2 Crown Court committals

As there will usually not be a further stage to prosecution disclosure in the magistrates' court, the identification of material that might undermine the prosecution case should be interpreted as widely as possible, as anything capable of having an impact on the case.

In the defence statement, the accused should do all of the following:

1. Set out the nature of the defence, including any particular defences on which the accused intends to rely.
2. Indicate the matters of fact on which the accused takes issue with the prosecution.
3. Set out, in the case of each such matter, why the accused takes issue with the prosecution.
4. Indicate any point of law (including any point as to the admissibility of evidence or an abuse of process) which the accused wishes to take, and any authority on which he or she intends to rely for that purpose.
5. Comply with any regulations made by the Secretary of State as to the details of matters that are to be included in defence statements.

If the defence statement discloses an alibi the accused must give particulars of the alibi in the statement, including:

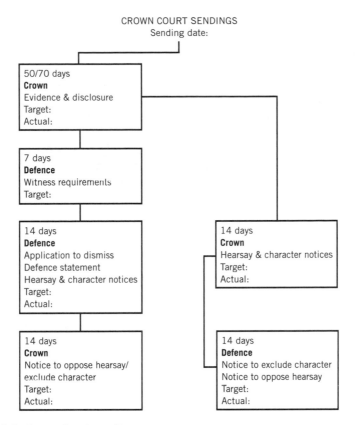

Figure 13.3 Crown Court sendings

(a) the name, address and date of birth of any witness the accused believes is able to give evidence in support of the alibi, or as many of those details as are known to the accused when the statement is given; and

(b) any information in the accused's possession which might be of material assistance in identifying or finding any such witness if the above details are not known to the accused when the statement is given.

Where an accused's solicitor purports to give a defence statement on behalf of the accused, the statement shall, unless the contrary is proved, be deemed to be given with the authority of the accused (CPIA 1996, s.6E as amended by CJA 2003, s.36).

Take time in the preparation of the defence statement and obtain your client's agreement to the document before it is served on the prosecution and the court. As a precaution you should ask your client to personally sign a copy of the statement for you only to retain, confirming that it corresponds with his instructions to you. This should avoid the risk of your client later maintaining that there had been a mistake in the statement (*R.* v. *Wheeler* [2001] 1 Cr App R 10).

Remember that evidence obtained as a result of inquiring into a defence statement may be used as part of the prosecution case or to rebut the defence and that detail which is not consistent with evidence given at trial may be put to your client in cross-examination.

However, you should provide sufficient detail to ensure that you receive any further disclosure not previously disclosed that will assist your case.

You should meet the statutory requirements but carefully consider the amount of detail required. Do not plead inconsistent defences. There is only a small risk of adverse inferences being raised against the defendant at trial. You should observe the time limit and apply for more time if required before the time limit expires (see Appendix 2.8).

Instructing advocates to draft the defence statement

The Bar Council has issued guidance to counsel about the circumstances that should exist before counsel agrees to draft a defence statement. It reminds counsel about the significance of this document and the need to obtain the client's informed agreement before it is sent. This guidance is set out in **Appendix 16**.

Applying for further time

Be ready to apply for further time to file a defence statement when this is required (see **Appendix 2, 2.9**). CPR 25.7 requires the application to be made by notice in writing to the court officer, with a copy to the prosecutor. If the prosecutor wishes to make representations, he must do so in writing within 14 days of service of the notice upon him.

A defence statement given late is still a defence statement for the purposes of CPIA 1996 (*DPP* v. *Wood and McGillicuddy* [2006] EWHC 32, QBD).

Sanctions

Faults in defence compliance may attract an adverse inference at trial under CPIA 1996, s.11 as amended by CJA 2003, s.39. The court and any other party may make such comment as appears appropriate and the court or the jury may draw such inferences as appear proper in deciding whether the accused is guilty of the offence where the accused is required to provide a defence statement and:

- fails to do so;
- does so out of time;
- sets out inconsistent defences in the defence statement;

or at trial:

- puts forward a defence not mentioned in or different from that in the defence statement;
- relies on a matter that should have been mentioned in the defence statement but was not (leave must be sought if that matter is a point of law);
- calls an alibi witness of whom the required details have not been supplied.

To assist the court in deciding whether to allow comments to be made or whether the jury should be allowed to draw inferences, the prosecutor should put the contents of the defence statement to the accused in cross-examination to elicit the differences between it and the actual defence relied upon and any justification for those differences.

Identification of issues

In a summary trial, where no defence statement is given, the defence must identify all the issues in the case before the close of the prosecution case (*Malcolm* v. *DPP* [2007] EWHC 363 (Admin)). To avoid unnecessary adjournments you should consider disclosure of the defence issues at an early stage. This requires your clients authority or the information is privileged.

13.3   BAD CHARACTER

'Bad character' is defined in CJA 2003, s.98 as evidence of, or a disposition towards, misconduct. CJA 2003, s.112(1) defines misconduct as the commission of an offence or other reprehensible behaviour.

The scheme in CJA 2003 is as follows:

1. Evidence of bad character is defined so as to exclude evidence directly connected with the offence with which the defendant is charged and any misbehaviour during the course of the investigation (s.98).
2. The common law rules governing the admissibility of evidence of bad character in criminal proceedings are abolished (s.99) and so are the rules contained in the Criminal Evidence Act 1898 about cross-examining defendants as to character (Sched.37, Part 5).
3. Evidence of the bad character of a person other than the defendant is admissible only with judicial leave, to be granted only on certain stated grounds (s.100).
4. Evidence of the defendant's bad character is admissible if any of the following gateways are open, but not otherwise (s.101(1)):

   (a) all parties to the proceedings agree to the evidence being admissible,
   (b) the evidence is adduced by the defendant himself or is given in answer to a question asked by him in cross-examination and intended to elicit it,

(c) it is important explanatory evidence,
(d) it is relevant to an important matter in issue between the defendant and the prosecution,
(e) it has substantial probative value in relation to an important matter in issue between the defendant and a co-defendant,
(f) it is evidence to correct a false impression given by the defendant,
(g) the defendant has made an attack on another person's character.

The meaning of matters 'in issue between the defendant and the prosecution' (gateway (d)) is explained in CJA 2003, s.103 to include matters that the court should take into account when reaching its decision: the question whether the defendant has a propensity to commit offences of the kind with which he is charged. This may be proved in any of the three ways above (i.e. evidence of the commission of the offence; evidence of other reprehensible behaviour; or evidence of the defendant's disposition towards this). But the evidence of the commission of an offence may take the form of a previous conviction for any offence.

The defence can apply to the court to exclude evidence of bad character under gateways (d) and (g) if its admission would have such an adverse effect on fairness that the court ought not to admit it. On an application to exclude evidence the court must have regard to the length of time since the matters it relates to occurred and the matters themselves. PACE, s.78 may be used to exclude evidence.

Examples that have been given of important explanatory evidence (gateway (c)) are: evidence of the two accused having been convicted of offences together in the past; or evidence in a case of violence that the accused had acted violently towards the victim in the past.

Where gateway (d) is relied upon the court must first be satisfied that any of the following apply:

1. The offence is in the same category as the previous matters. Categories exist in relation to Theft Act offences and sexual offences against children under 16.
2. The description of the offence is the same as that of the previous matter(s).
3. The facts of previous matter(s) have such a relevance to the matter(s) now alleged that the court should be made aware of them (*R.* v. *Somanathan* [2005] EWCA Crim 2866).

If the court is so satisfied, there are three questions which the court must ask itself: (i) whether the history of conviction(s) establishes a propensity to commit offences of the kind charged; (ii) whether that propensity makes it more likely that the defendant committed the offence charged; and (iii) whether it is unjust to rely on the conviction(s) of the same description or category. There is no minimum number of events necessary to demonstrate such a propensity. The fewer the number of convictions, the weaker is likely to be the evidence of propensity. A single previous conviction for an offence of the same description or category will often not show propensity. But it may do so where, for example, it shows a tendency to unusual behaviour, or where its circumstances demonstrate probative force in relation to the offence charged. If the *modus operandi* has significant features shared by the offence charged, it may show propensity. The judge may also take into consideration the respective gravity of the past and present offences; and consider the strength of the prosecution case (*R.* v. *Hanson* [2005] EWCA Crim 824).

When courts make decisions about the admissibility of previous convictions, they will need to know details of the offence to decide how similar they are to the present offence. The judge should look for similarities between what the defendant has done in the past and what he is now charged with. Those similarities do not have to be striking in the way that similar fact evidence has to be, but there must be a degree of similarity. The fact that the convictions are for offences of the same description or category does not automatically mean that they should be admitted (*R.* v. *Tully and Wood* [2006] EWCA Crim 2270 referring to and endorsing the judgment in *Hanson* above).

In *R.* v. *Tully and Wood* [2006] EWCA Crim 2270 the appellants had been tried for robbery in 2005 where a knife had been used to threaten a taxi driver. Wood had one conviction for robbery in 1995, four in 1997 and two in 1998 and he had more recent convictions for other offences of dishonesty. Tully had five convictions for robbery, the most recent in 2000. Several of his robbery convictions involved threats with a knife. The trial judge admitted all the offences of dishonesty of both appellants. Lady Justice Smith, giving the Court of Appeal's judgment that only the offences of robbery should have been admitted, said that evidence of the other dishonesty convictions had little probative force when considering whether that would make it more likely that they had committed this robbery as there were a great many people who had a propensity to acquire other people's property by one means or another.

Matters in issue also include (CJA 2003, s.103(1)(b)) the question whether the defendant has a propensity to be untruthful. This is not the same as propensity to dishonesty. Previous convictions, whether for offences of dishonesty or otherwise, are therefore only likely to be capable of showing a propensity to be untruthful where, in the present case, truthfulness is in issue and, in the earlier case, either there was a plea of not guilty and the defendant gave an account (on arrest, in interview or in evidence) which the jury must have disbelieved, or the way in which the offence was committed shows a propensity for untruthfulness, for example by the making of false representations (*R.* v. *Bovell and Dowds* [2005] EWCA Crim 1091).

The bad character of a non-defendant is admissible only with leave in the following circumstances (CJA 2003, s.100(1)):

(a) it is important explanatory evidence,
(b) it has substantial probative value in relation to a matter which –

     (i)   is a matter in issue in the proceedings, and
     (ii) is of substantial importance in the context of the case as a whole,

or if all parties to the proceedings agree to the evidence being admissible.

Normally, this will require the witness to be giving evidence as to an important issue and the bad character significantly reduces the witness's credibility. The conviction must be material to the credit of the witness: being grave and recent.

It is necessary for all parties to have appropriate information about and adequate notice of an application to admit bad character evidence (*R*. v. *Hanson* [2005] EWCA Crim 824). The procedure set out in CPR Part 36 must be followed and the appropriate forms completed and served on the clerk to the justices in the magistrates' court or the appropriate officer of the Crown Court and all other parties to the proceedings. The prosecutor must give notice of intention to introduce evidence of a defendant's bad character when he gives initial disclosure in the magistrates' court or within 14 days of committal in the Crown Court. In either case, the defence has 14 days to apply for the evidence to be excluded. A party who wishes to introduce evidence of a non-defendant's bad character or cross-examine a witness to elicit that evidence must apply within 14 days of the prosecutor giving initial disclosure in the magistrates' court or Crown Court or from the information becoming available, whichever is later. Notice of opposition to the application must be given within 14 days.

The court must consider:

1. Have the notice requirements been complied with?
2. What is sought to be adduced:

    • the fact of a conviction?
    • the details of an offence?

3. Why it is being relied upon:

    • do adequate records exist?
    • can they be proved?
    • do they relate to the defendant?
    • are the facts in dispute or can they be agreed?

4. Should the prosecutor's application be delayed until later in the proceedings?[1]

If an application for bad character evidence is made out of time, although time limits must be observed and a culture of non-compliance not permitted to take root, if the defendant was not prejudiced by the late application it should be allowed. But the court should not take account of the details of the conviction which the prosecutor seeks to admit when reaching their decision (*R. (on the application of Robinson)* v. *Sutton Coldfield Magistrates' Court* [2006] EWHC 307).

The Court of Appeal has held that while a defendant's previous convictions could be proved as a 'business and other document' under CJA 2003, s.117 the facts of the underlying offences could not be proved in that way and other evidence of this would be required (*R.* v. *Ainscough* [2006] EWCA Crim 694, applying *R.* v. *Humphris* [2005] EWCA Crim 2030).

13.4 HEARSAY

Is the evidence hearsay?

When considering whether evidence may need to comply with the provisions that make hearsay admissible, the first question to be answered is whether the evidence is hearsay. 'Hearsay' is defined in CJA 2003, s.114 as 'a statement not made in oral evidence in the proceedings [which] is admissible as evidence of any matter stated'. Section 115 defines a 'statement' as any representation of fact or opinion made by a person by whatever means (including a sketch, photofit or other picture) and a 'matter stated' as a statement made by a person with the intention of causing someone else to believe the matter, or of causing another person to act or a machine to operate, on the basis that the matter is as stated.

It follows that if the purpose of admitting the statement is not to prove its truth then it is not hearsay. Also, if the purpose of the person making the statement was not to persuade someone about what he was saying, then it is not hearsay.

If the evidence is hearsay, is it admissible?

CJA 2003, s.118 preserves the following rules of law which allow the admission of hearsay evidence:

- public information;
- reputation as to character;
- *res gestae*;
- confessions or mixed statements;
- common enterprise;
- expert evidence.

Hearsay evidence may also be admitted under CJA 2003, s.114 which provides that it may be admitted if:

- all the parties agree (s.114(1)(c));
- it is in the interests of justice (s.114(1)(d)).

171

In deciding whether the statement may be admitted under s.114(1)(d) there are a number of safeguards that the court must have regard to:

(a)   the probative value of the statement;
(b)   whether other evidence has been or can be given on the matter;
(c)   how important the matter is in the context of the case as a whole;
(d)   the circumstances in which the statement was made;
(e)   how reliable the maker of the statement appears to be;
(f)   how reliable the evidence of the making of the statement appears to be;
(g)   whether oral evidence of the matter can be given and, if not, why not;
(h)   the amount of difficulty in challenging the statement;
(i)   the extent to which that difficulty would be likely to prejudice the party facing it.

By CJA 2003, s.116 where the witness is not available, that person's statement is automatically admissible (apart from (e) below) if it would have been admissible if he had given oral evidence, he is identifiable and if the person is:

(a)   dead; or
(b)   unfit because of their bodily or mental condition; or
(c)   outside the UK and it is not reasonably practicable to secure his attendance; or
(d)   cannot be found despite reasonably practicable steps having been taken; or
(e)   afraid to give oral evidence and the court gives leave.

Leave may be granted under (e) above only if the court considers that the statement ought to be admitted in the interests of justice, having regard to:

(a)   the statement's contents;
(b)   any risk that its admission or exclusion will result in unfairness to any party to the proceedings (and in particular how difficult it will be to challenge the statement if the relevant person does not give oral evidence);
(c)   the fact that special measures may be taken for the giving of evidence by that person.

Under CJA 2003, s.123 the person who is unavailable must have been capable of making the statement. Under s.124 evidence can be given to attack that person's credibility.

By CJA 2003, s.117 evidence in a business document can also be admitted.

The court retains a general discretion to exclude evidence under PACE, s.78 when it would be unfair to admit it.

There is no absolute rule that prohibits the reading of a complainant's statement which is compelling and is the sole or decisive evidence, where the complainant is afraid to give evidence or cannot be traced and brought before the court. The court should consider what procedures may counterbalance any handicap to the defence (*R. (on the application of Robinson)* v. *Sutton Coldfield Magistrates' Court* [2006] EWHC 307).

A previous inconsistent statement may be admissible as evidence of any matter stated in it of which oral evidence by that person would be admissible (CJA 2003, s.119). So the earlier statement of a witness who has been intimidated may be admitted. Both the witness's earlier statement and his evidence on oath may be accepted as evidence of their truth.

A previous consistent statement by a witness who is called to give evidence can be admitted as evidence to rebut a suggestion of fabrication or as evidence of a recent complaint. It is admissible as evidence of the truth of any matter stated in it of which oral evidence by that person would be admissible (CJA 2003, s.120).

Advocates who cross-examine witnesses on their earlier statements risk admitting other evidence contained in those statements, to the detriment of the cross-examining party, which the witness omitted to give in the witness box.

Before multiple hearsay can be admitted, one of the statements must be a business document (CJA 2003, s.117) or a previous statement by a witness in the case (CJA 2003, s.119 or s.120) or the court must be satisfied that the value of the evidence in question, taking into account how reliable the statements appear to be, is so high that the interests of justice require the later statement to be admissible.

By PACE, s.78A (as inserted by CJA 2003, s.128), where a defendant relies upon a co-accused's confession, it is for the defendant to prove on the balance of probabilities, if the suggestion is made, that the confession was not obtained by oppression or in consequence of anything said or done that is likely to impact upon the reliability of the confession.

By CJA 2003, s.125 a Crown Court judge can stop a case that depends significantly upon hearsay evidence if that evidence is unconvincing.

By CJA 2003, s.126 a court can exclude hearsay evidence that would result in a waste of time but this provision is being very widely interpreted. PACE, s.78 is also available.

13.5   AGREEING THE CONTENTS OF STATEMENTS IN SUMMARY TRIALS

The written statement of a witness for the prosecution or defence should be properly signed, dated and prefaced by a caption in accordance with CJA 1967, s.9, MCA 1980, s.102 and the Magistrates' Courts Rules 1981, SI 1981/552, r.70 (see **Appendix 2, 2.7**).

A witness statement in s.9 form can be served upon the prosecution or the defence. If its contents are agreed and accepted, then the statement may be read to the court and becomes evidence in the same way as live evidence given at the trial. The witness need not attend; cross-examination is not possible.

173

However, acceptance does not prevent the party tendering the evidence from calling the witness to give oral evidence.

The Attorney General's Guidelines on Disclosure (see **Appendix 1** for website link) state in para.57 that the prosecutor should provide the defence with all the evidence on which the Crown proposes to rely in a summary trial. This should be done to allow the defence sufficient time to consider the statements before the evidence is called (*R. (on the application of Cleary)* v. *Highbury Corner Magistrates' Court* [2006] EWHC 1869 (Admin)).

Service of statements in your possession should be made within seven working days from entering a not guilty plea in the magistrates' court, to allow proper consideration. A lesser period may be agreed between the parties if the statement is uncontroversial.

An agreed statement is not conclusive, but if the opponent party then calls contradictory evidence, the proponent would normally be allowed to call the witness who made the statement to rebut the contradiction, even if an adjournment is necessary.

Prosecution witness statements served under CJA 1967, s.9 should be considered with careful regard to the defendant's comments upon their contents, if any. The prosecution may be prepared to agree to some editing or addition to such statements, so as to put them into an acceptable form.

Failure to reject the statement within seven days is treated as acceptance. Later application may, however, be made to the court to require a witness to attend and give oral evidence, but you are then at risk of refusal and/or costs.

Consider with care whether service of a defence witness statement, or detailed response to a prosecution witness statement, will disclose too much of your client's defence case. Generally, disclose only what you know is uncontroversial or formal, e.g. statements by a photographer, doctor, plan-drawer.

13.6 FORMAL ADMISSION

At any stage a formal admission of facts may be made, providing conclusive evidence of those facts. Admissions can be made orally at trial or in writing before trial, in accordance with CJA 1967, s.10. This should be made in writing within seven working days of knowledge of the facts.

This is a potentially useful cost-saving device; consider it carefully, with your client as appropriate, before using it. An admission can be withdrawn, but only with leave of the court. You should be slow to make an admission unless you are satisfied that the Crown could, if necessary, prove the relevant facts.

13.7   SPECIAL MEASURES

The Youth Justice and Criminal Evidence Act 1999 defines vulnerable and
intimidated witnesses (ss.16 and 17, respectively) and contains a number of
special measures for them including:

(a)   the use of screens around the witness box;
(b)   clearing the public gallery in sex offences and intimidation cases;
(c)   intermediaries and other assistance with communication;
(d)   video-recorded evidence-in-chief;
(e)   video-recorded cross-examination and re-examination (not commenced);
(f)   live TV links;
(g)   the removal of wigs and gowns.

Witnesses for prosecution or defence (and the defendant under the provisions
below) are eligible for assistance for any of the following reasons:

(a)   their age;
(b)   their incapacity;
(c)   the fear or distress which they are likely to suffer;
(d)   the witness is the complainant in respect of a sexual offence (this is a sub-
      category of 'fear or distress' for which the witness is eligible automatically
      for special measures assistance unless they do not wish to be).

Age

Witnesses under 17 years of age at the time of the hearing when the court
makes a determination about the need for assistance are eligible automatically
for special measures simply by virtue of their age.

Incapacity

The quality of evidence given by the witness (in terms of completeness,
coherence and accuracy) is likely to be diminished (the court must consider
any views expressed by the witness) where the witness has or suffers from any
of the following:

(a)   mental disorder within the meaning of the Mental Health Act 1983;
(b)   a significant impairment of intelligence and social functioning;
(c)   a physical disability or is suffering from a physical disorder.

Fear or distress

The quality of evidence given by the witness is likely to be diminished by
reason of the witness's fear or distress in connection with testifying. The
court must take into account:

(a) the nature and alleged circumstances of the offence to which the proceedings relate;

(b) the age of the witness;

(c) if relevant:

- the social and cultural background and ethnic origin of the witness;
- the domestic and employment circumstances of the witness;
- any religious beliefs or political opinions of the witness;
- any behaviour towards the witness on the part of the accused, members of the family or associates of the accused, or any other person who is likely to be an accused or a witness in the proceedings.

General tests and presumptions

One of the parties to the proceedings must make an application for the court to give a 'special measures direction' or the court may make a direction of its own motion. A special measures direction is binding other than in the event of a material change in circumstances.

A witness must be an eligible witness as outlined above. The special measure, or combination of measures, must be likely to improve and maximise the quality of the witness's evidence. In deciding whether this test is satisfied the court will consider all the circumstances of the case including any views expressed by the witness (wish to use an intermediary) and whether a special measure might inhibit testing of the evidence.

Child witnesses may be classified as either 'in need of special protection' or 'all other child witnesses':

1. The child witness is 'in need of special protection' if the proceedings relate to one of the offences listed in Youth Justice and Criminal Evidence Act 1999, s.35(3). The consequence is that the child's evidence must be given by video-recorded evidence-in-chief, if such a video exists (unless the court decides that this is not in the interests of justice), and cross-examination must be pre-recorded or by live link. In addition, if the case is a sexual one and evidence-in-chief is presented by video recording, the court must direct pre-recorded cross-examination and re-examination. These presumptions are subject to the specific special measures being available in that court. The offences listed in s.35(3) are:

    (a) any offence under:

    - the Sexual Offences Act 1956;
    - the Indecency with Children Act 1960;
    - the Sexual Offences Act 1967;
    - the Criminal Law Act 1977, s.54;
    - the Protection of Children Act 1978;

(b) kidnapping, false imprisonment or an offence under the Child Abduction Act 1984, s.1 or s.2;

(c) any offence under the Children and Young Persons Act 1933, s.1;

(d) any offence involving an assault, injury or a threat of injury to any person.

2. In the case of all other child witnesses, the court must make a 'special measures direction' admitting a video recording as evidence-in-chief and other evidence to be given by live link, providing that the special measure is available, that it is in the interests of justice to admit the video recording – unless the court determines that the special measure is not likely to maximise the quality of the witness's evidence.

Special measures for a defendant

Since January 2007, the Youth and Criminal Evidence Act 1999, s.33A has allowed the use of live link on application by the defence or at the Crown's own initiative for the evidence of witnesses if it is in the interests of justice and:

(a) if the defendant is under 18 at the time of the application, the inability to participate effectively as a witness giving oral evidence is compromised by their level of intellectual ability or social functioning and the link would enable participation more effectively;

(b) if the defendant is 18 or over and (i) suffers from mental disorder or otherwise has significant impairment of intelligence and social functioning; (ii) is unable as a result to participate effectively as a witness; and (iii) live link would assist.

A court may rescind an order.

Intermediaries

Examination of a witness through an intermediary (Youth and Criminal Evidence Act 1999, s.29) is being tested out in six areas as a pathfinder for national implementation.

The function of an intermediary is to communicate:

(a) to the witness, questions put to the witness; and

(b) to any person asking such questions, the answers given by the witness in reply to them,

and to explain such questions or answers so far as necessary to enable them to be understood by the witness or person in question.

Emerging best practice includes the setting of 'ground rules' in advance of trial based on the intermediary's report about the witness's communication needs and abilities. These ground rules include guidelines on appropriate questioning for that witness and practical issues such as how the intermediary will signal the need for a break or that the witness has not understood. The defence advocate should meet the intermediary before the trial begins.

NOTE

1. Where it appears that there may be weaknesses or potential weaknesses in the prosecution case, it is unwise to rule on the admission of previous convictions until the court is able to make a better assessment of the strengths or weaknesses of the prosecution case, such as when the Crown has called all its evidence but not closed its case: *R.* v. *Gyima and Adjei* [2007] EWCA Crim 429.

CHAPTER 14

Preparing for a contested hearing: process issues

Objectives of this chapter

- To explain how you can argue that your client should be discharged
- To describe the range of pre-trial issues and how you should respond to them
- To show how the trial advocate should be instructed
- To list the pre-trial checks that should be carried out

For useful checklists for Crown Court and magistrates' court trials see **Appendix 2**.

Throughout this chapter references in square brackets are to the LSC Transaction Criteria.

14.1 MAGISTRATES' COURT PRELIMINARY HEARINGS

Either-way cases: application to discharge at committal

When a defendant is to be tried in the Crown Court for an either-way offence you will need to consider whether the prosecution evidence discloses a case to answer. If the evidence is strong you should consider again with your client whether a plea might be entered in the magistrates' court to any either-way offence. This will necessitate an application under MCA 1980, s.25. This will normally be granted, particularly if the defendant has not formally entered a plea (consider *R. v. Warrington Justices, ex p. McDonagh* [1981] Crim LR 629, DC).

If the case is to continue to trial, you should then consider with your client whether applications should be made to discharge the defendant from all or any of those offences. There are tactical issues to bear in mind. If raising the matter will merely give the prosecution notice of an error that they can easily correct, or result in the substitution of another offence triable on indictment, it may be better not to do so. In that event it is good practice to obtain your client's written consent. If, however, the case will be discharged or the prosecution persuaded to discontinue or substitute a lesser charge, a submission should be prepared. Submissions as to the admissibility of evidence may be made at a committal hearing but not if they raise issues under PACE, s.78 as such argument may only be raised at trial. Defence evidence may not be called. Documentary hearsay may be introduced for the prosecution on a certificate from the prosecutor.

You must not agree to commit a case for trial until you have had time to consider evidence fully and to discuss in confidence with your client any tactical issues arising. You should, if necessary, seek an adjournment so that proper consideration may be given to these issues.

Indictable-only offences

CDA 1998 makes provision (in ss.51 and 52 and Sched.3) for adult defendants charged with an offence that is triable only on indictment to be sent straight to the Crown Court for trial following a preliminary hearing in a magistrates' court. The purpose of this hearing is to determine whether there is an indictable-only offence charged and whether there are related offences that also fall to be sent under s.51, to decide the defendant's remand status and to deal with any Representation Order.

An adult accused falls to be dealt with under CDA 1998, s.51 where the offence in respect of which he is appearing:

(a)   is indictable only; or
(b)   is an offence that in certain circumstances is so triable, including offences of trafficking of a Class A drug or a domestic burglary where the accused has two previous convictions for such an offence (PCC(S)A 2000, ss.110, 111) and offences listed in the Firearms Act 1968, s.51A;
(c)   is an either-way offence (or a summary offence which is imprisonable or carries disqualification) which is related to an indictable-only offence in respect of which he is sent to the Crown Court under s.51; or
(d)   is an either-way offence with which he is jointly charged with another defendant who is sent to the Crown Court in respect of a related indictable-only offence.

An adult accused appearing on an indictable-only charge must be sent forthwith to the Crown Court to be tried for that offence. There is, likewise, no discretion in respect of any related offences for which he, or any other person who is jointly charged with him for a related either-way offence, appears at the same time.

But the court does have a discretion whether to send to the Crown Court under s.51 a defendant who appears charged with either-way offences that are related to an indictable-only offence for which he has previously been so sent, or another person who is jointly charged with such a defendant.

Juveniles

Juveniles charged with an indictable-only offence are not liable to be sent to the Crown Court in their own right. But where a juvenile is charged jointly with an adult with any indictable offence in respect of which the adult is sent to the Crown Court under s.51 the magistrates may send the juvenile to the Crown Court as well if they consider that it is in the interests of justice for him to be tried jointly with the adult defendant. Where they do so, the magistrates may also send the juvenile to the Crown Court to be tried for any related offences. In accordance with your instructions, you should consider the argument as to where the interests of justice lie, particularly in the case of a juvenile suffering from mental disability.

Adjournments

CDA 1998, s.52(5) provides that the hearing in the magistrates' court may be adjourned. But it is envisaged that, given the limited nature of the court's function under s.51 it will seldom be considered necessary to adjourn. Circumstances in which it might be necessary to do so are set out below:

1. Normally only the first bail application will be made in the magistrates' court. However, if there is a lack of essential information, it may be appropriate to adjourn for long enough to obtain it.
2. The court need only satisfy itself that the defendant is an adult who is charged with an indictable-only offence. It is not the purpose of the preliminary hearing for the magistrates to determine whether there is a prima facie case. The Crown has the option of withdrawing if it is clear that the indictable-only charge cannot be sustained. Where there is doubt, it would not normally be appropriate to seek to adjourn the hearing unless a short adjournment (of days, not weeks) is likely to resolve the issue.
3. It may be appropriate to adjourn the preliminary hearing where the prosecution requests further time to investigate alleged related offences and it is desired to invoke the power to commit the accused to police detention under MCA 1980, s.128(7) to allow this further investigation.

14.2   CROWN COURT PRELIMINARY HEARINGS

Preliminary hearings for sent cases are not mandatory. They may still be held but (subject to the discretion of the resident judge) should only normally take place in the circumstances set out in the guidance to the standard directions for sent cases contained in Annex E to the Consolidated Criminal Practice Direction as amended on 22 March 2005; available on the Ministry of Justice website (see **Appendix 1** for website link).

Where a preliminary hearing takes place in cases which have been 'sent' to the Crown Court, the court will determine a future timetable for the case including, if appropriate, fixing a date for plea and case management hearing and/or trial date or warned period. Detailed guidance is given with the form in **Appendix 17**.

Bail

An accused whom the magistrates have sent in custody to the Crown Court may make an application for bail to the Crown Court, although many courts require a formal written notice (see **Appendix 2, 2.6**), and the first hearing affords an early opportunity for him to do so. There is nothing to prevent a defendant from seeking to make a bail application on a date before that fixed for the first Crown Court hearing; it is then for the Crown Court to decide when to allow an earlier hearing. If the court so decides, it will depend on the circumstances of the case whether at that hearing it is possible for the court to determine the timetable for the case (in effect bringing forward the date of the preliminary Crown Court hearing), or whether it will still be necessary to hold a hearing for that purpose on the date originally fixed. If an earlier hearing is arranged, the CDA 1998, s.51(7) notice and associated documents should be sent by the magistrates' court to the Crown Court in time for the date set for the hearing, and the CPS should be given as much notice of the date as possible.

Where the magistrates decide to send the accused on bail to the Crown Court, it is open to the prosecution to appeal to the Crown Court under the Bail (Amendment) Act 1993 against the grant of bail. Where this is done, the appeal must be heard within 48 hours. Again the CDA 1998, s.51(7) notice, etc., should be sent to the Crown Court in time for the appeal hearing, although in the time available it may not be possible for the court to do more than to resolve the remand issue.

CPR 16.11 allows the preliminary hearing in the Crown Court to take place in chambers.

Applications to dismiss

CDA 1998, Sched.3, para.1 requires the Attorney General to make regulations containing provision for the date by which the prosecution case must be served. The Crime and Disorder Act 1998 (Service of Prosecution Evidence) Regulations 2005, SI 2005/902 set 50 days (which is extendable) from the date the case is sent to the Crown Court where the defendant is in custody and within 70 days of sending in other cases.

Some defendants wish to indicate their intention to plead guilty at an early stage, although they are not able to enter a plea until the indictment has been preferred.

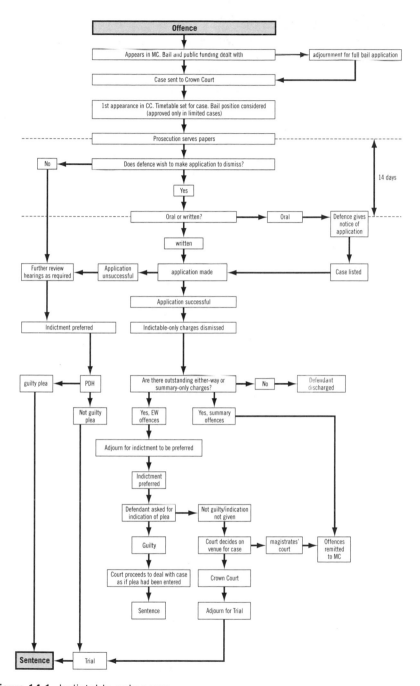

Figure 14.1 Indictable-only cases

The evidence served forms the prima facie case. It is generally convenient for the evidence to be served in one bundle. In a complex case it may be appropriate to serve it as it becomes available, in order to reduce delay. If so the prosecution should notify the defence that more evidence is to be served later. Where the prosecution evidence is served sequentially, the prosecution should advise the defendant and the court whenever the evidence served to date is adequate to constitute service of the prosecution case. This may be before all prosecution evidence has been served.

The date of service of the prosecution case is relevant to the timing of the applications for dismissal, disclosure and the preferment of the indictment. Where the institution of proceedings requires the consent of the Attorney General or the DPP, this is likely to be given after the prosecution case is ready, but before it is served.

Once the prosecution case has been served, the defence may make an application for dismissal under CDA 1998, Sched.3, para.2. Detailed provision for this is made in CPR Part 13. The defence may give notice of intention to make an oral application, or make an application in writing (to which the prosecution may respond with a request for an oral hearing). The notice or written application, accompanied by copies of any material relied on, must be copied to the prosecution, which is allowed 14 days from receipt in which to make comments or adduce further evidence. There is provision for the 14-day period to be extended. The case will be dismissed if the prosecution fails to prove an essential ingredient of the offence or a judge is persuaded that no reasonable jury would convict on the evidence disclosed. Arguments as to admissibility (including under PACE, ss.76 and 78) may be raised.

Like the dismissal rules for transfer cases, the CPR include provision for evidence to be given orally, but only with the judge's leave, which may be given where the interests of justice require. This will often be appropriate in situations where a case has been inadequately investigated and further information may assist the defence in preparing its case, for instance by identifying relevant issues.

If a defendant succeeds in having the case against him dismissed, CDA 1998, Sched.3, para.2(6) provides that no further proceedings on the dismissed charge may be brought other than through a voluntary bill of indictment.

The Prosecution of Offences Act 1985, s.22A (as inserted by CDA 1998, Sched.8) allows the prosecution to discontinue a case that has been sent to the Crown Court under CDA 1998, s.51, at any time before the indictment is preferred.

The Crown Court will deal with a summary offence only if the accused pleads guilty to it and has been convicted of the indictable-only offence to which it is related; in so doing the court's powers are restricted to those that would have been available to a magistrates' court. In any other circumstances the summary offence will either be relisted in the magistrates' court for trial or (if the prosecution does not wish to proceed) be dismissed.

Where (following a successful application to dismiss or discontinuance, or for any reason) the indictable-only offence which caused a case to be sent to the Crown Court is no longer on the indictment, but there remain either-way offences for which the defendant has not been arraigned, the procedures for dealing with them are set out in CDA 1998, Sched.3, paras 7–12 for adult defendants and in para.13 for cases involving juveniles.

In order to avoid unnecessary transfers between the Crown Court and the magistrates' courts, the Crown Court should deal with outstanding either-way offences where there is a guilty plea, or where the case appears suitable for trial on indictment, or where the defendant elects Crown Court trial. Cases should be remitted to the magistrates for trial only where a not guilty plea is indicated (or no indication is given), the case is suitable for summary trial and the defendant is content to be so tried.

The procedure amounts to an adapted plea before venue/mode of trial hearing, at which the Crown Court determines mode of trial in much the same way as the magistrates would do.

First, the outstanding counts on the indictment which charge either-way offences are read to the defendant and the court invites him to indicate a plea, explaining that if he indicates that he would plead guilty, the court will proceed to deal with him as if he had been arraigned and had actually pleaded guilty.

If the defendant indicates that he would plead not guilty or fails to give any indication, the court must next consider whether the case is suitable for summary trial or trial on indictment, having regard to any representations made by the prosecution or the defendant, the nature of the case, the seriousness of the offence, whether magistrates' sentencing powers would be adequate, or any other circumstances.

If the court decides that the offence is more suitable for trial on indictment, the case will proceed in the usual way. If on the other hand it decides that the case is more suitable for summary trial, the court must give the defendant the option of electing Crown Court trial.

Where the indictable-only offence that caused a case to be sent to the Crown Court is no longer on the indictment, cases involving children or young persons should be remitted to the magistrates' court unless it is necessary that they should be tried at the Crown Court. The circumstances in which the Crown Court should deal with juvenile defendants are where:

(a)   the accused faces a specified offence or serious specified offence or is charged with an offence which is a grave crime for the purposes of PCC(S)A 2000, s.91 and the court considers that it may be necessary to use Crown Court sentencing powers; or

(b)   the juvenile is charged jointly with an adult with an either-way offence, and it is necessary in the interests of justice that they should be tried at the Crown Court.

Where a young person is charged alone with an offence which is not a specified, serious specified or grave crime, there is no provision for the Crown Court to retain the case.

14.3   PLEA AND CASE MANAGEMENT HEARING (PCMH)

The case management regime introduced by the Consolidated Criminal Practice Direction handed down on 22 March 2005 is designed to avoid, as far as possible, the need to adjourn hearings, and to reduce to a minimum the number of pre-trial hearings. The emphasis is on the prosecution and defence preparing properly prior to the PCMH to ensure that the PCMH is an effective hearing and that, as far as possible, no further hearings are required prior to trial. You must check that you have gathered all the required information. The relevant forms and guidance appear at **Appendix 17**.

Actions to take before the PCMH

1.   Advise the defendant about sentence discount for a guilty plea [54.6] and inform the Probation Service about an intended guilty plea not less than 15 days before the PCMH.
2.   Draft (and obtain the client's consent to) a defence statement for submission under CPIA 1996, s.5 once initial disclosure has been made.
3.   Select a named trial advocate to be the 'instructed' advocate to whom any payment from public funds will be paid.
4.   Send a brief to the trial advocate within seven days of the committal in a custody case and 21 days in a bail case, allowing the trial advocate seven days to read the brief.
5.   Hold a conference with the intended trial advocate within 14 days of the committal in a custody case and 28 days in a bail case [67].
6.   Ensure that the brief to the intended trial advocate is sufficiently complete to enable him to advise on all matters relevant to the PCMH and contains [58] at least a summary of the evidence, the prosecution committal bundle, the defendant's full instructions, the defence witness statements and the tapes of any interviews with the defendant. Comment on which witnesses should attend court, details of previous convictions, the date of primary disclosure (if any) and details of disclosure already made by the defence.
7.   In all publicly funded cases the Representation Order should be included with the brief as this is the authority for the advocate to be paid from public funds.

8. Submit a list of prosecution witnesses required at the trial, having consulted with the trial advocate, to the court and the prosecution not less than 14 days after committal and again 14 days before the PCMH.
9. Ensure that if the PCMH advocate is not the intended trial advocate, he has clear instructions from the intended trial advocate about conduct of the PCMH and the answers to be given to the judge's PDH questionnaire. Note the provisions of the Consolidated Criminal Practice Direction regarding desirability of trial advocate attending the PCMH.
10. Ensure that if the PCMH advocate is not the trial advocate, he has a note of the intended trial advocate's availability.
11. Decide whether there is a need for the advocate to be instructed during the substantive hearing and if necessary identify the grounds on which the judge may grant a certificate for that purpose.

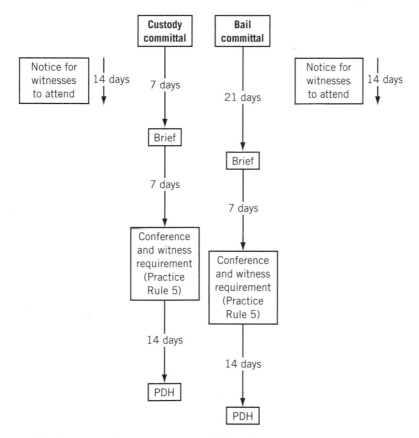

Figure 14.2 Summarising the timescale of the hearing

Timetable after committal (C)

Before

C + 7	Brief to advocate (custody cases)
C + 14	Conference with advocate (custody cases)
C + 14	Serve list of prosecution witnesses required to attend trial
C + 21	Brief to advocate (bail cases)
C + 28	Conference with advocate (custody cases)

Require witnesses to attend trial

Prosecution witness statements used at committal may be read, instead of those witnesses being called, unless a party objects.

The written statements and depositions of the prosecution witnesses will be read out at trial without oral evidence being given, unless the accused informs the Crown Court and the prosecutor within 14 days of the committal. If notice is not given in time, the accused will lose the right to prevent the evidence only being read, unless the court gives leave to require the attendance of the witness.

Asking about intended pleas

The Probation Service may ask about intended pleas either in person at committal or in forms handed out at committal or for the Crown Court probation team or court administrator to send a form to the solicitor for completion and return before the PCMH, requesting the solicitor to notify them about the intended plea(s).

Considering evidence

In co-operation with the advocate consider:

(a)   proofs and observations on evidence and which witnesses will be called;
(b)   CJA 1967, s.9 statements;
(c)   CJA 1967, s.10 admissions;
(d)   what exhibits will be required.

Ensure defence statement and expert evidence, character, hearsay and special measures notices are served at appropriate times.

Considering pleas

In co-operation with the advocate and as necessary:

1.   Discuss appropriate pleas, bearing in mind the gravity of charge, the weight of the evidence, sentencing options and policy including discount for guilty plea.

2. In the event of guilty plea ensure contact is made with the Probation Service (at least 15 days before the PCMH) so that pre-sentence reports are prepared and that any medical or psychiatric reports are available, and remember to obtain any necessary authorities.
3. Obtain written consent from the client before suggesting the tendering of alternative pleas to the prosecution as this may be admissible in evidence if rejected.
4. Consider obtaining written confirmation from your client if he is tendering a plea on a particular version of the facts.

Relevance of statement made in plea and directions hearings

Statements in the course of such a proceeding, which have no force of law, or the contents of the questionnaire should not be used for evidential purposes without the consent of the party affected (*R. v. Hutchinson* [1985] Crim LR 730). What is said at such a hearing is not expected to form part of the material used at trial and it is rarely appropriate to refer to it. Instead hearings are meant for the efficient disposal of business in the Crown Court (*R. v. Diedrich and Aldridge* [1997] Crim LR 58).

However, care must be taken to avoid the prosecution treating the matter as an exceptional case and admissions made by you as the advocate or agent being admissible under common law hearsay rules.

Custody time limits

An appearance at a PCMH does not bring a custody time limit to an end unless your client is arraigned. Sureties must normally attend a PCMH.

14.4 OTHER PRE-TRIAL ISSUES

Pre-trial reviews

Both magistrates' courts and the Crown Court can hold pre-trial reviews to check on progress in a case or to deal with specific issues. Liaise with the case progression officer.

Binding rulings

Magistrates or a Crown Court judge may make at any pre-trial hearing a ruling (MCA 1980, s.8A; CPIA 1996, ss.39–43) as to:

(a) the admissibility of evidence; and/or
(b) any question of law.

You should identify any such issue and provide sufficient material for the advocate to argue the case. The judge's ruling is binding unless later discharged or varied in the interests of justice.

However, a party cannot apply to discharge or vary unless they can show a material change of circumstances. Such hearings are particularly suitable to deal with character and hearsay applications so that all parties are aware by the time of trial of the relevant admissible evidence.

Preparatory hearings

Formal preparatory hearings (which are the start of the relevant trial and end a custody time limit) may be held in cases where the indictment involves a serious or complex fraud case or reveals a case of such complexity, seriousness (CJA 2003, s.309) or length that substantial benefit is likely to accrue from:

(a)   identifying the material issues;
(b)   assisting the jury's comprehension of the case;
(c)   expediting proceedings;
(d)   assisting the judge's management of the case.

Sureties should attend.

At a preparatory hearing the judge may:

(a)   adjourn the proceedings;
(b)   rule on admissibility or law (from which ruling all parties may appeal);
(c)   order a prosecution case statement, the service of schedules and consideration of CJA 1967, s.10 requests;
(d)   order a defence case statement.

A case statement will include:

- principal facts;
- witnesses;
- exhibits;
- propositions of law and consequences of these;
- the nature of the defence and principal matters in dispute;
- objections to the prosecution case statement;
- points of law to be argued;
- CJA 1967, s.10 admissions.

Preparatory hearings also take place:

(a)   when the Crown seeks a trial without a jury in intimidation cases;
(b)   where charges are to be treated as specified allowing a trial on the remaining matters without a jury;
(c)   where there has been a preparatory hearing: both sides may lodge interlocutory appeals to the Court of Appeal.

Defence witnesses

The defence need not disclose witnesses (except expert or under the disclosure rules) until CJA 2003, s.34 is brought into force. This cannot be done until a code of practice has been agreed. A case statement under these provisions cannot normally be used as part of the prosecution case.

Attending the advocate at preliminary court hearings

A representative may always attend the advocate at any preliminary hearing. At those hearings, consideration must be given as to whether a representative should attend the trial or sentencing hearing. A judge's certificate will be required in many cases. However, if fixed litigator's fees are introduced, careful consideration will be required as to the real necessity for such a certificate.

Representation Order

An RDCO Form B statement of means must be supplied to the Crown Court within four days of the first date of hearing in publicly funded cases.

14.5   REPRESENTATION FOR TRIAL

Level of representation

Consider appropriate level of representation:

1. Who is the most suitable advocate for the type of case and personality of client?
2. In the magistrates' court, consider application for certificate for counsel in appropriate cases.
3. In Crown Court, if appropriate, consider whether suitable solicitor has rights of audience.
4. If not, consider choice of suitable counsel.

Be aware of the complex provisions of the Criminal Defence Service (General) (No.2) Regulations 2001, SI 2001/1437 (as amended) as to the number of advocates who may be instructed in different situations and ensure that your Representation Order covers exactly the levels of representation that you require.

A QC may accept instructions in the Crown Court to appear without junior counsel in cases such as:

(a) pleas of guilty worthy of silk representation where the plea is certain in advance of the hearing;

(b)   appeals to the Court of Appeal, Criminal Division, worthy of silk representation which can properly be undertaken by a silk alone;

(c)   otherwise straightforward matters which have some sensitive overlay, whether political, local or other.

See the Solicitors' Code of Conduct 2007, guidance notes 8 and 9 to Rule 11 (Attending advocates at court) (**www.sra.org.uk**).

Conferences

The object of a conference is to enable your client to meet his advocate to establish confidence and to be advised jointly by the trial advocate and solicitor. A conference with the trial advocate should normally be held in the following cases and a record kept of the decision whether to do so [67.1]:

(a)   where there is a not guilty hearing;

(b)   where your client needs to be advised about plea(s);

(c)   where the case is complicated by a particular factor or involves serious consequences;

(d)   where the case requires careful consideration of tactics, evidence, plea, experts, exhibits, witnesses.

Your client should be informed of the date and time of the conference. Consider holding the conference at your office so as to ensure his attendance at the conference and that time is not wasted waiting unnecessarily for him.

The solicitor should take an active part in the conference and not merely take notes. Full notes of the conference are essential however, and should be typed up afterwards and sent to the advocate and to the client.

At the end of the conference the solicitor should prepare a list of action points to be taken and confirm this with the advocate. These matters should be prepared as soon as possible. If you anticipate any difficulties then contact the court to ensure sufficient time is given.

If your client fails to attend two conferences then consider listing the case before a judge, without attendance of the witnesses, so as to obtain the client's instructions. Solicitors should write to the client to this effect before taking this action.

Brief to trial advocate

A brief to the trial advocate (whether in-house or solicitor advocate/counsel) should contain full and detailed information concerning the case and be prepared as soon as possible after committal proceedings. In the case of any unusual preparation or expenditure it may be prudent to seek the advice and support of the advocate to justify any application for authorities from the Legal Services Commission and ultimately to assist in any problems that may arise on determination. Such advice could cover the cost of transcripts, enquiry agent's fees, expert witnesses and the like, where the solicitor has any doubt that they may be required.

Other relevant documents should be included as enclosures with the brief. The backsheet to the brief should contain the name of the court, name of the case (including co-defendants), the case number (if known), which defendant the advocate is instructed to act for, whether remuneration is by public funding or fee and the name, address, telephone number and reference of the instructing solicitor.

Information to be included in brief to advocate [58]

Heading: to include next hearing date and court and case number.

1. Enclosures.
2. Details of charges in indictment.
3. Pleas to be entered.
4. Case history including committal date/date sent or transferred/date of PCMH.
5. Detail of co-accused.
6. Any relationship with prosecution witness or co-defendants.
7. Bail history in the case.
8. Periods of time in custody.
9. Background information on accused.
10. Full antecedents of the defendant.
11. Previous convictions [58.5].
12. TICs and any disputes over compensation arising on charges or TICs.
13. An outline of the prosecution case [58.1].
14. A summary of what each prosecution witness deals with [73.1].
15. Outline of the defence case, possible witnesses and exhibits.
16. Defence statement (detail of any disclosure already made by the defence) [73.7].
17. Witness list submitted (CPIA 1996, s.68) (and comments on which witnesses should attend court) [58.3] to include adviser at police station if relevant.
18. Expert reports.
19. Plans/photographs.
20. An analysis of the major issues, factual and evidential, in the case.
21. Any particular problems and any particular area on which the advocate advice is sought.
22. Whether or not a conference is required.
23. Directions sought at PCMH or pre-trial review.
24. Public or private funding and details of any applications in relation to costs.
25. Instructions to the advocate to advise on appeal at end of case.

Backsheet must include:

(a)   date prepared;
(b)   identity of allocated litigator;
(c)   identity of allocated advocate;
(d)   AIM number.

Enclosures to be included with brief to advocate

1. Indictment/charge sheet/committal documents.
2. Prosecution statements and exhibits (including police station interview tape) [58.2].
3. Additional evidence.
4. Client's proof on allegation and investigation.
5. Client's observations on prosecution evidence.
6. Statement of defendant's personal circumstances.
7. Additional background information on client references, etc.
8. A list of previous convictions [73.5].
9. A schedule of TICs.
10. Defence statement.
11. Statements of defence witnesses [58.4].
12. Expert reports.
13. Unused material:

    (a)   initial disclosure, with date given, and MG6C schedule [58.6];
    (b)   continuing disclosure (if any, and/or request for continuing disclosure).

14. Hearsay notices.
15. Character notice.
16. Bail/custody time limit application.
17. Copy of correspondence with prosecution and details of any disclosure made by defence.
18. Copy of Representation Order.
19. Standard brief to unattended advocates.
20. Standard brief in relation to appeal.

Attending the advocate at the hearing

Payment from public funding for providing support for the advocate at court for a case listed for trial (including Newton hearings and what turn out to be cracked trials); hearings of cases listed for pleas of guilty (following a plea and directions hearing); sentence hearings following a committal for sentence; appeals against conviction and/or sentence and bring backs for breach of a Crown Court order can only be authorised where the proceedings, or the personal circumstances of the legally assisted person, fall within one or other of five exceptions, or the litigator has obtained a certificate of attendance to provide support for the advocate at court: see the Solicitors' Code of Conduct 2007, guidance notes 8 and 9 to Rule 11 (Attending advocates at court). The exceptions are:

(a) the defendant is charged with a class 1 or 2 offence;
(b) the proceedings have been brought or taken over by the Serious Fraud Office or are before the Crown Court by reasons of a notice of transfer under the Criminal Justice Act 1987, s.4 (serious or complex fraud transfers);
(c) the legally assisted person is or was at the time when the Crown Court acquired jurisdiction of the case (by committal, transfer or otherwise) a child or young person within the meaning of the Children and Young Persons Act 1933, s.107;
(d) the legally assisted person is unable to understand the proceedings or give instructions because of an inadequate knowledge of English, mental illness, other mental or physical disability; or
(e) the legally assisted person, if convicted, is likely to receive a custodial sentence whether suspended or to take immediate effect. This exemption is only available for the days when a sentence of imprisonment is likely to be imposed.

These provisions do not affect the situation where solicitors attend court for a conference with the advocate where a conference is necessary. The Law Society advises that where practitioners consider it necessary to attend or arrange for the attendance of a responsible representative, a certificate should be applied for. Careful consideration will be required if fixed litigators' fees are introduced and more may be expected of advocates than has historically been the case.

A certificate may be granted at PCMH and after on any ground that satisfies the judge, but regulations include examples of suitable situations where:

(a) there are numbers of defence witnesses;
(b) there are quantities of defence evidence;
(c) the defendant is disruptive;
(d) there is more than one defendant;
(e) there is a need for note taking.

14.6 FINAL PREPARATION

Review before the hearing

You should review readiness for the hearing sufficiently in advance to enable steps to be taken if shortcomings are discovered.

Prosecution case

Check receipt (as appropriate) and keep a record of dates of receipt of:

(a)   record of previous convictions;
(b)   advance information;
(c)   tapes of interviews;
(d)   custody records;
(e)   committal bundle;
(f)   notices of additional evidence;
(g)   prosecution initial disclosure: undermining material and schedule;
(h)   prosecution continuing disclosure: material that may assist the defence case;
(i)   expert's report.

Check that the CPS has been told:

(a)   which witnesses are required (and confirmed in writing);
(b)   whether the record of interview required editing;
(c)   if tape recording of police interview is required to be played in court;
(d)   of any agreement as to s.9 statement or s.10 admissions;
(e)   of any expert evidence to be called.

Defence case

Check that the defendant has been:

(a)   proofed adequately and that he understands the practicalities of giving evidence [61.1];
(b)   advised whether to give a defence statement in the magistrates' court and the implications of doing so [63.1, 63.2];
(c)   advised of the implications of giving a defence statement in the Crown Court or not doing so and whether and when it should be signed [64.1, 64.2, 64.3];
(d)   warned of hearing date/time/place [59.1];
(e)   given access to his proof of evidence;
(f)   advised of court procedures, behaviour [59.2] and of evidence to be given by both prosecution and defence [60];
(g)   advised whether or not to give evidence [59] and the implications of not giving evidence [62.1].

Check that defence witnesses have been:

(a)   proofed adequately;
(b)   warned of hearing date/time/place [66.1];
(c)   reminded of evidence if appropriate;
(d)   advised of court procedures, behaviour [66.2].

Check defence statement (if appropriate) has been given to the CPS and the court [65.1]. If it is known in advance that the defence is unable to proceed ensure that the court is given notice [68.1].

Brief to unattended advocate

In cases where an advocate is unattended:

1. Deal with advocate's early arrival at court to see the client.
2. Include sufficient details about the defendant and any witnesses to enable the advocate to contact them if they do not appear.
3. Require the judge's comments on sentence to be fully recorded.
4. Require notes to be provided of the headings of the advocate's speech in mitigation.
5. Require a telephone report to the solicitor after the case ends.
6. Require the advocate to deal with witnesses' expenses.
7. Require the advocate to deal with the client and any relatives who may be present after the case has been concluded.
8. Require the advocate to find out where the client has been taken if in custody, and pass that information to the solicitor.
9. Require the advocate to endorse the brief within two days with what oral advice on appeal has been given to the client.

Notification of trial

If a date for trial is fixed notify your client promptly of the name and address of the court and the date and time attendance is required and the date and time of any conference arranged and seek confirmation of receipt by enclosing an addressed pre-paid envelope.

If a date is not fixed the matter will be placed in the warned list. Write a letter to your client informing him of the warned list procedure. Clients may not otherwise understand the procedure.

As soon as you are notified that a case is on the warned list notify your client. Practices as regards notification will vary depending on a client's communicability (distance, telephone, etc.); ask your client to provide a telephone number where he can be contacted, or where somebody else can contact him, at short notice, if possible. It is your duty to take reasonable steps to ensure your client attends court on time. Failure by your client to attend will necessitate further adjournments and could lead to arrest.

Be sure to notify sureties when a trial is listed. They will have to attend.

Attendance at trial

1. Where a solicitor or representative attends the advocate, he must be fully appraised of the case.
2. The role of the solicitor is an active one ensuring that the advocate represents the client's case fully at court, and offering assistance when appropriate.
3. Ensure defence witnesses are available/contactable.
4. Take as full notes of evidence as possible and with particular care when the advocate is on his feet. Always make full notes of the judge's comments. The advocate will often require notes of evidence overnight or during the trial. Make them legible and ensure that there are gaps between lines so that the advocate can identify relevant sections.
5. You can and should take instructions from your client during the trial. Be aware your client may wish to speak to you from the dock. You may not however advise your client or otherwise discuss the case from the time he starts giving evidence, until he has left the witness box, without leave of the court. Advise him of this rule in advance. This rule also applies to all other witnesses.
6. Obtain witness expense forms, assist witnesses to fill them in and take them to the accounts department.
7. If your client is convicted and/or sentenced to a term of imprisonment or otherwise, ensure that you attend your client with the advocate.
8. Contact the family/friends after the case and with your client's authority inform them of result.
9. When seeing a client who has been sentenced to a term of imprisonment, ensure that he signs relevant documents, e.g. a letter of authority regarding any property to be returned or otherwise.
10. Ensure that sureties attend court on the first day of trial.

CHAPTER 15

Youths

Objectives of this chapter

- To enable you to work within the distinct ideology, law, practice and procedures of the Youth Court
- To identify relevant issues around bail, place of trial and sentencing
- To emphasise the factors specific to preparing a case with a young client
- To show when youths should be diverted from the criminal justice system

15.1   GENERAL CONSIDERATIONS

Your duty to your client

Your primary duty is to your client (Solicitors' Code of Conduct 2007, 1.04). This is the child or young person. Some parents or appropriate adults purport to be giving instructions or try to interfere with your client's instructions. They have no right to do so and it is the solicitor's responsibility to ensure that the roles are made clear right from the start of the professional relationship. The criminal justice system is new to many clients and their families and they are understandably confused, and afraid. First and foremost you are responsible for representing your client; working with the family and appropriate adult is ancillary, but should of course be approached with respect for their possible anxiety. Although sometimes this causes difficulties, usually most family members will co-operate and be supportive when the difference in duties and roles is explained and understood. Any confusion in your primary duty to your client can risk you failing in your professional duty and, more importantly, failing your client.

Speaking to your client alone

You should talk to your client alone, both at the outset and at various stages in the case. This is because an appropriate adult is not bound by a duty of confidentiality and is a potential prosecution witness. You should specifically advise your client of this. The Law Society Criminal Law Committee issued guidance on this: see [1993] *Gazette*, 19 May. Some clients may be less forth-coming with you in the presence of the appropriate adult, especially if the appropriate adult is a parent or guardian.

You can speak to the parent/appropriate adult alone or with the client afterwards, depending on what the client's instructions are. Some legal repre-sentatives are anecdotally reported to ignore their client, particularly where the appropriate adult is another 'professional', for example, a social worker. Remember to explain your role to the client and to the appropriate adult as necessary.

Client's age

The age of the child or young person at the date of the offence and at stages throughout the case is of vital importance. Age impacts on criminal respon-sibility, where the case is dealt with, bail, sentencing and mitigation. It partic-ularly influences expectations about the child's emotional and intellectual maturity, although age and physical development are not usually conclusive of maturity. You should keep a regular note of the child or young person's age in years and months.

Throughout your dealings with a young person he/she is likely to be devel-oping physically, intellectually, emotionally and socially, but changes in different areas of development do not necessarily happen at the same time. Be alert to this.

Using appropriate language

You should always use language and give explanations that will be under-stood by the particular client – as you would for adult clients who may some-times find it difficult to understand some of the language in the criminal process – it may be even harder for some children or young people and those who have not previously experienced the criminal justice system. 'Putting the case back' or 'adjournment' can be meaningless phrases to the client.

Young people usually have a short attention span. They are unlikely to take in a large amount of information at one time. This should be borne in mind when both imparting and collecting information.

Using an interpreter

The necessary use of a language interpreter inevitably reduces the ease of communication. You must put aside extra time to ensure effective communi-cation with the young person through an interpreter. Sometimes the client does not require an interpreter but his/her parent does. The client may be used to interpreting or translating for a parent and automatically attempt to take on this role. Where the court hasn't arranged an interpreter, for example where the client speaks English but his/her parent does not, beware the client interpreting to the parent. It is not appropriate for a non-English speaking parent to act as the appropriate adult at the police station or at court unless a suitable interpreter is available. The officers at the police station or the court will be responsible for arranging for an interpreter for the appropriate adult.

Balancing client, court and statutory duties

CDA 1998, s.37 states that:

(1) It shall be the principal aim of the youth justice system to prevent offending by children and young persons.
(2) In addition to any other duty to which they are subject, it shall be the duty of all persons and bodies carrying out functions in relation to the youth justice system to have regard to that aim.

The qualification in the legislation was sought by the Law Society Criminal Law Committee in recognition of the defence solicitor's primary duty being to the client. The current ethos and culture of government policy is to reduce offending and the defence solicitor may feel under pressure to minimise their defence role. The balancing of the duties to the client, the court and the statutory duty is not usually in conflict but sometimes can be complex. If in doubt as to your position, contact the Professional Ethics Department at the Solicitors Regulation Authority on 0870 606 2577.

Welfare of the child

Any client under 18 is a child for the purposes of the Children Act 1989 (it is recommended that you are familiar with Parts III and IV in particular and the duties of local authorities to provide services to safeguard the welfare of children in need, and the various duties to accommodate). The principal consideration of the Children Act 1989 is the welfare of the child (s.1(3) the 'welfare checklist'). The welfare of the child or young person, although not the paramount consideration on sentencing, is also a statutory consideration under the Children and Young Persons Act 1933, s.44 which provides that:

Every court in dealing with a child or young person who is brought before it, either as an offender or otherwise, shall have regard to the welfare of the child or young person, and shall in a proper case take steps for removing him from undesirable surroundings, and for securing that proper provision is made for his education and training.

This applies to both the defendant and young witnesses when before the court.

International standards

You should be aware of the United Nations Convention on the Rights of the Child (1989) (**www.unhcr.ch/html/menu3/b/k2crc.htm**) and the United Nations Standard Minimum Rules for the Administration of Juvenile Justice – the Beijing Rules (1985) (**www.unhcr.ch/html/menu3/b/h_comp48.htm**). These conventions have been ratified by the UK but do not have direct effect. They are rarely referred to in most Youth Courts or cases. However, international standards will become increasingly important in our jurisprudence, as they already have in the European Court of Human Rights (**www.echr.coe.int**).

Youth offending teams

You should be prepared to challenge information shared by youth offending teams (YOTs) as necessary. The YOT will often provide information to the court in relation to bail issues, or by way of pre-sentence or specific sentence report. The information collected by them can be provided by agencies other than the client, and it should not be assumed that all information will be accurate.

Diversion: those under 18

When young people first get into trouble, behave anti-socially or commit minor offences, they can be dealt with outside the court system. If children are behaving anti-socially, the police and local authority can use a variety of pre-court orders including:

- acceptable behaviour contracts;
- anti-social behaviour orders;
- local child curfews;
- child safety orders.

The purpose of these pre-court orders is to stop young people getting sucked into the youth justice system.

Publicity

Reporting restrictions automatically apply to most proceedings in the Youth Court so that the name, address or school of a child or young person is not published. But if your client is being prosecuted for being in breach of an ASBO or an order is made on conviction, the automatic restrictions do not apply and you will need to ask the court to make an order if you wish to restrict what is published.[1]

15.2   THE REPRIMAND AND FINAL WARNING SYSTEM

If the young person has committed a first or second minor offence, a system of reprimands and final warnings under CDA 1998, ss.65 and 66 can be used by the police. Where the police consider that the Threshold Test (as set out in the Code for Crown Prosecutors; see **Chapter 5**) is met in a case, other than an indictable-only offence, and determine that it is in the public interest instead to administer a reprimand or final warning, the police may do so without referring the case to a Crown Prosecutor.

A reprimand is a formal verbal warning given by a police officer to a young person who admits they are guilty of a minor first offence. You should be satisfied that there is sufficient evidence of that guilt. Sometimes the young person can be referred to the YOT to take part in a voluntary programme to help them address their offending behaviour.

A final warning is a formal verbal warning given by a police officer to a young person who admits their guilt for a first or second offence. Again, you should be satisfied that guilt can be proved. Unlike a reprimand, however, a final warning also means the young person is assessed to determine the causes of their offending behaviour and a programme of activities is identified to address them.

A reprimand or warning must be given in person by a police officer. Where the young person is aged under 17, the reprimand or warning must be given in the presence of a parent or guardian or other appropriate adult (which cannot be the person's legal representative), and any written information must also be issued to the adult.

However, prosecutors must also consider what course of action will meet the statutory duty to prevent offending. Prosecutors should ensure that a youth is prosecuted through the courts only where there are clear public interest factors in favour of prosecution. Having applied the evidential test and arrived at the appropriate charge(s), Crown Prosecutors should consider the public interest criteria. Primarily this is as set out in the Code for Crown Prosecutors (see **Appendix 1** for website link).

A decision whether to prosecute a youth offender is open to judicial review if it can be demonstrated that the decision was made regardless of, or clearly contrary to, a settled policy of the DPP developed in the public interest such as the Code for Crown Prosecutors. See also *R.* v. *Chief Constable of Kent, ex p. L*; *R.* v. *DPP, ex p. B* (1991) 93 Cr App R 416. The judgment in this case highlights the importance of the prosecutor obtaining in appropriate cases as much information as possible from sources such as the police and YOTs, about the youth offender's home circumstances and background before reviewing a case. The court held that an application for judicial review could be successful if the decision to prosecute was made against a background of lack of, or insufficient, inquiry into the circumstances and general character of the accused.

The final warning scheme has replaced cautions for children and young people. Once a young offender has received a warning a further offence will usually result in a criminal charge. The process involved and the criteria that must be met before a reprimand or warning can be considered are set out in **Chapter 5**.

In the ACPO Youth Offender Case Disposal Gravity Factor System, the offences listed are each scored at entry point levels of one to four, with aggravating and mitigating factors that may take the offence up or down on the scale by a maximum of one point.

- Level 1: Always the minimum response applicable to the individual offender, i.e. reprimand, warning or charge. Example offence: obstructing police.
- Level 2: Normally reprimand for a first offence. If offender does not qualify for a reprimand but qualifies for a warning then give warning. If offender does not qualify for a warning, then charge. Example offence: criminal damage.
- Level 3: Normally warn for a first offence. If the offender does not qualify for a warning then charge. Only in exceptional circumstances should a reprimand be given. The decision maker needs to justify remand. Example offence: burglary (non-dwelling).
- Level 4: Always charge. Example offence: Burglary (dwelling).

15.3   COURT PROCEEDINGS

You owe the same duty to a youth as to any other client. You should meet with or at least telephone the client before their first appearance. The client often assumes there will be a full trial at the first hearing, and may not have absorbed any information given after charge and so will need early reassurance and information. In addition, taking instructions and giving advice is more time consuming when dealing with children than it is with most adults, and the office environment is less stressful and distracting than the police station or court environs. It is rarely possible to give or obtain sufficient information at one appointment sitting, but young clients can be erratic in keeping appointments, so you will need to make the best use of the client's presence at any time. Be prepared to seek an adjournment in the client's interests.

Client's ability to understand

You should undertake your own assessment of the client's ability to understand the proceedings and their situation. You might wish to adapt the format now used by police (this will be attached to the custody record) which sets out a series of questions, for example, 'did you go to a special school?'.

Some clients will have learning or emotional difficulties and will require psychological or psychiatric reports.

Some clients are open about their literacy but many are embarrassed and can fake literacy very skilfully. All information must be gone through verbally with the client.

However, even if the client is illiterate, they must still be sent a copy of the evidence and their draft proof. The client may be able to read this through with, for example, their parent or social worker. Some firms have links with local groups to whom they can refer young people for this purpose.

Reports relevant to the case

If the client has previously had contact with the criminal justice system resulting in a conviction or a final warning the likelihood is that there will be a report from a YOT. You should obtain a copy as soon as possible.

If the client has not previously been involved in the system, you should consider obtaining relevant school or medical reports, any statement of special educational needs, social services records and/or contact any other professional who has had dealings with the client. You may also wish to contact a favourite teacher, or other professional for a character reference to use in any mitigation. However, you will require the client and their parent's/guardian's consent in writing and you should have blank consent forms with you in the file. You should explain to the client and the parents why such information may be of use. Remember to keep explaining your role. The family may often have had so much contact with so many professionals that they no longer distinguish between them.

The need for your client to understand

The client may also be embarrassed to admit to not understanding or may be passive in the face of official proceedings and not consider it necessary to understand. It is your responsibility to impress on them that they are 'employing' and instructing you, and that therefore they need to engage with the proceedings and the process.

Appropriateness of the charge

You will in any event be considering the appropriateness of charge both against the evidence and against the Code for Crown Prosecutors. Be aware that the Threshold Test requires only reasonable suspicion and be prepared to argue that no further action should be taken. Check in particular whether the case is suitable for a reprimand or formal warning based on an informed decision by your client. The CPS may be more persuaded if representations are supported by medical or psychiatric evidence but this is not always appropriate and the client's instructions should first be obtained. Where the CPS is not prepared to reconsider the charge, you may, in extreme cases, wish to consider an application for leave to apply for judicial review.

Preparing for mitigation

Obtaining reports and information is part of preparation of mitigation at sentence.

Action at court

It is vital to speak to the YOT officer at court. The YOT will have up-to-date antecedents which is the copy the bench will see and which you will need to obtain. The CPS will generally have a copy, but it is not always up to date (as in the adult courts). It is particularly helpful to speak to the YOT member if there is to be a bail application (see below) to obtain information on availability of local bail packages, and to ensure no additional information has arisen that you and/or the prosecutor are unaware of.

15.4   REPRESENTATION ORDERS

Finances

In the Youth Court or the magistrates' court, means are not an issue for youths under 18. The Crown Court has power to order that the defendant pay their defence costs. The Youth Court or magistrates' court does not. It is only if youths are transferred/sent/committed to the Crown Court for trial or there is an appeal against conviction that a Form B has to be completed. It is the means of the youth that are in issue.

Interests of justice

The same criteria apply as for adults, but stress the age of the defendant (and of the witnesses who may well also be young persons). In practice it is rare for the order to be refused. You should be prepared to appeal if necessary – children and young people cannot be expected to represent themselves in criminal courts.

15.5   PREPARING THE CLIENT

The Youth Court is not an open court. You will need to remind the court about reporting restrictions (Children and Young Persons Act 1933, s.49) where the client appears in the adult magistrates' court, for example where charged with an adult and appearing there or in relation to breach of bail conditions.

You should explain the procedure you expect at the hearing to the client but warn them that sometimes other issues come up and the procedure may change. Prepare the client for what their involvement might be. For example, where you are trying to persuade the bench to adopt a community disposal, some benches routinely ask the defendant's advocate if they can address the client direct, and in some cases permission is not sought at all. Technically you can decline permission or intervene but this approach may not always assist the client's best interests. Unless there is good reason such as mental health problems or communication problems, you should prepare the client for this possibility. Your clients are increasingly expected to engage with the court.

The informality of the Youth Court is generally observed but within limits. You should also advise the client about the impact of their body language and physical attitude – it won't help your client if he or she is slouching, chewing or apparently ignoring the proceedings, even if their attitude is clearly a result of fear or bravado.

In the atmosphere of the court a youth may behave in a disruptive manner, including in the public area to impress other youths in the vicinity. You should advise such a client that excessive disruptive behaviour may lead to exclusion from the court building and will not make a good impression on the court. However, you should seek to avoid creating the perception with your client that you are someone who is not on their side, who is in authority and only wishing to reprimand him/her. Being seen to tell the client off can create difficulties between the practitioner and the client later.

15.6   PLACE OF TRIAL

Those under 18 do not normally have a right to elect jury trial but issues can arise as to the preferred place of trial for them (see **Figure 15.1**). You should be aware of your client's age at all stages:

1.   If a youth attains 18, a case may be remitted from the Youth Court to the adult magistrates' court. Consider relevant arguments.
2.   If a youth is jointly charged with an adult, they must normally appear in the adult magistrates' court: be aware of the limitations this imposes on sentence without remittal to the Youth Court.
3.   If a youth is jointly charged with an adult who is committed, transferred or sent to the Crown Court the youth may also be committed, etc., if it is in the interests of justice. Consider with your client the preferred place of trial and relevant arguments.

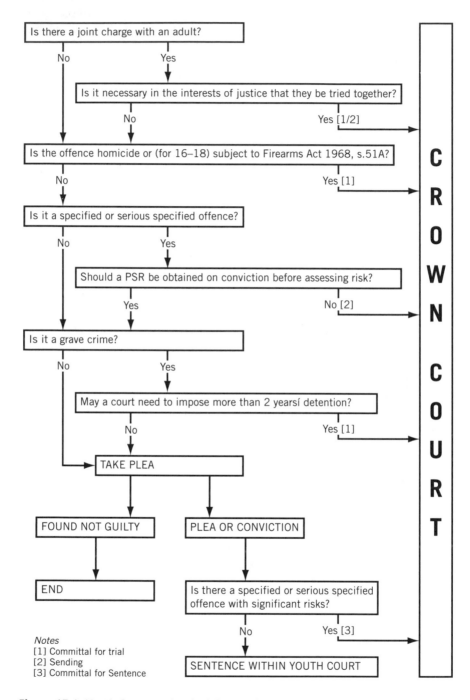

Figure 15.1 Youth Court mode of trial procedures

4. Youths charged with homicide or (if 16 but under 18) with offences covered by the Firearms Act 1968, s.51A must be tried at the Crown Court.
5. Youth offenders charged with an indictable-only offence are not liable to be sent to the Crown Court in their own right. But where a youth is charged jointly with an adult with any indictable offence in respect of which the adult is sent to the Crown Court under CDA 1998, s.51, the magistrates may send the youth to the Crown Court as well if they consider that it is in the interests of justice for him to be tried jointly with the adult defendant. Where they do so, the magistrates may also send the youth to the Crown Court to be tried for any related offences. In accordance with your instructions, you should consider the argument as to where the interests of justice lie, particularly in the case of a youth suffering from mental disability.
6. If a youth faces a charge of a grave crime (those crimes listed in PCC(S)A 2000, s.91; see below) or is a dangerous young offender (as defined by CJA 2003) consider whether the magistrates' court or the Youth Court may decline jurisdiction because they may not have sufficient sentencing power; your client's preferred place of trial; and all relevant arguments. In the event of a guilty plea it will be usual to seek to have the matter tried at the summary level as this significantly limits the court's sentencing powers.
7. Grave crimes are (PCC(S)A 2000, s.91):

   (a) an offence punishable in the case of a person aged 21 or over with imprisonment of 14 years or more not being an offence for which the sentence is fixed by law; or
   (b) an offence under the Sexual Offences Act 2003, s.3 (sexual assault); or
   (c) an offence under the Sexual Offences Act 2003, s.13 (child sex offences committed by children or young persons); or
   (d) an offence under the Sexual Offences Act 2003, s.25 (sexual activity with a child family member); or
   (e) an offence under the Sexual Offences Act 2003, s.26 (inciting a child family member to engage in sexual activity.

8. The issue in relation to a grave crime is whether the Youth Court will have sufficient sentencing power and the test is whether it may be necessary to impose detention in excess of two years on the facts of the particular case. You should have regard to the relevant guidelines.
9. Specified and serious specified offences are set out in **Appendix 9.**
10. In *R. (on the application of Crown Prosecution Service)* v. *South East Surrey Youth Court* [2006] Crim LR 367 the court had to reconcile statutory provisions that do not present a coherent picture. The court held:

    (a) The policy of the legislation is that youths should be dealt with in the Youth Court.
    (b) The decision of the court in *R. v. Lang* [2006] Crim LR 174 should be particularly noted in relation to youths who commit non-serious specified offences.

(c) There is a need for rigour before finding significant risk of serious harm. Such a conclusion will almost always require a pre-sentence report by the youth offending team.

(d) It is therefore unlikely to be appropriate to find dangerousness before the conviction. If the defendant is convicted there may be a committal for sentence then.

15.7   COURT BAIL AND REMAND

Children and youths under 18

Young people of 17 years old are treated by the courts as if they were adults. On refusal of bail, 17-year-olds will be sent to a Young Offenders Institution (YOI) or remand centre.

For those who are 10–16 years old the court may bail with or without conditions. If bail is refused there may be remand to local authority accommodation, as a starting point, with or without conditions (conditions may be, for example, non-association and curfew); and secure remand. Secure remand can be secure local authority accommodation if certain criteria are met (see CDA 1998, ss.97 and 98 and Children and Young Persons Act 1969, s.23(4A) and (5A)) or custody. Remand to custody should be an absolute last resort – see Home Office Circular 30/1992, *Criminal Justice Act 1991: Young People and the Youth Court*, para.49, which strongly encourages the use of local bail support programmes. A 15- or 16-year-old boy who is not vulnerable (i.e. not less mature emotionally or physically than his peers such as to cause difficulties or the likelihood of self-harm in a prison setting) may be remanded to a YOI or remand centre.

When conditional bail is relevant you should have first canvassed with your client any problems that likely conditions may cause for the child and his or her family, in order to ensure that there are conditions with which your client and his/her parents or any other named person can comply (and with which others agree to comply), which will not impact on schooling or other acceptable extra-curricular activity. The court should consider the client's welfare under the Children and Young Persons Act 1933, s.44 in making conditions. When conditions are read out check with the client or parent/guardian if these are likely to cause any real problems in making decisions.

Secure remands

The local authority may apply to the court to hold young persons aged 10–16 years old in secure accommodation under the Children Act 1989, s.25.

However, the Children and Young Persons Act 1969, s.23 (as amended) gives the courts power to remand certain categories of 12–16-year-olds direct to local authority secure accommodation: all 12–14-year-olds; 15- and 16-year-old girls; and 'vulnerable' 15- and 16-year-old boys: in each case if a place has been identified in advance. Alternatively, courts may remand 15- and 16-year-old boys direct to prison accommodation. In all these cases, the criteria in the Children and Young Persons Act 1969, s.23(5) have to be met. Eventually courts will have power to remand all categories of 12–16-year-olds to local authority secure accommodation.

The s.23(5) criteria as amended are:

(a) the child or young person is charged with, or has been convicted of, a violent or sexual offence, or of an offence punishable, in the case of an adult, with imprisonment for a term of 14 years or more; or

(b) the child or young person has been charged with or convicted of an imprisonable offence which together with other imprisonable offences of which he has been convicted amount or would amount to a recent history of repeatedly committing imprisonable offences while remanded on bail or to local authority accommodation;

and in either case the court must be of the opinion that only remanding the child or young person to local authority secure accommodation/prison accommodation would be adequate to protect the public from serious harm from him or that such a remand would prevent the commission by him of further imprisonable offences.

Local provision

Provision of local bail supervision and support (BSS) schemes and secure accommodation varies from region to region. You should be familiar with the provision of secure accommodation in your area and with the local BSS and make contact with the local scheme where there is a risk that bail will be refused. You will need to know what is offered as a matter of practice by the YOT covering the area of your local court.

The availability of secure accommodation in the area can become a determining factor if the case gets to the stage of considering a remand to secure local authority accommodation.

15.8 TRIAL AND PREPARATION FOR TRIAL

In addition to the usual issues, there are some factors specific to youths including the following:

1. You should stress the welfare principle when trying to get disclosure from the Crown, although most prosecutors will not refuse disclosure. If necessary, refer to the Attorney General's Guidelines on Disclosure (see **Appendix 1** for website link) or enter a not guilty plea.
2. Use every hearing to obtain as much information from the client as possible, either through direct questions or from general conversation.

211

Young people are generally the worst attendees at the office to give instructions. All the agencies in the criminal justice system are under pressure to reduce unnecessary delay and benches are increasingly robust in refusing adjournments. If you apply to adjourn in order to take instructions you should expect to have the application refused, unless there are exceptional circumstances, and the matter put back for you to take the instructions you need to progress the case.

3.   Where the client had declined to answer questions at the police station, the same considerations generally apply as for adults. However, when making representations that no adverse inferences should be drawn, stress the client's age and reliance on legal advice. In fact it is rare that adverse inferences are drawn in Youth Courts as it is always unreasonable to expect a child or young person to choose not to follow legal advice while under arrest and in a police station. You should always argue that no adverse inference should be drawn.

4.   The parent must normally be present at court at all stages if the child or young person is under 16, unless this is unreasonable, for example if the parent is a witness (Children and Young Persons Act 1933, s.34A(1)(b)). You should argue against the court ordering the attendance of the parent where the client does not want them there in the event of estrangement. If the young person is over 16, parental attendance may be required. Be alert to the 'inappropriate' adult – for example the parents who seek to intervene in the solicitor–client relationship.

5.   Where the prosecution witnesses are youths, their evidence-in-chief may be given by pre-recorded video evidence. Your client may need to make a similar application. You should make sure that the 'putting at ease' part of any video is edited. This could be prejudicial to your client.

6.   You should be familiar with the Practice Direction (Crown Court: Trial of Children and Young Persons) [2000] 1 Cr App R 483 issued by the Lord Chief Justice. This applies to Crown Court trials and a number of cases have been stayed as a result of this Practice Direction. Although it is rarely relevant in the Youth Courts, the principle should apply in relation to all youths and you should be alert to circumstances that risk breach.

15.9   SENTENCING

Remember that the relevant age for sentencing the offender for the offence is the age at conviction (the date your client pleads guilty or is found guilty), not sentence (*R. v. T (A Juvenile)* [1979] Crim LR 588). Your client's age at the date of the offence may be relevant for the purposes of mitigation and it is the starting point for sentencing. Sentencing guidelines lay much emphasis on the level of maturity of the particular defendant.

Remitting to the Youth Court

You should remember that there is power to remit between Youth Courts – a Youth Court may remit the child or young person to the court for the area where he habitually resides. It is generally considered good practice for the local court to deal with sentence, which will mean the involvement of the local YOT and will be more convenient for your client.

Available sentences

Practitioners should know the range of currently available sentences in the Youth Court, their nature, preconditions, the age range of offenders to which they apply and procedural requirements.

Points to note on sentencing

The Youth Court has discretion to lift reporting restrictions after conviction if it is in the public interest to do so. Arguments against lifting reporting restrictions might include reference to international law on the basis of the United Nations Convention on the Rights of the Child 1989 and the Beijing Rules. Restrictions should only be lifted if there would otherwise be a risk of harm to the public.

The issue of the need for an interpreter for the parent but not the defendant (see above) can be particularly problematic at sentencing stage. For example, where a community sentence is contemplated, the parent will ultimately need to be involved in the sentence – and there may be a conflict if the client is effectively acting as interpreter.

Reports

You will need to be gathering information or reports, to be used in either the sentencing proceedings or mitigation, at an early stage of the proceedings. The requirements for a court to obtain a pre-sentence report vary (see PCC(S)A 2000, ss.8(1), (3) and 36). A specific sentence report is required before a court may sentence a young offender to a reparation order, action plan order or curfew order. Remember that the situation and circumstances of children and young people can change significantly over short periods of time – will it be safe to rely on a previous report?

You should always check the facts in the YOT pre-sentence reports and that the recommendations contain legally possible sentences for the child or young person's age.

It may be necessary for you to provide some background information on the child's personal and family history and welfare, and you are likely to need to look to sources of information beyond your client.

You should be prepared to challenge assertions in the pre-sentence report about lack of remorse – does the particular client have the necessary emotional development to understand the consequences of their actions and to feel remorse, or to express any remorse felt in a recognisable way?

Prepare a checklist for preparing personal mitigation and present positive character references. See sample bail and mitigation checklists at **Appendix 2, 2.12** and **2.14**.

Parents

It is vital that you remember throughout that your duties as solicitor are to your young client. You should always remember that there may be communication problems between your client and the client's parents, and you should particularly consider whether any representations you are planning to make in relation to the parents on sentencing will in fact be against your client's interests. Subject to your instructions, it is good practice to work closely with both client and parent. For example, it is often appropriate to send a copy of any correspondence to the client to the parent as well, in a separate envelope, in the same post. Parents, however, may need separate representation because:

1. Parents are normally liable for any fine if the offender is under 16. The court may order the parent to pay if the offender is over 16 unless certain exceptions apply. The parent has the right to be heard in respect of such an order and you need to consider whether any conflict of interests arises.
2. Parenting orders: again, there is a possible conflict of interest with the young offender. The making of an order may be in the child or young person's interests but not those of the parents, or a parent may want an order to be made but the young person has instructed you that he/she doesn't. If such a problem arises, the parent should be heard separately and should preferably be represented. Since the parent will not be eligible for public funding as an 'accused or convicted person' you should try to obtain assistance from the duty solicitor in the Youth Court.

NOTE

1. An application for a freestanding ASBO for a youth is made in the magistrates' court and there are no reporting restrictions unless the court imposes them in exercise of its discretion under the Children and Young Persons Act 1933, s.39. If an order is made on conviction, there are no reporting restrictions regarding the making of the order, unless the court imposes them, but automatic reporting restrictions still apply regarding the details of the criminal offence which led to the order being made. The principles concerning s.39 were set out in *R* v. *Winchester Crown Court ex parte B* [2000] Cr App R 11 and approved in the context of ASBOs by Elias J in *R (T)* v. *St Albans Crown Court and Others* [2002] EWHC 1129 (Admin).

CHAPTER 16

Clients at a disadvantage

Objectives of this chapter

- To enable you to recognise and meet interpretation needs
- To explain your role when acting for a mentally disordered client
- To show where you can go for assistance with a mentally disordered client
- To describe the possible outcomes for a mentally disordered client

---

16.1 INTERPRETERS

Attendance of interpreters

The Office for Criminal Justice Reform (OCJR) has issued a revised National Agreement on Arrangements for the Use of Interpreters and Language Service Professionals Investigations and Proceedings within the Criminal Justice System (see **Appendix 1** for website link).

Interpreters: general

Interpretation plays a far greater role in the criminal process than is realised and can potentially make all the difference between a defendant being found guilty or not guilty. An interpreter needs to have linguistic competence, a professional attitude, an understanding of the legal process and of his duties and the need for impartiality and confidentiality. The fact that a person calls himself an interpreter does not necessarily mean that he has these qualities. How often has the interpreter spoken the language recently? Does he or she understand a particular dialect and slang words?

In identifying your client's interpretation needs:

1. Establish if a defendant has difficulty understanding English, especially formal, legal registers, or has a hearing or speech impediment.
2. In the case of a foreign language speaker, find out the person's preferred language. Be aware that there can be immense variation in dialects of a

language, or within different communities so check the regional as well as national language spoken.

3. In the case of a deaf person, ascertain the preferred means of communication, e.g. sign language or lip speaker.

4. Discuss the person's preferences in the selection of an interpreter: religion; ethnic origin.

Selecting an interpreter

Interpreters should be of a recognised quality and wherever possible taken from the National Register of Public Service Interpreters (NRPSI) or the Council for the Advancement of Communication with Deaf People (CACDP). The starting point must be full or interim Diploma in Public Service Interpreting (DPSI) Law Option accreditation. Where this is not practicable then the interpreter should have some recognised skill or qualification, or be on the firm's internal list required by the LSC contracts as being of an acceptable standard. Where the client is vulnerable and wishes to have an initial consultation with a trusted person with no qualifications in interpreting, then the advantages in improving client confidence should be weighed against the risk of compromising the best evidence. A qualified interpreter should be used thereafter where possible.

At the police station

The defence solicitor is responsible for ensuring:

(a) that any interpretation needs of the client or appropriate adult in the police station not identified by the police are met;

(b) if a second interpreter is not available, that the interpreter employed by the police is appropriate for defence consultations and that the client consents to the use of the same interpreter.

If you use a separate interpreter for defence consultation, the defence is responsible for obtaining and paying for the interpreter's services, either under existing contracting arrangements or through prior authority from the LSC. The LSC has issued the following advice.

When a defence solicitor requires an interpreter to facilitate the provision of advice between a solicitor and a client, a different interpreter, where practicable, should be used. Where this is not practicable the client may, through his or her defence solicitor, consent to the use of a police-appointed interpreter.

As the interpreter is a potential prosecution witness (on client comprehension and accuracy of interpretation) it is appropriate, where feasible, to have a separate interpreter for consultation.

It may also be necessary to have a second interpreter if the client is vulnerable, or knows the interpreter personally, or by repute. Interpreters employed by the police should be selected from the NRPSI or CACDP and therefore bound by the professional codes of impartiality and confidentiality, but community relations can mean that the client has little confidence in the interpreter–police relationship. This may affect the quality of the solicitor–client consultation if a separate interpreter is not used.

However, these issues need to be weighed against the client's interests in waiting in custody for a second interpreter. This can be a lengthy period especially if interpreters for that language are rare.

Where the police-employed interpreter is used, it is good practice to advise the client of the interpreter's independence from the police.

Ask the interpreter to sign the following confirmation if the conversation is privileged:

> In interpreting the conversation between the lawyer and his client, I agree to interpret everything discussed and I acknowledge that this conversation is privileged and cannot be disclosed to any third party.

> Signed _____

Preparing the case

The defence is responsible for obtaining interpreters for attendance on clients and witnesses. The defence solicitor is responsible for arranging payment of the interpreter's fees, although in unusual circumstances it is advisable to obtain prior authority from the LSC.

The key documents should be translated for the client.

In court

Responsibility for arranging a foreign language or sign language interpreter for court proceedings lies with:

(a)   the police or other prosecuting agency, for a defendant who is charged with an offence and first appears in court within two working days (not including Saturdays) of charge;

(b)   the court (magistrates' court, Crown Court or Court of Appeal) for a defendant in all other circumstances;

(c)   the prosecution, for a prosecution witness;

(d)   the defence for a defence witness.

Youth Courts

In Youth Court cases parents or other appropriate adults requiring interpreters must have that facility which is provided by and at the expense of the court.

Helping the court to organise an interpreter for the defendant

The magistrates' court will usually be informed by the police before the first hearing that an interpreter is required for a defendant. If the need for an interpreter only becomes apparent after the defendant has been released from the police station or the case has been committed, transferred or sent for trial, the defence solicitor should inform the magistrates' court or Crown Court of this as early as practicable.

The defence solicitor should be able to help the court to appoint a suitable interpreter. The solicitor should collect relevant information about the defendant and pass this on to the court. The information to be collected is the same information that a solicitor must obtain to organise an interpreter for a defence witness. That information will have been obtained if the solicitor has already employed an interpreter to enable the solicitor to communicate with the defendant. If the solicitor considers that the same interpreter could be employed to interpret for the defendant in court (providing that the interpreter was not used at the police station), the solicitor should inform the court of the interpreter's details as early as practicable. It is the court's decision whether this or another interpreter is used in court. The court will inform the defence of the name of the person whom it has appointed.

Materials to be supplied to the interpreter

The interpreter will be helped by having sight of a copy of the statement made to you by the person whose evidence is to be interpreted, as well as copies of any prosecution witness statements that are likely to be put to the witness in cross-examination.

More than one interpreter at court

Each co-defendant must have a separate interpreter. In some cases it will be appropriate to engage a separate court interpreter for the witnesses, defendant and the appropriate adult, for example, if there are a large number of witnesses or co-defendants to make separate interpreters necessary. Arrangements should be agreed with the court and in some cases, prior authority obtained from the LSC.

Defence witnesses

The defence solicitor is responsible for arranging for interpreters for defence witnesses. The interpreter should be taken from the appropriate register, and qualified to interpret and translate to the satisfaction of the defence solicitor.

The solicitor should inform the court and the prosecution of the name of the interpreter to be employed to interpret for a defence witness, to avoid duplication.

Where the solicitor considers there should be a separate interpreter for the defence for consultations during the proceedings then the solicitor is responsible for employing and paying that interpreter. In unusual circumstances prior authority should be obtained from the LSC.

The court-appointed interpreter will interpret or translate the evidence to the court during the proceedings. In some cases the defendant may wish to give evidence through the interpreter he or she has used in previous consultations rather than through the court-appointed interpreter. This may be the case if the defendant is vulnerable or has language or speech needs and the existing communication between the known interpreter and defendant will improve best evidence. The court should be notified of this application in good time.

Keeping a record

It is good practice to keep a record on your case file of the details of the client/witness for whom an interpreter is required; a person who is instructed to interpret on the client/witness's behalf; any briefing given to an interpreter about any special terminology or procedure involved in the conduct of the case; and previous hearings when an interpreter has been involved (see **Appendix 7** for an example).

16.2 MENTALLY DISORDERED DEFENDANTS

Mental disorder

Be aware of the breadth of the statutory definition of mental disorder: 'Mental disorder' means mental illness, arrested or incomplete development of mind, psychopathic disorder and any other disorder or disability of mind (Mental Health Act 1983 (MHA 1983), s.1). This will be amended by the Mental Health Act 2007, s.1 (yet to be brought in force) to mean simply 'any disorder or disability of the mind'. Enquire if your client has been prescribed tranquillisers or anti-depressants; it may indicate a diagnosed depression.

Home Office Circulars

The Home Office Circular on services for mentally disordered suspects or offenders issued in May 1995 (12/95) offers guidance on when it may be appropriate to charge and prosecute a mentally disordered suspect. The Circular does not use the term 'diversion', in order to stress that diversion and prosecution are not necessarily mutually exclusive. It emphasises that the existence of mental disorder should not be the only factor considered, and the police and CPS should not feel inhibited from pursuing a prosecution if this is considered necessary in the public interest, particularly if the offence is serious or there is a risk to public safety. Where a prosecution takes place, the treatment and care needs of the individual must still be met.

An accompanying booklet, *Mentally Disordered Offenders: Inter-Agency Working*, gives examples of good practice as well as setting out the main responsibilities of those working in the criminal justice system, including the police, probation service, the courts and the prison service. It also recognises that solicitors, particularly those acting in the defence of mentally disordered suspects, have an important role to play in effective inter-agency working and they are encouraged to become involved in local schemes. As well as assisting mentally disordered suspects to obtain the care and treatment they need, you must ensure that they have the same rights and opportunities as any other suspects to clear their names against wrongful allegations, and where appropriate to take responsibility for their actions. With these aims in mind, the booklet contains a separate section giving advice on the role of legal representatives, which was prepared in conjunction with the Law Society's Mental Health and Disability Sub-Committee.

Readers are also referred to D. Postgate and C. Taylor, *Advising Mentally Disordered Offenders* (Law Society Publishing, 2000).

Circular 12/95 provides information about central and local initiatives and developments in inter-agency working and advises against diversion from the criminal justice system where the offence is serious or the defendant represents a danger to the public.

You should try to arrange the most favourable course of action for the defendant, having regard to the following:

(a) the urgency of obtaining treatment;
(b) the seriousness of the offence;
(c) whether a lesser charge would suffice;
(d) whether a defendant is in custody, or on bail;
(e) whether a hospital is available and is willing to offer treatment.

Note that, in discussing an appropriate disposal, the prosecution may request sight of a copy of any medical report. Beware the potential dangers of disclosing confidential or damaging information; obtain the views of the psychiatrist. If medical reports are required you will retain control if you obtain the report rather than allowing the court to order one.

It is essential to establish where your client last lived or usually lives. In case of difficulty you can contact the regional forensic psychiatry adviser at the regional health authority. Courts can assist by requiring the authority to provide information about possible arrangements.

Obtaining instructions

You may find yourself in serious doubt about your client's mental capacity because of your own observations, or those of police or court staff.

You may be unable to obtain any sensible instructions or any communication from your client. It is a matter for your professional judgement whether you consider yourself 'instructed' to act. Explain your difficulty to and try to obtain additional information from the following sources, which may enable you to make an informed decision:

1. **Legal adviser.** If you cannot obtain a signature to the Representation Order application, ask the legal adviser to consider granting it without a signature. He may know of the defendant from previous appearances.
2. **Prosecutor.** Ask for full access to all case papers. Note in particular any account by witnesses of bizarre behaviour, verbal responses, interview, medical problems, evidence of drugs, etc. Note any previous recorded Mental Health Act orders among any previous convictions.
3. **Police.** If necessary, you may need to contact the police to obtain a copy of the custody record, to trace any relatives who were in contact during your client's detention in the police station, or to trace doctors called in to advise during the detention.
4. **Probation Service/social services authorities/local mental health services.** They may be aware of your client from previous contact with court including diversion schemes and community mental health teams and may have access to previous relevant reports.
5. **Family or relatives.** They may be present at court or available by telephone to give history and practical assistance – in particular to offer accommodation.

Psychiatrist's report

Consider the following possible means of access to a psychiatrist at short notice:

1. **Court duty scheme.** Some courts have psychiatrists available at short notice. Transfers between courts may be desirable to gain access to a scheme. The community psychiatric nurse is available at most courts and some police stations and can summon a psychiatrist if necessary.
2. **Police referrals.** Ascertain from the police details of any doctors or psychiatrists who saw the defendant in police custody.
3. **Prison doctors.** If the defendant has already spent a period in custody on remand, contact the prison medical staff for an opinion.
4. **Private referral.** If you seek a psychiatric opinion of your own accord, you will need a psychiatrist who is able to provide prompt assistance. You

will wish to find a psychiatrist with relevant expertise and you may require him to provide a bed if hospital treatment is to be considered as an alternative to prison. Make contact first by telephone to explain the position and obtain an estimate of costs. Obtain your client's consent if possible and use your Representation Order to cover costs. Obtain an extension or authority as appropriate. This option is to be preferred as it gives you control of the report and choice of psychiatrist.

5. **Court order.** Generally, the court will not be in a position to order reports until after conviction, or hearing evidence sufficient to establish the act or omission charged was done (see PCC(S)A 2000, s.11). Courts will often order fitness to plead reports. Note that the court will have an obligation to obtain a medical report if considering a custodial sentence for a defendant who is, or appears to be, mentally disordered. Be aware that reports can be subject to considerable delay and consider the more appropriate way forward.

In some areas, court-ordered reports can be quicker; also, the responsibility for the delay lies solely with the court. The practitioner will need to weigh up local practice, the court's use of preferred psychiatrists and the advantages mentioned in point 4 above.

Fitness to plead

Home Office Circular 93/91, on the Criminal Procedure (Insanity and Unfitness to Plead) Act 1991, gives guidelines to all relevant agencies on this issue.

Magistrates' courts

The magistrates have no jurisdiction to try an issue of fitness to plead, but for imprisonable cases see below. If your client is apparently unfit to plead the following choices arise:

1. Discuss with the prosecution the discontinuance of proceedings or reduction of charges so as to allow summary trial wherever the sentencing powers of magistrates are sufficient (Code for Crown Prosecutors; see **Appendix 1** for website link).
2. The use of MHA 1983, s.37(3). This can only be used if the defendant is suffering from mental illness or severe mental impairment. It cannot be used if the defendant is suffering from psychopathic disorder or mental impairment that is not severe.
3. For a summary offence, advise the court of the position; the court will enter not guilty pleas and order a trial.
4. The magistrates may be persuaded to order a report on the question of fitness if there is a possibility that the defendant may recover in the near

future. Alternatively, you could seek authority under a Representation Order for a report to be obtained. If someone is unfit to plead but with appropriate medication and treatment can become fit to plead within a reasonable time, adjournments should be sought until that point is reached.

Crown Court

At the Crown Court the fitness of the client to plead will, in appropriate cases, be tried by the court as a distinct issue (see the Criminal Procedure (Insanity) Act 1964, as amended, the Criminal Procedure (Insanity and Unfitness to Plead) Act 1991 and Home Office Circular 93/91 referred to above). You may wish to seek a specialist report on fitness. Careful preparation and detailed medical advice will be required. You should obtain the necessary authority to incur the relevant expenditure and give instructions to your experts at the earliest opportunity. You should seek to obtain disclosure of all relevant medical records.

If a client may be acquitted of the offence you should not raise the issue of fitness to plead until the judge has held that there is a case to answer.

Remember that insanity is a defence if the defence can prove McNaughten insanity to negative the necessary mental element. You should refer to an appropriate practitioner text on this.

If the client is found unfit to plead or acquitted by reason of insanity, the court may impose:

(a)   an absolute discharge;
(b)   a hospital order, with or without restrictions, without limit of time or (until the Mental Health Act 2007 comes into force) for a specified period (except in cases of murder);
(c)   a guardianship order;
(d)   a supervision and treatment order.

Suicide risks

If you suspect (by reason of your own observations or those of the police, prosecution or family) that your client is suicidal, consider with your client:

(a)   where your client will be most or least at risk;
(b)   an urgent need for psychiatric referral (you should be aware of the arrangements available at courts in your area);
(c)   an urgent need to warn the police and prison authorities by telephone and in writing of the issue.

If appropriate, request prison medical authorities to consider the use of their suicide risk procedure.

You should also consider carefully your ethical position and your relationship of confidentiality with your client. This is a difficult area of potential conflict of duty. Seek the advice of a professional colleague and/or a psychiatrist in confidence. Keep careful notes.

Subject to the above, beware the 'false alarm' raised on some occasions by the prosecution in a bail application, which is vigorously denied by the defendant and contradicted by others, e.g. family doctor, etc.

Readers are referred generally to D. Postgate and C. Taylor, *Advising Mentally Disordered Offenders* (Law Society Publishing, 2000).

Information on hospitals

In finding hospital accommodation for a mentally disordered defendant, it is essential to establish where your client last lived or usually lives. Health authorities will not normally accept responsibility for a patient from outside their area.

Health authority services

1. **Local psychiatric hospitals.** These are run by mental health NHS trusts. Local health authorities are the commissioning 'purchaser'. They provide facilities for patients who may from time to time need treatment and care in hospital, sometimes in a secure setting. The provision of secure wards for patients who are disruptive or difficult to contain in open wards varies greatly. Health authorities or trusts provide detailed information about provision of local psychiatric services.
2. **Medium secure units.** These provide treatment and care in a secure setting for patients whose disruptive or possibly harmful behaviour constitutes a risk to others. Generally a period of up to 18 months' or two years' treatment is provided. Detailed information is available from regional forensic psychiatry advisers.

Private health services

There are psychiatric hospitals in the private sector, known as registered mental nursing homes, whose facilities and services fill gaps in the state scheme. It may be that a regional authority will pay for the cost of providing accommodation at a private hospital for a patient within its responsibility whose needs cannot be otherwise met.

Special hospitals

There are three special hospitals, run by Broadmoor, Ashurst and Rampton hospital authorities, which provide special security for patients subject to

MHA 1983 detention because of their dangerous, violent or criminal propensities. Generally, they will only admit those who cannot be accepted anywhere less secure.

Court order

If you have a client who has been diagnosed by one doctor (perhaps at the prison) as suffering from a mental disorder that justifies a hospital order, but you cannot find a psychiatric hospital willing to admit him, you should contact the regional forensic psychiatry adviser at the regional health authority.

In the event of a failure to respond, or a conflict between hospitals or authorities as to responsibility for your client, consider applying for an order from the court.

If a court is minded to make a hospital order or interim hospital order, it may require the health authority to provide information upon hospitals in its region or elsewhere at which arrangements could be made for admission of the defendant (MHA 1983, s.39).

Bail

Consider whether the likely sentence requires a report. If it does not, do not suggest it.

Conditions can be imposed requiring co-operation with arrangements to obtain medical reports (MCA 1980, s.30(2)). Clients should not be remanded in custody merely because they are mentally unwell (see Home Office Circular 6/90, para.7).

Summary trial of summary or either-way offences

Problems

The trial of the defendant who is mentally ill and incapable of giving proper instructions may present you with practical and ethical difficulties. You can only take your client's instructions as you find them, and make the court aware of the position.

It may be that a defence can be established upon the absence of *mens rea* at the time of the offence.

Non-imprisonable offences

If the offence is non-imprisonable, the court must convict before it can order medical or other reports or decide upon disposal.

Imprisonable offences

If the offence is imprisonable, the court may deal with the defendant without proceeding to full conviction providing it is satisfied that the defendant 'did the act or made the omission charged', but to do so it needs to be aware of the defendant's apparent illness. If satisfied that the necessary conditions are met, the court may then make a hospital order (MHA 1983, s.37(3)).

Non-summary cases

The magistrates have no jurisdiction to handle indictable-only crime. Under CDA 1998, s.51 no plea is entered, so the issue of fitness is left to the Crown Court. Either-way offences, where the court does not use MHA 1983, s.37(3) and declines jurisdiction, will be committed to the Crown Court.

Disposal

Consider the best disposal at each stage.

1. **Remand to hospital.** The court has the power if remanding a defendant in custody to remand to a hospital for reports (MHA 1983, s.35).
2. **Interim hospital order.** Upon a defendant's conviction for any imprisonable offence, in order to assist the court in deciding whether to make a hospital order, an interim hospital order may be made to enable the defendant's condition and response to be evaluated (MHA 1983, s.38).
3. **Community order.** If the court makes a community order with a mental health treatment requirement (CJA 2003, ss.177 and 207), it may attach a condition that the defendant submits to psychiatric treatment if the defendant consents (CJA 2003, s.207).
4. **Hospital order.** Upon a defendant's conviction for an imprisonable offence or after a finding the defendant did the act or made the omission charged, a hospital order may be made requiring the defendant to be detained in a suitable hospital for treatment: the order does not enforce attendance for a set period and the date of release is determined by doctors (MHA 1983, s.37). A hospital order can also be made without a conviction being recorded and if an order is likely to be made you should consider proceedings under the provisions of MHA 1983, s.37(3). Provided the Crown can prove by evidence that the act was done or omission made (and you may assist if appropriate under CJA 1967, ss.9 and 10), an order can be made without conviction if the court is satisfied that your client is suffering from mental illness or severe mental impairment.
5. **Guardianship.** As an alternative to a hospital order, but under the same provisions, a guardianship order may be made where appropriate by which the defendant is placed under the guardianship of the local social services authority. The purpose is to ensure care and protection is

provided. The guardian has powers to require the defendant to live where directed, attend for medical treatment, education, training, etc. (MHA 1983, ss.37, 40).

6. **Restriction orders.** The magistrates have no power to make restriction orders under MHA 1983, s.41 but may commit in custody to Crown Court for sentence for that purpose (MHA 1983, s.43).

7. **Hospital direction and limitation order.** This is a form of hospital order (under MHA 1983, s.45A) attached to a period of imprisonment. The court must be satisfied on the evidence of two medical practitioners (one of whom must give evidence orally) that:

   (a) the offender is suffering from a psychopathic disorder;
   (b) the disorder is of a nature or degree that makes it appropriate for him to be detained in a hospital for medical treatment; and
   (c) some treatment is likely to alleviate or prevent a deterioration to his condition.

An offender who is sentenced to a term of imprisonment with a hospital direction and limitation order will be conveyed to a specific hospital and treated as if he had been sentenced to imprisonment and transferred to hospital. If the offender ceases to be in need of treatment before the expiration of the sentence, he will be liable to be returned to prison. If he is still in hospital when the sentence expires, he will cease to be subject to restriction and will remain in hospital as if detained under MHA 1983, s.37. He will be eligible for release on the decision of the responsible medical officer.

The power to issue this order is only available in the Crown Court.

CHAPTER 17

Action after acquittal or conviction and sentence

Objectives of this chapter

- To list the cost issues that should be considered and explain how to deal with them
- To show how to give sound and timely advice about whether to appeal
- To ensure that all the necessary steps to appeal are taken
- To show how you can work with the Criminal Cases Review Commission so that it can help your client

---

Throughout this chapter references in square brackets are to the LSC Transaction Criteria.

17.1   COSTS

Defendant's costs on acquittal

If privately funded, or pre-public funding, work (including at the investigation stage) has been carried out, and your client is acquitted, or the case is discontinued or withdrawn, remember to apply for costs from central funds. A good practice guide on taxation of costs is available from the Justices' Clerks Society (**www.jc-society.co.uk**).

An order from central funds should be made where a case is not proceeded with or dismissed. An order should normally be made unless there are positive reasons against it: that is if the defendant's own conduct has brought suspicion on himself and misled the prosecution into thinking the case against him is stronger than it is.[1]

The bill must normally be lodged within three months of acquittal. Rates of remuneration that are considered reasonable in each area of the country are published annually by the Supreme Court Costs Office.

Witnesses' costs in all cases

The costs of attendance at court of a witness required by the defendant or the court, or of an interpreter, or of an oral report by a medical practitioner, are allowed out of central funds, unless the court directs otherwise.[2]

Such expenses cannot be claimed as disbursements under a Representation Order unless the court refuses to make an order from central funds. The court must, however, expressly order costs out of central funds in favour of a character witness.

Lodgement of bills

At the end of every stage of a case it is necessary to register a claim for publicly funded costs within three months. This applies whether or not the case ends at that stage. A claim should be registered if during criminal proceedings sentence is deferred or a warrant is issued for the defendant's arrest (in magistrates' court proceedings time for registering a warrant case claim begins to run six weeks after the warrant is issued). A claim must be registered whether or not an appeal is to be lodged.

Wasted costs

Wasted costs orders against legal representatives are made under POA 1985, s.19A.

'Wasted costs' are defined as costs incurred by a party as a result of any improper, unreasonable or negligent act or omission on the part of any representative or employee of a representative which the court considers it is unreasonable to expect that party to pay in the light of any such act or omission (POA 1985, s.19A(3)). The wasted costs jurisdiction does not affect the duties you owe to your client. It is a control on the way you carry out those duties.

A court intending to exercise the wasted costs jurisdiction must concisely formulate the complaint and grounds upon which such an order might be sought. It must consider:

- Has there been any improper, unreasonable or negligent act or omission?
- As a result, have any costs been incurred by a party?
- Should the court exercise its discretion to make an order? If so, what specific sum was involved? (See *Re Barrister (Wasted Costs Order) (No.1 of 1991)* [1992] 3 All ER 429.)

Further guidance was given by the Court of Appeal in *Ridehalgh* v. *Horsefield* [1994] 3 All ER 848:

- The key question will usually be whether the lawyer has been guilty of any 'improper or unreasonable or negligent act or omission' under the Supreme Court Act 1981, s.51. Improper conduct is not confined to conduct that violates the letter of a professional code of ethics, and negligence is not confined to actionable breaches of the lawyer's duty to his own client.
- Even when advocates are not liable in negligence over the way in which they conducted the case in court, they can still be liable to a wasted costs order. However, the courts should make full allowance for the fact that an advocate in court often has to make decisions quickly and under pressure. It is only when an advocate's conduct of proceedings is quite plainly unjustifiable that it could be appropriate to make a wasted costs order against him.
- Legal privilege is the client's, which he alone can waive. This can mean that lawyers are unable to tell the court the whole story. Judges should make full allowance for this. The lawyer is entitled to the benefit of any doubt.
- Save in the most obvious cases, the court should be slow to initiate the enquiry whether a wasted costs order should be made. No order can be made unless costs have actually been wasted as a result of the lawyer's conduct. If conduct was proved but no waste of costs was shown to have resulted, the court can do no more than refer the case to the professional body or the Legal Services Commission.
- Even if the court is satisfied that costs have been wasted as a result of the lawyer's conduct, the court is not bound to make an order. It should give sustainable reasons for its decision either way.

The power is thus to compensate, not punish; costs liable to be awarded are only those caused by the default. The amount of costs must be specified in the order (Costs in Criminal Cases (General) Regulations 1986, SI 1986/1335, reg.3B(1)). The representative must be allowed the opportunity of making representations before any order is made (reg.3B(2)).

Practice Direction (CA (Crim Div): Costs in Criminal Proceedings) [1991] 2 All ER 924 indicates (para.8.3) that hearings should normally take place in chambers. Because this may be difficult to arrange in a magistrates' court, consider requesting that the matter first be examined in writing.

While the court cannot delegate its decision, it may be desirable for the clerk to the justices to make enquiries of the representative and inform the court of the outcome. A simple explanation may put right misunderstandings.

Notwithstanding the words in POA 1985, s.19A a solicitor's first duty is (subject to the CPR) to his lay client, and the propriety or reasonableness of his conduct must be judged in the light of that paramount duty. A solicitor is under a duty to follow his client's lawful instructions,[3] although if these conflict with the rules the solicitor may have to withdraw.

A legal representative should not be considered to be negligent because he acted for a party who pursued a claim which was bound to fail unless to do so amounted to an abuse of the process of the court. A competent advocate might take a point which is fairly arguable and is under a duty to do so if it is in the interests of his client. Ultimately, the test is whether the point taken is 'fairly arguable' (*per* Aldous LJ in *Sampson* v. *John Boddy Timber Ltd* (1995) *Independent*, 17 May, CA).

Any potential liability for negligent acts applies to the way you carry out your professional duty to promote and protect the best interests of your client. It does not impose any limitation on that duty. These issues must be examined without the benefit of hindsight and not from a prosecution viewpoint.

Your duty to your client to keep information about him confidential prevents you, subject to the CPR, from revealing that information to any third party (including the court and the CPS) except to the extent that it is reasonably necessary where your conduct is under investigation. If your client is at risk, consider whether he should be separately advised and represented because of a possible conflict of interest between you.

A court may, if appropriate, postpone the making of a wasted costs order to the end of a case if it appears more appropriate to do so because the likely amount is not readily calculable or the legal representative concerned is unable to make full representations because of a possible conflict with the duty to his client (Practice Direction (CA (Crim Div): Costs in Criminal Proceedings) [1991] 2 All ER 924, para.8.4).

These considerations will normally require any contemplation of the making of a wasted costs order to take place at the end of a trial (which in the case of a sending will be at the conclusion of the Crown Court proceedings).

An appeal against a wasted costs order in the magistrates' court must go to the Crown Court within 21 days (Costs in Criminal Cases (General) Regulations 1986, reg.3C). From the Crown Court it goes to the Court of Appeal, Criminal Division.

A common problem is when a client on a serious charge, such as robbery, protests his innocence and instructs you to apply to the magistrates for bail. The client has numerous previous convictions and the court knows that he had absconded while on bail in the past. You are not surprised when the magistrates refuse bail. The client is anxious to try again for bail as soon as possible and instructs you to apply to the Crown Court. You hesitate. You know that your client has a right to apply for bail but consider it a hopeless application. How would the court react? What if the court also regards this application as hopeless? Would you face a wasted costs order for taking up the court's time unnecessarily? Should you consider your own position on receiving those instructions from the court?

The Law Society Criminal Law Committee's advice is that you act correctly by making the Crown Court application. On those clear instructions it is not improper, unreasonable or negligent and should not result in a wasted costs order against you. You are under an obligation to carry out your client's instructions (unless they would involve you in an unlawful act or a breach of the rules of the professional conduct of solicitors) and to represent your client fearlessly. You should ensure that everything the client wishes to say is before the court, regardless of your personal opinion about its lack of merit or chances of success

17.2 ACQUITTAL

Apply for defendant's costs and reasonable expenses. But it is not possible to recover any loss of earnings by the defendant. Apply also for restitution of any property seized from the defendant.

17.3 CONVICTION/SENTENCE

Correcting mistakes

A court may vary or rescind a sentence or other order (including replacing an invalid order) on the application of the prosecution or defence or on its own initiative. In the magistrates' court there is no time limit provided that it is in the interests of justice (MCA 1980, s.142). In the Crown Court the power must be exercised within 28 days from the day the order was made unless the amendment is purely administrative (*R. v. Norman* [2006] Crim LR 1072).

These powers should be used, rather than an appeal, when a decision has been made that is clearly wrong.

Immediate advice

You have a duty to advise all clients of their appeal rights. A useful reference guide is published by Justice.[4] If an appeal is to proceed, ensure that your client understands the basis for it [77.3.3, 77.4.1]. Consider whether any fresh evidence may be available [77.3.3, 78.8.2]. Ensure that you diarise the latest date for lodging any appeal and advise the client of this.

17.4 IMPRISONMENT

The advocate (where instructed) and you or your representative should see your client in the cells and provide preliminary advice on the question of appeal and check with your client if any matters need to be dealt with in his life as a result of imprisonment.

You should find out which prison your client will be taken to.

You should spend time with the family/friends of your client informing them of the whereabouts of your client, the procedure for prison visits, visiting orders and letters to the prison, and on appeal procedures.

The Prisons Handbook[5] contains full information about all the penal establishments in England and Wales, including their regimes, accommodation and facilities. It also contains penal case law, the Prison Act 1952, the Prison Rules, advice to prisoners and a list of helpful organisations and resources.

Your client and (with his permission) his family should be written to immediately after the court confirming the sentence and any advice, including any given at court.

Your client should be informed of the earliest release date and his responsibilities on licence explained.

In the event of later difficulties in locating your client, HM Prison Service may be contacted at Prisoner Location Service, PO Box 2152, Birmingham B15 1SD. You need to write to the Prison Service giving as much information as possible, including your client's:

(a)   name, age and date of birth;
(b)   offence;
(c)   the court of conviction/sentence and the date of conviction/sentence.

17.5   APPEALS AGAINST CONVICTION AND/OR SENTENCE

From the magistrates' court to the Crown Court

Appeals may be against conviction and/or sentence and are heard by a judge sitting with magistrates. Appeals against conviction are by way of re-hearing, and fresh evidence may be called. Obtain the notes of evidence given at the magistrates' court trial from the justices' clerk [73.3.1]. Note that magistrates' courts are not courts of record and notes kept by the clerk are not a record of the evidence given. There is no obligation on the court to provide such copy notes, although the Divisional Court has ruled that clerks should view sympathetically such requests from solicitors where a proper reason is given. A charge is likely where they are provided.

Warn your client that the Crown Court may award any sentence, whether more or less than that of the magistrates, providing it is not more than the maximum sentence the magistrates could have imposed [73.3.4, 77.4.2]. An RDCO may be made against a funded defendant in an appeal against conviction but not in an appeal against sentence (Criminal Defence Service (Recovery of Defence Costs Orders) Regulations 2001, SI 2001/856, reg.4(2)(c)).

Procedure

Appeal is by notice in writing (see **Appendix 2, 2.11**) to the magistrates' court and prosecutor within 21 days of sentence being passed. An appeal against conviction cannot begin earlier. The Crown Court may extend the period, i.e. give leave to appeal out of time, on receipt of a letter setting out the reasons (which will be put before a judge). Your magistrates' court Representation Order will cover you for time spent advising on appeal and completing the notice. An application for a new Representation Order should be made promptly for the appeal itself. Ensure that your client is aware of the procedure and time limit [77.1, 77.2].

Bail pending appeal

If your client is sentenced to custody, an application to the magistrates' court for bail pending appeal cannot be made until notice of appeal is served on the court and the prosecution.

Consider a possible appeal with your client [77.5] and if you are so instructed file notice of appeal. Apply with speed, otherwise you may prolong your client's time in custody. The notice can be lodged and application made the same day on which the sentence is passed.

If the application fails, make an application to a judge in chambers at the Crown Court on the prescribed form (see **Appendix 2, 2.6**) to be served on the Crown Court and prosecution; there is no time limit for making such an application. At least 24 hours' notice is normally required.

Even if bail is refused, the court may agree to expedite the appeal hearing.

Abandonment

Abandonment should be notified in writing to the magistrates' court, Crown Court and prosecution at least three days before the hearing.

High Court

Right to appeal by way of case stated to the High Court[6] is available to:

(a)   a party to magistrates' court proceedings (defence or prosecution);
(b)   any person aggrieved by a conviction, order, determination or other proceedings.

It is available to challenge the proceedings on grounds of:

(a)   error in law; or
(b)   an excess of jurisdiction.

Procedure

The case is drawn up at the request of a party or aggrieved person by the clerk to the justices.

The time limit for application is within 21 days of conviction or, only if case adjourned for sentence, within 21 days of sentence. The Divisional Court has no power to extend this time limit, but a defective application, made in time, may be corrected later.

Apply to the magistrates' court in writing, specifying grounds.

The magistrates' court may state a case conditionally on the applicant entering into a recognisance to pursue the matter.

It is important to appreciate that your client loses the right of appeal to the Crown Court if he applies for case stated.

In appropriate cases you will wish to consider whether judicial review is an alternative remedy. This does not carry with it the loss of the right to appeal to the Crown Court. Criminal funding is not available for such hearings (Criminal Defence Service (General) (No.2) Regulations 2001, SI 2001/1437, reg.3(4)) but holders of a General Criminal Contract may apply for appropriate funding from the Community Legal Service.

Appeal from the Crown Court[7]

An application for leave to appeal against conviction or sentence must be sent to the Crown Court within 28 days from conviction and/or sentence. The time limits are separate.

Within 14 days of conviction and sentence the advocate should have prepared a written advice in favour of or against appeal [78.4].

Within a further seven days your client should be sent a copy [78.5] of the advocate's advice and if it is negative your client should be advised that he can pursue the appeal but it is unlikely to succeed as a result of the advocate's advice.

An advice in favour of appeal and confirming the grounds of appeal should be included with the application for leave to appeal [78.6].

If the single judge refuses leave, your client is entitled to pursue his appeal to the full court and must do so within 14 days of receipt of the notice of refusal from the single judge.

You will be sent a copy of the notice of refusal. You should write to your client informing him of your advice on the refusal [78.7]. You should advise your client that if an appeal without merit is pursued, particularly beyond the single judge, that the appellant can forfeit up to a maximum of 90 days. This power is less likely to be used if the appeal was renewed on the advocate's advice and in practice the court tends to direct that only a maximum of 28 days shall not count towards the sentence. Ensure that your client is advised at all stages of the procedure on time limits for appeal [78.1, 78.2].

Always advise your client and his family that the appeal procedures take a long time [78.3].

The Representation Order will cover advice as to whether to lodge an appeal and whether to renew an application for leave after refusal by the single judge. It can also include a prison visit in an appropriate case. If leave is given by the single judge an application to the Court of Appeal for a new Representation Order is required. If one is granted, consider whether any transcript is required [78.8.1].

You should be familiar with *A Guide to Proceedings in the Court of Appeal Criminal Division*, which is available free of charge from all Crown Court centres and on the Courts Service website (see **Appendix 1** for website link). After setting out the initial steps to be taken at the conclusion of the case, it goes on to deal with the settling of grounds of appeal, the obtaining of transcripts, the perfection of grounds and the procedure which then follows. It contains useful information on which your client should be advised [78.8.3] about public funding, extension of time limits, bail pending appeal, abandonment and costs. Most of the guide is set out in the latest edition of *Archbold*.

Appendix 1 to the guide, which sets out specific instructions to the advocate to give advice and assistance on appeal in the event of a conviction and again following sentence, should have been included with every brief.

17.6 APPEAL AGAINST A JUDGE'S RULING

An order or ruling made by a judge at a preparatory hearing may be appealed against to the Court of Appeal (Criminal Division). Leave is required from the judge or the court. The judge may complete the preparatory hearing but the swearing in of a jury has to be delayed until the appeal has been determined. The Crown has other rights of interlocutory appeal against certain rulings made on other occasions.

17.7 RE-TRIAL FOLLOWING TAINTED ACQUITTALS

The prosecution may apply to the High Court to quash a tainted acquittal if a witness in the case is later convicted of perverting the course of justice or anyone is convicted of an offence of interference and the court finds there was a real possibility that the defendant would otherwise have been convicted; and that the matter is not so old or any other reason that it is not in the interests of justice to allow a re-trial. The Representation Order will cover such proceedings as they are regarded as incidental to the criminal proceedings from which they arose (Criminal Defence Service (General) (No.2) Regulations 2001, reg. 3(3)).

17.8   DOUBLE JEOPARDY/APPLICATIONS TO QUASH ACQUITTAL

CJA 2003, Sched.5 lists a series of 'qualifying offences' (all serious offences), the person's acquittal for which may, in defined circumstances, be quashed by the Court of Appeal, on application by a prosecutor (the written consent of the DPP is required), and a re-trial ordered.

17.9   CRIMINAL CASES REVIEW COMMISSION

The Criminal Cases Review Commission (CCRC) has jurisdiction to refer cases to the relevant Court of Appeal. Its jurisdiction includes referrals in respect of sentence as well as conviction. It may also refer convictions or sentences made or imposed in the magistrates' court to the Crown Court.

There are conditions to be satisfied before the CCRC can decide to refer a case to the Crown Court:

1. There must be a real possibility that the conviction, verdict, or sentence would not be upheld.
2. Conviction cases: there must be evidence or argument not previously raised (unless there are exceptional circumstances).
3. Sentence cases: there must be information or an argument on a point of law not previously raised.
4. There must have been a determined appeal or a refusal of leave to appeal (unless there are exceptional circumstances).

Court of Appeal investigation

The case must have been through the normal appeal process. Exceptionally, application and reference may be entertained even though the appellate process was not invoked, e.g. material on which an appeal might have been based may not come to hand until years later. 'Exceptional' has a clear, ordinary meaning and is not defined by the Criminal Appeal Act 1995.

Where it is possible to appeal out of time that route should be taken first.

The Court of Appeal may itself direct that the CCRC investigate a particular matter 'in such manner as the Commission thinks fit'. This extends to any matter which the CCRC thinks is related and relevant to the determination of a case by the Court of Appeal.

'Real possibility'

The CCRC is not to refer a case unless it considers that there is a real possibility that the conviction, finding or sentence would not be upheld were the reference to be made – could the new material cause the Court of Appeal to think the conviction unsafe (Criminal Appeal Act 1995, s.13(1)(a))?

The 'real possibility' must be judged (save in exceptional circumstances, e.g. flagrantly incompetent advocacy – counsel takes a decision in defiance of your client's instructions) on the strength of an argument or evidence not raised at trial, or on appeal, or on an application for leave to appeal as it should not give the defence the opportunity to run two different defences through appeal.

The review is not limited to fresh evidence. It is wider, as it can look at evidence available at the previous hearing but not used. Is there a reasonable explanation for failure to produce the evidence? What if the advocate failed to cross-examine a witness properly so that certain evidence did not come out?

Sentence

In the case of a sentence the CCRC must be able to point to an argument on a point of law, or information about the circumstances of the offence or the offender, that was not raised at trial.

Points of law include: 'wrong in principle'; failure to give a discount for early plea; a sentence that did not fall within the jurisdiction of the court imposing it; an erroneous interpretation of a statutory power. Adherence to tariff or disparity between offenders for equivalent offences is not a point of law, even if the tariff has changed over the years (*R. v. Graham* [1999] Crim LR 677).

When referring a case

The CCRC must provide the court to which the reference is made with a statement of the CCRC reasons for making the reference. The CCRC must supply a copy to every person likely to be a party to any proceedings in the appeal rising from the reference.

When not referring a case

The CCRC must give reasons for a decision not to make a reference to the person making the application.

Application form

The CCRC has produced an information pack which includes an application form (available from the Criminal Cases Review Commission, Alpha Tower, Suffolk Street, Queensway, Birmingham B1 1TT; DX 715466 Birmingham 41). It does not insist that a completed form is submitted or that it is completed in full. Material has been well presented by lawyers where there is a summary at the front backed up by the documentation in a folder, with a clear indication of what they think the issues are and what the next steps should be. However, the CCRC would prefer you to use the form to 'front up' an application, just so it can be sure that it has all the information it needs. It welcomes telephone calls seeking advice and guidance as to what other information or documentation would be beneficial (tel: 0121 366 1800). The CCRC is happy to discuss a potential application.

Your role

Your role is to:

(a) advise on an application to the CCRC;
(b) prepare an application (including taking witness statements, obtaining experts' reports and opinions);
(c) continue to advise and do work for that client while the CCRC is reviewing the case.

There is no particular limit on your role while the investigation and review is being undertaken.

The CCRC encourages legal representation of applicants. You can emphasise the strengths of an application while ignoring irrelevant detail. You should emphasise to your client that the CCRC's role is investigative and that an adversarial approach at this stage is unlikely to assist.

A key role of yours is to advise the CCRC on the merits of the application. You should be realistic in your assessment of what points raised by your client and identified by you – even if resolved in your client's favour – are likely to make a difference to the safety of the conviction; process failure does not automatically make a conviction unsafe. Don't be afraid to put forward meritorious grounds just because they cannot yet be supported by evidence; the CCRC has an investigative role.

You should identify the issues of concern:

1. In what respect is it suggested that the conviction is unsafe?
2. What evidence is (or may be) available to support that contention?
3. If there are a number of issues, assess their relative weight and pertinence.

You should obtain your client's case papers from the solicitors who have previously represented him in the case so that you can confirm the instructions which he gave them and see what investigations they undertook and decisions they made.

A well-constructed and well-supported application in which the grounds are clearly identified and argued and the case mapped out for the CCRC will help your client. An application that is structured similarly to the way in which the CCRC prepares a statement of reasons in support of its conclusion is very helpful: a summary of the prosecution and defence case at trial; the

239

appeal history (date, grounds and outcome); and the grounds of application to the CCRC. The use of chronologies, summaries and skeleton arguments in support of the grounds is encouraged by the CCRC.

In relation to the incident giving rise to the conviction, you should set out your understanding of the sequence of events and give details of the witnesses involved and the extent of their involvement, their full names, contact addresses, or last known location and the role (if any) played by the client.

Although there is no entitlement to have information received by the CCRC disclosed to you while the CCRC investigates and reviews the application, where the CCRC recognises that it is dealing with a solicitor who understands its independent role and responsibilities and criteria for referring a case to an appeal court, it is more likely to consider it of value to actively involve you.

If the CCRC is going to interview someone, you may want to attend the interview.

You should respond promptly to correspondence and keep your client informed about the work being done on his case. You should manage your client's expectations; explain at the outset the CCRC's work position.

There are criteria by which individual cases can be assessed for priority ranking. The CCRC is happy to explain them as they are at any given time. If there may be grounds for priority ranking, representations about this may be prepared for submission with the application.

In your application, make clear whether there was an application for leave to appeal or a full appeal and whether the appeal was against conviction/sentence or both.

Alert the CCRC to where pertinent documentation can be found including forensic tests conducted – when they were conducted and location and availability of material the CCRC may wish to test.

Public funding

Advice and assistance from firms holding a General Criminal Contract are available to clients who are financially eligible. The General Criminal Contract contains guidance for miscarriage of justice applications and the LSC can in appropriate cases grant an extension on that for all relevant activities (form CDS5). This guidance applicable to a CCRC application is separate from advice and assistance given in respect of the original trial and any other appeal.

NOTES

1. Prosecution of Offences Act 1985 (POA 1985), s.20(3); Costs in Criminal Cases (General) Regulations 1986, SI 1986/1335, reg.16(1); Practice Direction (Sup Ct: Crime: Costs in Criminal Proceedings) [1999] 4 All ER 436.
2. Ibid.
3. 'We take the view that notwithstanding the words in s.19 the solicitor's first duty is to his lay client and the propriety or reasonableness of his conduct must be judged in the light of that paramount duty. If he (the solicitor) is instructed to ask for a witness, whether this witness comes from Halifax or abroad, the solicitor is under a duty to act in accordance with his client's interest and he is under a duty to follow his lay client's instructions. At the end of the day the interest of the lay client is paramount and if there is a conflict between the two (the interests of the court and the interests of the client) it seems that in accordance with the best legal tradition, the first duty is to the client and any other duty takes second place' *per* HHJ Atkinson (see *Criminal Practitioners Newsletter*, July 1992).
4. *How to Appeal: A Guide to the Criminal Appeal Process* (Justice, 2003), available from Justice, 59 Carter Lane, London EC4V 5AQ.
5. M. Leech, *The Prisons Handbook* (Waterside Press, 2007, published annually).
6. Applications are to the Divisional Court until the relevant provisions of the Access to Justice Act 1999 are brought into force.
7. See Justice publication in note 4 above.

APPENDIX 1

Criminal justice system websites and forms

Attorney-General's Office
(www.attorneygeneral.gov.uk)

Guidelines on the Acceptance of Pleas and the Prosecutor's Role in the Sentencing Exercise

Guidelines on Disclosure

Guidance on the Common Law Defence of Conspiracy to Defraud

Criminal Justice Online
(www.cjsonline.gov.uk)

Code of Practice for Conditional Cautions

Out-of-Court Disposals for Adults: A Guide to Alternatives to Prosecution

Courts Service
(www.hmcourts-service.gov.uk)

A Guide to Proceedings in the Court of Appeal Criminal Division

Criminal Appeal Forms

Crown Prosecution Service
(www.cps.gov.uk)

Conditional Cautioning Code of Practice

The Code for Crown Prosecutors

The Director's Guidance on Conditional Cautioning

Legal Guidance

Director's Guidance

Disclosure Manual

Home Office
(www.homeoffice.gov.uk)

Home Office Circulars

If you need a pre-2003 circular, you can request it by hard copy by contacting the Direct Communications Unit at: Public.Enquiries@homeoffice.gsi.gov.uk; tel: 020 7035 4848.

Home Office Circular 93/91 on the Criminal Procedure (Insanity and Unfitness to Plead) Act 1991

Home Office Circular 12/95 on services for mentally disordered suspects or offenders

Home Office Circular 24/98 on reducing delays

Home Office Circular 30/1999 and Memorandum of Good Practice Re Early Release of Bodies (see App. 4 to the Criminal Bills Assessment manual below)

Home Office Circular 30/2005 on cautioning of adult offenders

ACPO Youth Offender Case Disposal Gravity Factor System: see Annex D to Home Office Circular 14/2006 on the reprimanding/warning of offenders (**www.knowledge network.gov.uk/ho/circular.nsf**)

PACE Codes (**http://police.homeoffice.gov.uk**)

Prosecution Team Manual of Guidance (**http://police.homeoffice.gov.uk/operational-policing/prosecution-manual-guidance**)

Judicial Studies Board
(**www.jsboard.co.uk**)

National Mode of Trial Guidelines

A Guide to the Award of Costs in Criminal Proceedings

Law Commission Reports
(**www.lawcom.gov.uk**)

Law Commission Report 269 Bail and the Human Rights Act 1998

Law Society
(**www.lawsociety.org.uk**)

Criminal Law Committee guidance

Criminal Litigation Accreditation Scheme

(See Solicitors Regulation Authority for new Solicitors' Code of Conduct 2007 and archived rules and guidance)

Legal Services Commission
(**www.legalservices.gov.uk**)

CDS forms   (**www.legalservices.gov.uk/criminal/forms.asp**)

CDS1: Client's details form

CDS2: Application for advice and assistance

CDS3: Application for advocacy assistance

CDS4: Application for prior authority to incur disbursements in criminal cases

CDS5: Application for extension of upper limit

CDS6: Contract work report form

CDS7: Contract work assessment form

CDS8: Assigned counsels' fee note in criminal cases

CDS9: Police station standby report

CDS10: Application for review of refusal or withdrawal of advocacy assistance or representation

CDS11: Generic costs form

CDS12: Duty solicitor application form

CDS13: Application form for contribution towards fees for accreditation for duty solicitor or accredited representative

FR1: This form allows contracted suppliers to claim for file reviews of reported crime and civil matters on an annual basis

File review letter: This letter contains guidance on claiming for file reviews

Criminal Bills Assessment Manual (and Appendices) (**www.legalservices.gov.uk/ criminal/guidance_fees_funding.asp#integrated**)

Criminal Defence Service remuneration rates (**www.legalservices.gov.uk/criminal/ current_payrates.asp**)

Duty Solicitor Manual
(**www.legalservices.gov.uk/criminal/police_stations.asp#info**)

General Criminal Contract (**www.legalservices.gov.uk/criminal/crime_contracts.asp# about**)

Public Defender Service Guidance (**www.legalservices.gov.uk/docs/pds**)

The Code of Conduct for Employees of the Legal Services Commission who provide services as part of the Criminal Defence Service

Guidance on the Code of Conduct

PDS Manual, forms and guidance (**www.legalservices.gov.uk/criminal/pds/reports_ guidance.asp**)

Specialist Quality Mark (**www.legalservices.gov.uk/criminal/forms/specialist.asp**)

Ministry of Justice
(**www.justice.gov.uk/criminal/procrules_fin/index.htm**)
Criminal Procedure Rules 2005

Protocols:

    Control and management of heavy fraud and other complex criminal cases protocol

    Disclosure: a protocol for the control and management of unused material in the Crown Court

The Consolidated Criminal Practice Direction

Prescribed forms:

    Application for dismissal of transferred charge(s) following a sending

    Application relating to bail in the Crown Court

    Statement of a witness

    Application for a witness summons Rule 28

    Application for special measures direction

    Notice of intention to introduce hearsay

    Notice of opposition to the introduction of hearsay

    Application for leave to adduce non-defendant's bad character

    Notice of intention to adduce bad character evidence

    Application to exclude evidence of the defendant's bad character

    Plea and case management hearing

    Crown Court preliminary hearing

Magistrates' court – directions for case committed to the Crown Court

Magistrates' court – directions for case sent to the Crown Court

Magistrates' court – case progression

Youth Court – directions for case committed to the Crown Court

Youth Court – directions for case sent to the Crown Court

Youth Court – case progression

**National Offender Management Service
(www.noms.justice.gov.uk)**

**Office for Criminal Justice Reform
(http://police.homeoffice.gov.uk/news-and-publications/publication/operational-policing/
national-agreement-interpret.pdf)**

Agreement on Arrangements for the Use of Interpreters

**Sentencing Guidelines Council
(www.sentencing-guidelines.gov.uk/guidelines/index.html)**

Sentencing Guidelines Council guidelines

The Court of Appeal sentencing guidelines

Magistrates' court sentencing guidelines

Practice Directions

Guideline Judgments Case Compendium

Dangerous Offenders: Guide for Sentencers and Practitioners

**Solicitors Regulation Authority
(www.sra.org.uk)**

Solicitors' Code of Conduct 2007

**Victim Support
(www.victimsupport.org.uk)**

APPENDIX 2

Sample forms, checklists and letters

2.1 STATE OF CASE FORM

UFN:	**NI no:**	**File ref:**
Name:	**Tel:**	**Fee earner:**
Address:		**Date of birth:**
Marital status:	**Occupation:**	**Job:** Kept/Lost
Court:	**Conflict check:** Yes/No	**Linked file:** Yes/No
Offence(s):	Summary/Either-way/Indictable	**Custody no:**
	Guilty/Not guilty	**Date of offence:**
	Elect CCT/Consent ST	**Date of charge:**
Custody time limit expires (committals – 70 days, summary trials – 56 days):		
Bail conditions:		**Surety name/address:**
Co-defendants and solicitors:		
Special features:	Juvenile Expert evidence	Interpreter Mental Health
Expert instructed: Yes/No	**Expert on register:** Yes/No	**Expert satisfactory:** Yes/No
Police station advice: Yes/No	**Advice and assistance:** Yes/No **Extension:** Yes/No **Hours:**	**Narey hearing:** Yes/No
Legal aid: Yes/No	**LA application made:** Yes/No	**Granted:** Yes/No
Private: Yes/No	**Funds on account:** Yes/No	**Amount:** £
Discontinuance:	**Appropriate:** Yes/No	**Requested:** Yes/No
Documentation:	**Requested:**	**Received:**
Advance Information	Yes/No	Yes/No
Custody record and tapes	Yes/No	Yes/No
Committal bundle	Yes/No	Yes/No
Medical/psychiatric report	Yes/No	Yes/No
Unused material	Yes/No	Yes/No
Client care letter: Yes/No	**Advice on case:** Yes/No	**Sent on:**
Proof taken: Yes/No	**Date:**	
ADVICE AND ASSISTANCE	**Sufficient benefit test met:** Yes/No	
ADVOCACY ASSISTANCE	**Merits test met:** Yes/No	

Date of appointments:	Kept?	Chased?	Date of appointments:	Kept?	Chased?
1.			3.		
2.			4.		

Date of hearings:	Result:		Fee earner:	Days in custody:
1.				
2.				
3.				
4.				
5.				
6.				

247

2.2 CRIMINAL FILE PROCEDURAL REVIEW FORM

Client name		Fee earner	
UFN		Supervisor	
Date			
File type	Magistrates' court	Crown Court	Court duty	Police station advice and assistance

File management		Comments	Score
Is the file orderly?			
Opened within how many days?			
GFM 1/2 completed?			
State of case form completed?			
Record of advice form completed?			
Conflict check (if appropriate)?			
Key dates recorded on timeline?			
Undertakings recorded?			
Case plan (if appropriate)?			
Linked files identified?			
Summary of evidence prepared?			
Brief/Note to advocate for each hearing?			
Client care			
Client care letter sent?			
Within how many days?			
Instructions, advice and action recorded?			
Confirmed in writing?			
Client seen within 10 days (Custody)?			
Client seen within 15 days (Bail)?			
Proof of evidence taken?			
Observations on evidence taken?			
Non-attendances chased?			
Devolved powers			
Used appropriately?			
Recorded correctly on forms?			
Funding			
Representation Order?			
CDS 1 & 2 correctly completed?			
Evidence of means if advice and assistance?			
Time recorded?			
Disbursements paid within 7 days?			
Authority for disbursements approved?			

Use of experts		
Expert on register?		
If no – file note of reason and evaluation?		
End of case		
Outcome letter sent?		
Closure procedures followed?		
CDS11 on file?		
Complaints		
File free from complaints?		
If no – appropriate response/follow-up?		

Observations on legal/procedural issues	

Corrective action required?	
Action required	
Date action required by	
Date of further review	
Corrective action carried out?	

2.3 PEER REVIEW OF CRIMINAL CASES

PEER REVIEW FORM
Client name:
UFN:
Fee earner:
Case complexity/difficulty: exceptional/demanding/routine/minor
Case seriousness: most serious/moderately serious/least serious

1 = excellent

2 = competence plus/good

3 = threshold competence

4 = below competent/poor

5 = non-performance/very poor

X = insufficient information to make a judgement

N/A = not applicable

Lead charge:	
Other charge(s):	
A. The file	
1. Is the composition of the file compliant with office manual?	1 2 3 4 5
2. How appropriate is the level of information recorded:	
(a) at investigation stage?	1 2 3 4 5 X N/A
(b) post-charge?	1 2 3 4 5 X N/A
3. How appropriate was the management of the case throughout?	1 2 3 4 5 X N/A
Comments:	
B. Communication	
1. How appropriate were the lawyer's communication and client-handling skills?	1 2 3 4 5 X
2. How appropriately was the client informed of:	
(a) the merits (or not) of their defence/case?	1 2 3 4 5 X N/A
(b) all developments (including conclusion)?	1 2 3 4 5 X N/A
3. How appropriate was the lawyer's communication with others, including the CPS, defence counsel, etc.?	1 2 3 4 5 X N/A
4. How timely was all communication?	1 2 3 4 5 X N/A
Comments:	
C. Information and fact-gathering	
1. How effective was the lawyer in seeking relevant information from the client?	1 2 3 4 5 X
2. How effective was the lawyer in seeking relevant information from the police and/or prosecution:	
(a) at investigation stage?	1 2 3 4 5 X N/A
(b) post-charge?	1 2 3 4 5 X N/A
3. How effective was the lawyer in seeking relevant information from others?	1 2 3 4 5 X N/A
Comments:	
D. Advice and assistance	
1. How good was the advice?	1 2 3 4 5 X N/A
2. (a) How appropriate was advice on plea?	1 2 3 4 5 X N/A
(b) If (at any stage) the client was advised to plead guilty, was the timing of the advice:	
(i) too early?	
(ii) appropriate?	
(iii) too late?	
3. How appropriate was advice on appeal?	1 2 3 4 5 X N/A
Comments:	

E.	**The work/assistance**	
1.	Was all work done that should reasonably have been done? If no, specify:	Y N X
2.	How effective was the work done in achieving the client's (reasonable) objectives?	1 2 3 4 5 X
3.	What was the impact of the lawyer on:	1 2 3 4 5 X N/A
	(a) bail: better than expected/as expected/worse than expected?	X N/A
	(b) mode/venue: better than expected/as expected/worse than expected?	X N/A
	(c) the process: better than expected/as expected/worse than expected?	X N/A
	(d) verdict: better than expected/as expected/worse than expected?	X N/A
	(e) sentence: better than expected/as expected/worse than expected?	X N/A
4.	Was the client prejudiced in any way by the work done or not done? (If yes, specify)	Y N

Comments:

E.	**Efficiency**	
1.	How efficiently was the work carried out?	1 2 3 4 5 X
2.	Throughout the file, how effectively did the organisation use resources (including experts)?	1 2 3 4 5 X
4.	Were any disbursements incurred appropriate?	Y N N/A

Comments:

F.	**General**	
1.	Where ethical issues arise were they dealt with appropriately?	Y N N/A

Overall mark	
(a) At investigation stage	1 2 3 4 5 X
(b) At magistrates' court stage	1 2 3 4 5 X
(c) At Crown Court stage	1 2 3 4 5 X
(d) Overall file score	1 2 3 4 5 X

2.4 POLICE STATION FORMS

(a) Attendance form

POLICE STATION ATTENDANCE FORM		
UFN:	Book no.:	Own/Duty
Date:	GFM/1 completed:	Yes/No
Fee earner with conduct:	AIM no.:	

CLIENT DETAILS	
Name:	Address:
Date of birth:	
Tel.:	
E-mail address	
Referral from third party: Yes/No	Family contact details:
Name: Tel.:	Name: Tel.:
Address:	Address:
Relationship to client:	Relationship to client:
Has the client received advice in this matter from another firm in the last six months? Yes/No	
If Yes, justify a new claim for payment:	

ARREST DETAILS	
Police station:	Custody no.:
Tel.:	Arrest/Voluntary:
Officer in case:	Tel.:
Time and date of arrest:	Relevant time:
Allegation (including date):	
F/E	F/E
Time of first call:	Time of request for attendance:
Time of first contact with client:	Time of attendance:
Time between call and contact: mins	Time between request and attendance: mins
Delay in contact/attendance: Yes/No	If yes, reason:
Access to client delayed: Yes/No	Extent of delay: hours
Reason:	Representations made: Yes/No

Appropriate adult required:	Yes/No	Name:	
Address:		Relationship to client:	
		Police contacted AA:	Yes/No
		Tel:	
		Client advised on AA's role:	Yes/No

If attendance sufficient benefit test met: Yes/No	Interview/ID procedure/Complaint/Charge
If no attendance, reason:	

INFORMATION FROM POLICE
Inspected custody record: Yes/No

Search of client: Yes/No	Intimate: Yes/No	Client's consent given: Yes/No
Legal authority and reason: s.32/s.54 (including strip)/s.55 (intimate)		
Evidence obtained:		

Search of premises:	Yes/No	Address:
Legal authority and reason:	s.18/s.32	
Evidence obtained:		

Samples taken:	Yes/No	Client's consent given:	Yes/No
Type: FP (s.61) DNA (s.63) Photo (s.64A)		Intimate (s.62):	
Retention explained:	Yes/No	Reason:	

Previous questioning/interview:	Yes/No	
Details:		
Previous attendance at PS: Yes/No	Legal advice received: Yes/No	Legal advice sought: Yes/No

Co-accused:		Yes/No			
Name:	Solicitor:		Known to client?	In custody?	Conflict

Significant statement or silence:	Yes/No	Advised client to comment on this in interview: Yes/No

Consultation with officer:	Name:

CONSULTATION WITH CLIENT			
Eligible for: Advocacy Assistance/Advice and Assistance/Ineligible			
CDS 1 & 2 completed:	Yes/No	**Requested evidence of means:**	Yes/No
Previous convictions/cautions:	Yes/No		
Details:			
Outstanding criminal cases/on bail: Yes/No			
Details:			
Language needs:	Yes/No	**Language preferred:**	
Health problems:	Yes/No		
Details (include nature and effect of illness, and medication taken:			
Name and address of GP:			
FME called:	Yes/No	**Note in custody record:**	Yes/No
Social worker/probation office:	Yes/No	**Name:**	
Address/organisation			
Injuries:	Yes/No		
Details (include description and cause):			
Witness to injuries:	Yes/No	**Name:**	
FME called:	Yes/No	**Affects fitness for IV:**	Yes/No
Note on custody record:	Yes/No	**Photographs required:**	Yes/No
Attitude to TICs?			
Witness(es):	Yes/No	**Alibi:**	Yes/No
Alibi where and when:			
Witness name:	**Address of witness:**		
Advised client on implication of silence under:	s.34: Yes/No	s.36: Yes/No	s.37: Yes/No
Advised client to:	answer questions/remain silent/issue prepared statement		
Reasons:			
In interview, client:	answered questions/remained silent/issued statement/mixed		
Complaint against police:	Yes/No	**Advised client on procedures for complaint:**	Yes/No
Make complaint prior to release:	Yes/No		

254

IDENTIFICATION PROCEDURES			
Obtained original description provided by each witness: Yes/No			
Advised client on methods of identification and procedure: Yes/No			
Advised client of right of refusal and implications thereof: Yes/No			
Advised client to consent to:			
Client consented to:		Representations made:	Yes/No
Date of ID procedure:		Place:	Type:
Witness:	Identified?	Witness remarks	
1.	Yes/No		
2.	Yes/No		
3.	Yes/No		

HISTORY OF CASE		
Date of attendance	Result:	Fee earner attending:
1.		
2.		
3.		

OUTCOME	
No further action:	Yes/No
Caution/warning/reprimand/fixed penalty/reported for summons: Yes/No	Caution conditions:
Conditional caution: Yes/No	
Advised client of implications of diversion:	Yes/No
Charge: Yes/No	
Advised client on implications of reply to charge and inferences from silence: Yes/No	
Advice to client: reply to charge/remain silent	
Reasons:	
Time of charge:	Reply:
Advised clients on prints, photos and DNA:	Yes/No
Bail refused: Yes/No	Representations made: Yes/No
Procedure for future applications explained: Yes/No	Prospects of success: Yes/No
Bail granted: Yes/No	Explained consequences of FTA: Yes/No
Conditions:	Explained consequences of breach: Yes/No
	Charge (inc date):
Court:	Date: Time:
Costs form completed: Yes/No	File allocated to:

255

(b) Telephone consultations: attendance cases

POLICE STATION TELEPHONE CONSULTATIONS				
Client				
Date:				
UFN:				

Date	Time	Person	Police station	F/E	Duration
		Standard advice (see below)			
		Standard advice on non-attendance cases (see below)			

STANDARD ADVICE

1. Introduced myself and explained status. ❏

2. Confirmed service at police station is free. ❏

3. Warned of the lack of confidentiality. ❏

4. Advised that answers should normally be 'yes' or 'no' ❏

5. Outlined reason for arrest. ❏
   Give short detail:

6. Checked on welfare and vulnerabilities [details endorsed on folder]. ❏

7. Advised that we would attend the police station. ❏

8. Warned against any discussions with the police, particularly against answering any questions during a search. Nor should he/she sign any further document. ❏

9. Explained rights to Code and phone call. ❏

10. Explained how to make further contact with us. ❏

11. Counter any police ploys suggesting you will delay release. ❏

12. Identify any further action required and time of next contact/attendance. ❏
    Give detail here:

2.5 NOTICE OF APPLICATION TO VARY BAIL CONDITIONS

TO the Clerk to the Justices of the Magistrates' Court sitting at [*place*]

AND TO the Branch Crown Prosecutor, Crown Prosecution Service, [*address*]

Name of defendant:

Address:

Offence(s) alleged:

Next bail date:

Name(s) of co-defendant(s):

TAKE NOTICE THAT I intend to make application to the Court at 10.00 a.m./

2.00 p.m. on [*date*] to vary the defendant's bail conditions as follows:

Reason for application:

Date: Signature of Solicitor

Unique case reference no:

Note: At least one full working day's notice of application is normally required. The defendant must usually attend the hearing in person.

2.6 NOTICE OF APPLICATION RELATING TO BAIL TO BE MADE TO THE CROWN COURT

At: ....

Unique case reference no.: ....

Crown Court number: ....

or

Serial number: ....

Name and location of Magistrates' Court: ....

....

TAKE NOTICE THAT an application relating to bail will be made to the Crown Court

at

on   or to be notified

at   or to be notified

on behalf of the defendant

1. Defendant

Surname: ....

Date of birth: ....

Forenames: ....

Home address: ....

2. Solicitor for the applicant

Name: ....

Address: ....

3. If defendant is in custody state:

Place of detention: ....

Prison number: ....

Length of time in custody: ....

Date of last remand:..

4. State particulars of proceedings during which the defendant was committed to custody or bailed unconditionally including:

(a) the stage reached in the proceedings as at the date of this application:

....

....

(b)   the offences alleged:

....

....

5.   Give details of next appearance in court of case pending before magistrates

Place: ....

Date:...

Time: ....

Give details of any previous applications for bail or variations of conditions of bail

....

....

6.   Nature and grounds of application

(a)   State fully the grounds relied on and list previous convictions (if any):

....

....

(b)   Give details of any proposed sureties and answer any objections raised previously:

....

....

2.7   STATEMENT OF WITNESS

(Criminal Justice Act 1967, s.9
Magistrates' Courts Act 1980, s.102
Magistrates' Courts Rules 1981, r.70)

STATEMENT OF [*name of witness*]:

Age of witness (If over 21, enter over 21):

Address:

This statement (consisting of [*specify*] pages each signed by me) is true to the best of my knowledge and belief and I make it knowing that, if it is tendered in evidence, I shall be liable to prosecution if I have wilfully stated in it anything which I know to be false or do not believe to be true.

Dated the .... day of .... 20 ....

Signed: Signature witnessed by:

[*Set out statement*]

2.8 WITNESSES AT COURT

TO:

Crown Prosecution Service
Prosecution of [*name*]
[*Specify*] Magistrates' Court
URN:

We act for the defendant whose case was committed to the [*specify*] Crown Court on [*date*].

Please treat this letter as notice that all witnesses [*except*] should attend to give evidence at the trial unless we notify you in writing to the contrary.

2.9 APPLICATION TO EXTEND TIME FOR SERVICE OF DEFENCE STATEMENT (REG.3(3) AND RULE 8)

TO [*specify*] Court

CPS/R. v. [*name*]

Unique reference case number

CC to CPS

Application for extension of time under the Criminal Procedure and Investigations Act 1996 (Defence Disclosure Time Limits) Regulations 1997.

We act for the accused named above.

Please treat this letter as our application for an extension of the period during which the accused may serve the defence statement.

(a) The accused believes, on reasonable grounds, that it is not possible for him/her to give a defence statement under section 5(6) of the Criminal Procedure and Investigations Act 1996 during the period of 14 days from (purported) compliance by the prosecution of its obligation under s.3 of that Act [or the period ordered by the court on [*date*]].

(b) The grounds for so believing are:

  •

  •

  •

(c) The number of days by which the accused wishes the period to be extended is [*specify*].

(d) A copy of the notice was served [today] on the prosecutor.

2.10   EXTENSION OF SERVICE LETTER (CPS)

[Firm details]

CPS (*specify section*)
DX

[Reference]   *[Date]*

Dear Sir

Name of defendant:
Court:
Next appearance:
Main charge:

We enclose a copy of the letter to the court requesting an extension of time for service of the defence statement.

Yours faithfully

2.11   NOTICE OF APPEAL TO CROWN COURT, AGAINST CONVICTION, ORDER OR SENTENCE

TO the Justices' Clerk of the Magistrates' Court sitting at *[place]*

AND TO the Branch Crown Prosecutor, Crown Prosecution Service, *[address]*

TAKE NOTICE THAT I, *[name and address of appellant]*

intend to appeal to the Crown Court at *[address]* against:

* my conviction
* the sentence which was passed upon me *[state sentence]*
* the order made against me *[state order]*

(*delete as appropriate)

on *[date]* by the Magistrates' Court above for the offence(s) set out below:

[state offence(s)]

Dated: ....   Signed: ....

Unique case reference no.:

2.12 BAIL CHECKLIST

Name:

Date of birth:

Likely objections to bail:

    Fail to appear   ❑
    Further offence   ❑
    Obstruct justice   ❑

Available addresses:

Time there:

Nature of occupation:

    Community ties
    Plea
    Strength of evidence
    Likely outcome
    Previous convictions
    Bail record/explanation
    Offences on bail/explanation

Possible conditions

Sureties:

    Names
    Amount

Security:

    Amount

Residence:

Reporting:

Curfew:

Surrender travel documents:

No contact:

Exclusion from area:

2.13   REQUEST TO BAIL INFORMATION SCHEMES

[*This pro forma can be handed to your client so that he may make it available to the officer to address relevant concerns.*]

FROM: [*solicitors*]

TO: Bail Information Officer

Date:

I should be grateful if you could interview my client named below and, if appropriate, produce a bail information report to the court setting out the factors that you consider stand in favour of or against bail. I attach a copy of the pre-convictions provided by the CPS.

Client's name:
Date of birth:

Remanding court:
Date of hearing at which remanded in custody:

Date of next hearing:

Reasons court gave for refusal of bail (please tick all that were given).

❑   Risk of failure to attend

❑   Risk of offending during bail

❑   Risk of interfering with witnesses or victims

❑   Self-protection

❑   Not practical to obtain sufficient evidence

I can provide the following information about why the court came to this decision or any indications the court gave as to what conditions might allow bail to be granted:

Contact telephone number, e-mail or fax:

2.14   MITIGATION CHECKLIST

A.   Nature of offence

    1.1.   Culpability

    1.2.   Harm

2.   Reasons for offence

3.   Consequences of offence

B.   Personal mitigation

4.   Attitude to offence

5.   Disabilities/medical issues

6.   Personal circumstances

7.   Steps awaiting sentence

8.   Consequences of sentence

C.   Guilty plea discount

D.   Conclusion

Is there a relevant guideline?   Y N

If No, is there a compendium case?   Y N N/A

2.15   WITNESS CHECKLIST

FACT/EXPERT/CHARACTER?

Witness name:

Address:

Contact numbers:

Disabilities:

Interpreter required? If yes, language/dialect:

Dates not available:

Court details provided:

2.16   CROWN COURT CHECKLIST

Client:	Aim:
Allocated to:	Supervisor:

Action	Target date	Actual date
❑ Has Magistrates Class Work been sent for billing?	❑	
❑ Conflict check completed	❑	
❑ Form B submitted	❑	
❑ Bail:	❑ Yes (see Sched.4) ❑ No Prison:	
❑ Sureties:	❑ Yes (see Sched.3) ❑ No	
❑ Interpreter required:	❑ Yes Language: ❑ No	
❑ Proof	❑	
❑ Personal statement	❑	
❑ Observations on evidence	❑	
❑ Advocate briefed	❑	
❑ Name (in-house or other)	❑	
❑ Contact details	❑	
❑ On expert list	❑	
❑ Witness requirements notified	❑	
❑ Unused schedule received	❑	
❑ Initial disclosure received	❑	
Defence statement served:		
❑ CPS	❑	
❑ Court	❑	
❑ Further disclosure requested	❑	
❑ Further disclosure received	❑	
❑ Conference arranged	❑	
❑ Medical expert instructed	❑ Yes Name: Contact details: ❑ N/a	
❑ Report received	❑	
Report sent:		
❑ Advocate	❑	
❑ Client	❑	
❑ CPS	❑	
❑ Court	❑	
❑ Appraisal completed	❑ Yes	

❑ Expert instructed	❑ Yes　　Name: Contact details: ❑ N/a	
❑ Report received	❑	
Report sent:		
❑ Advocate	❑	
❑ Client	❑	
❑ CPS	❑	
❑ Court	❑	
❑ Appraisal completed	❑ Yes	
❑ Defence witnesses	❑ Yes (see Sched.1)　❑ No	
❑ Witnesses proofed	❑ Mark in Sched.1	
❑ Witnesses warned for trial	❑ Mark in Sched.1	
❑ Witness summons	❑ Mark in Sched.1	
Hearsay notices served:		
❑ Court	❑	
❑ CPS	❑	
Hearsay counternotice served:		
❑ Court	❑	
❑ CPS	❑	
Character notices served:		
❑ Court	❑	
❑ CPS	❑	
Character counternotice served:		
❑ Court	❑	
❑ CPS	❑	
❑ Advice from advocate/supervisor	❑	
❑ Advice from advocate/supervisor	❑ Received　❑ Actioned	
❑ **Litigator's certificate**	❑ Required　❑ Received	
❑ VHCC	❑ Yes　❑ Notified　❑ No	
Custody time limit	**Committal date**	
❑ Committal to trial (112 days)	❑　　　　　(please calculate)	
❑ Section 51 committal to trial (182 days)	❑　　　　　(please calculate)	
❑ Advice on appeal	❑	
❑ Appraisal of external advocate	❑ Yes	

Schedule 1   Witnesses

Name	Proof Section 9 Statement	Availability	Summons	Warned Y/N Date (letter sent)

Schedule 2   Defence requirement prosecution witnesses

Name	Notified to CPS	Insept F/C

Schedule 3   Sureties

Name	Address	Contact No.

Schedule 4   Bail conditions

1

2

3

4

5

267

2.17   MAGISTRATES' COURT TRIAL CHECKLIST

Client:	Aim:	

Action	Target date	Actual date
❏ Proof	❏	
❏ Personal statement	❏	
❏ Observations on evidence	❏	
❏ Witness requirements notified	❏	
❏ Unused schedule received	❏	
❏ Initial disclosure received	❏	
Defence statement served if appropriate:		
❏ CPS	❏	
❏ Court	❏	
❏ Further disclosure requested	❏	
❏ Further disclosure received	❏	
❏ Medical expert instructed	❏ Yes ❏ N/a	
❏ Report received	❏	
❏ Expert instructed	❏ Yes ❏ N/a	
❏ Report received	❏	
❏ Defence witnesses	❏ Yes (see Sched.1) ❏ No	
❏ Witnesses proofed	❏ Mark in Sched.1	
❏ Witnesses warned for trial	❏ Mark in Sched.1	
❏ Witness summons	❏ Mark in Sched.1	
Hearsay notices served:		
❏ Court	❏	
❏ CPS	❏	
Hearsay counternotice served:		
❏ Court	❏	
❏ CPS	❏	
Character notices served:		
❏ Court	❏	
❏ CPS	❏	
Character counternotice served:		
❏ Court	❏	
❏ CPS	❏	

Schedule 1   Witnesses

Name	Proof Section 9 Statement	Availability	Summons	Warned Y/N Date (letter sent)

Schedule 2   Defence requirement prosecution witnesses

Name	Notified to CPS	Insept F/C

2.18   CLIENT CARE LETTER (PUBLIC FUNDING)

Dear

Your case:
Next hearing date:

Thank you for asking us to assist you.

I am a solicitor [I am a trainee solicitor/paralegal and I work under the supervision of [*name*] who is a solicitor]. I will do most of the work in this matter myself. If I am not in, you may speak to other members of my team. A message will always be taken from you.

I enclose our leaflets 'Information for Clients' and 'Criminal Law', which tell you about this firm and about criminal proceedings. The first leaflet also tells you what you should do if you have any concerns about the way we are handling your case.

Your case

You have been accused of [*specify*]. The allegation against you is that [*give details*].

Your instructions are [*summarise*].

I advised you that [*specify advice*].

What will happen now is [*give details and chronology*].

If you plead guilty or are convicted the sentence will be in the range [*specify*]

Based on the information I currently have, I would expect your case to be concluded within [*number*] months.

I must advise you that, if you are guilty, you will obtain a reduction in the length of any sentence that you might otherwise receive if you plead guilty at an early opportunity. This will normally be a discount of one-third if you plead guilty at the first opportunity, but the discount will reduce as the case progresses.

If you plead not guilty and are on bail at the time of the trial and you do not appear in court, then the court may proceed to try you in your absence.

The advice we have given you above cannot normally be disclosed. Under the Criminal Procedure Rules 2005 we can be required by the court to confirm that we have given you advice about those matters and also about whether we have had any difficulty in receiving instructions from you. We may not disclose, without your authority, details of the actual instructions we do receive or of any advice that we give you as a result.

Bail

If you fail to attend court when required to do so without reasonable cause you may be arrested and found guilty of the offence of failing to appear which is an imprisonable offence. Your bail may also be withdrawn.

Bail conditions

You have been bailed with the following conditions:

[*List any conditions*]

If you breach any of these conditions you are liable to arrest. Your bail may be withdrawn and you may then be held in custody until the conclusion of your case.

[*Or*: You have been released on unconditional bail. Your only obligation is to attend court at the correct time and date.]

Fees

Our charge will be calculated mainly by reference to the time spent by me and by other solicitors and executive staff dealing with this matter. This includes advising, attending on you and others, dealing with papers, correspondence, telephone calls, travelling and waiting time. This rate does not include VAT or disbursements, which will be added to the bill.

Our hourly rates are £[. . .] for a partner, £[. . .] for a solicitor over four years' qualification, £[. . .] per hour for any other solicitor and £[. . .] per hour for a trainee or clerk.

In matters such as this, it is difficult to estimate how many hours of work will be necessary to complete the matter. If you are concerned to have a more precise estimate of the possible costs you should please speak to us.

Order for costs

If your matter concludes at court and in the event that you are acquitted, I will apply for the payment of your costs from central funds. Payment is not automatic and will be subject to such an order being granted by the court. It is possible that, if such an order is made, it may not be for the full amount of the costs actually incurred.

If you are convicted, you may be ordered to pay a contribution towards the prosecution costs. This will be in addition to our costs. In the Crown Court you may also be ordered to pay defence costs depending on your means at that time.

Terms of business

It is normal practice to ask clients to make payments on account of anticipated costs and disbursements. It is helpful if you can meet requests promptly, as your case may otherwise be delayed. If you have any difficulty in meeting any request for payment, please let me know immediately. At this stage please could you let me have £[. . .] on account?

We shall deliver bills to you at regular intervals for the work carried out during the conduct of the case. This assists our cash flow and enables you to budget for costs. I am sure you will understand that in the event of a payment not being made we must reserve the right to decline to act further and that the full amount of the work done up to that date will be charged to you. Accounts should be settled within 28 days. Interest will be charged on bills that are not paid within that time.

I am required by legislation to make certain enquiries under the money laundering regulations and I have to reserve the right to serve appropriate notices. I am not then permitted further to discuss money laundering issues with you.

As confirmation that you would like us to proceed on this basis, I would be obliged if you would sign the extra copy of this letter enclosed and return it to me in the envelope provided. Please also forward the cheque as requested for payment on account.

Yours sincerely

2.19 CLIENT CARE LETTER (PUBLIC FUNDING)

Dear

Your case:
Next hearing date:

Thank you for asking us to help you.

I am a solicitor [I am a trainee solicitor/paralegal and I work under the supervision of [*name*] who is a solicitor]. I will do most of the work in this matter myself. I am a [*specify*]. If I am not in, you may speak to other members of my team. A message will always be taken from you. The Legal Services Commission requires all solicitors and legal advisers to be supervised by another solicitor in their firm.

I enclose our leaflets 'Information for Clients' and 'Criminal Law', which tell you about this firm and about criminal proceedings. The first leaflet also tells you what you should do if you have any concerns about the way that we are handling your case.

Your case

You have been charged with [*specify*]. The allegation against you is that [*give details*].

Your instructions are [*summarise*].

I advised you that [*specify advice*].

What will happen now is [*give details and chronology*].

If you plead guilty or are convicted the sentence will be in the range [*specify*].

Based on the information I currently have, I would expect your case to be concluded within [*number*] months.

I must advise you that, if you are guilty, you will obtain a reduction in the length of any sentence that you might otherwise receive if you plead guilty at an early opportunity. This will normally be a discount of one-third if you plead guilty at the first opportunity, but the discount will reduce as the case progresses.

If you plead not guilty and are on bail at the time of the trial and you do not appear in court, then the court may proceed to try you in your absence.

The advice we have given you above cannot normally be disclosed. Under the Criminal Procedure Rules 2005 we can be required by the court to confirm that we have given you advice about those matters and also about whether we have had any difficulty in receiving instructions from you. We may not disclose, without your authority, details of the actual instructions we do receive or of any advice that we give you as a result.

Bail

If you fail to attend court when required to do so without reasonable cause you may be arrested and found guilty of the offence of failing to appear, which is an imprisonable offence. Your bail may also be withdrawn.

Bail conditions

You have been bailed with the following conditions:

[*List any conditions*]

If you breach any of these conditions you are liable to arrest. Your bail may be withdrawn and you may then be held in custody until the conclusion of your case.

[*Or*: You have been released on unconditional bail. Your only obligation is to attend court at the correct time and date.]

Fees

Your application for legal aid has been sent to the court and you will receive a separate letter when we know the result of the application. The court will consider whether or not your application is in the interests of justice and, if your case is dealt with in the magistrates' court, whether or not your financial circumstances are such that you should receive legal aid. In the Crown Court, legal aid is not dependent on your financial circumstances.

Whether or not you are granted legal aid, you must attend court on the date shown above. If legal aid is refused I will discuss with you appealing the decision where appropriate or advise you of our private costs.

If you are granted legal aid, we will be able to attend court for you but you must report to the court any change in your address or financial circumstances.

Order for costs

If you are convicted, an order that you pay all or some of the prosecution costs may be made against you. You may also be ordered to contribute to the costs of your defence if your matter is tried in the Crown Court. This will depend on your financial circumstances.

If you have any queries at any time, please contact me.

Yours sincerely

APPENDIX 3

Conflict of interest

(Source: Criminal Law Committee of the Law Society)

Guidance was issued by the Standards Board and Criminal Law Committee in July 2005 to help criminal practitioners identify conflicts of interests and potential conflicts of interests when asked to act for co-defendants. The guidance is followed by a step by step guide which is intended to be used as a quick conflict check when interviewing defendants.

1. The Criminal Defence Service Regulations were amended recently to require one solicitor to be appointed to act for all co-defendants in a legal aid case unless there is, or is likely to be, a conflict. The purpose of this was to ensure economy in the use of public funds by ensuring that a single solicitor represented co-defendants where it was proper to do so. The current professional conduct obligations which deal with conflicts of interest (and a new conflict rule which will replace these obligations, but which is not yet in force) prevent a solicitor or firm acting for two or more clients where there is a conflict or significant risk of a conflict arising between the interests of two or more clients. They do permit a solicitor to act for co-defendants where conflict is not a factor. The difficulty often lies, however, in spotting potential conflict and deciding whether it is sufficiently real to refuse instructions. This guidance is intended to help you make these decisions.

2. Your starting point when considering conflict should always be your fundamental professional obligation to act in each client's best interests. Can you discharge this obligation to each client? This means firstly asking each client if they are aware of any actual or potential conflict between them and then, if they indicate that there is no such conflict, asking yourself whether you feel there are any constraints on the advice you would want to give to one client – or the action you would want to take on that client's behalf – which is likely to arise because you act for another co-defendant.

3. A conflict of interest arises wherever there is a constraint of that sort, for example where it is in the best interests of client A:

   - to give evidence against client B
   - to make a statement incriminating client B
   - to implicate client B in police interview
   - to provide prejudicial information regarding client B to an investigator
   - to cross examine client B in such a manner as to call into question his or her credibility
   - to rely upon confidential information given by client B without his consent
   - to adopt tactics in the course of the retainer which potentially or actually harm client B.

274

4. If these obligations actually come into conflict when acting for two or more clients you will have to cease to act for one and often both. This can cause considerable disruption and expense, which is why the rules require that you should not accept instructions if there is a significant risk of this happening.

5. Many criminal clients will, of course, have retained you at the police station prior to a police interview and are thus not at that stage defendants. The obligations referred to above obviously apply at this early stage and you must be satisfied that in accepting instructions on behalf of a client prior to a police interview this does not place you in conflict with another client who is also to be interviewed. In order to assess whether you can act for both clients it is important that you do not interview the clients together and that you get instructions which are as full as possible from the first client before any substantive contact with the second client. However, never let the police deter you from seeing the second client because they think there is a conflict – that decision must be yours.

6. A further consideration when taking instructions at the police station, especially out of office hours when an immediate conflict check is not possible, is that the firm may already act for another defendant in that matter or information obtained at the police station may be relevant to another client on an unrelated matter. For example, the firm may be acting in divorce proceedings for a wife where violence is alleged and information that her husband has been charged with an offence involving violence would be relevant and may make it impossible to continue acting for the wife. This highlights the importance of carrying out a conflict check at the earliest opportunity.

7. When considering accepting instructions from more than one client in the same matter you need to assess not only whether there is a conflict at the outset, but whether events are likely to arise which will prevent you from continuing to act for one or both at a later stage in the proceedings. In almost all cases there will be some possibility of differences in instructions between the clients but the rules do not prevent you acting unless the risk of conflict is significant. Assessing the risk is often not easy. It is also important that where you have accepted instructions from co-defendants you remain alert to the risk of conflict arising as the case progresses.

8. When considering whether there is an actual conflict there are obvious indicators such as whether the clients have differing accounts of the important relevant circumstances of the alleged crime or where one seems likely to change his or her plea. There are also less obvious indicators. These would include situations where there is some clear inequality between the co-defendants which might, for example, suggest that one client is acting under the influence of the other rather than on his own initiative. If you are acting for both this may make it difficult for you to raise and discuss these issues equally with them. In trying to help one, you might be undermining the other. If you believe you are going to be unable to do your best for one without worrying about whether this might prejudice the other you should only accept instructions from one.

9. The risk of future conflict can be an even more difficult issue to assess. It may be that you have two clients who are pleading not guilty and who are apparently in total agreement on the factual evidence. Should they both be found guilty, you need to consider at the outset whether you would be able to mitigate fully and freely on behalf of one client without in so doing harming the interests of the other. It may be that one has a long list of convictions and is considerably older than the other. If so, it may be that the younger client with a comparatively clean record was led astray or pressurised into committing the crime and would want

you to emphasise this in mitigation. If there is a significant risk of this happening you should not accept instructions from both.

10. Even where care is taken when accepting instructions from more than one client in the same matter there will inevitably be situations where a conflict subsequently arises. This will commonly happen where one defendant changes his or her plea or evidence. A decision will then have to be taken as to whether it is proper to continue to represent one client or whether both will have to instruct new firms. In making this decision you need to consider whether in the changed circumstances your duty to disclose all relevant information to the retained client will place you in breach of your duty of confidentiality to the other client. In other words, you need to decide whether you hold confidentially any information about the departing client which is now relevant to the retained client. If you do have such information then you cannot act for either client.

11. Following the changes to the Regulations, some practitioners have reported pressure from some court clerks on solicitors to represent co-defendants even where there is a clear risk of conflict. Similar pressure has been applied by police at police stations prior to interviews. However, the professional rules of conduct preclude you acting for both clients in those circumstances, and the Regulations are not intended to put solicitors in a position where they are asked to act contrary to their professional responsibilities. If asked by the court for your reasons why you cannot act for both defendants, you must not give information which would breach your duty of confidentiality to your client(s). This will normally mean that you can say no more than that it would be unprofessional for you to continue to act.

12. For the avoidance of doubt, you cannot resolve a conflict by instructing another firm or counsel to undertake the advocacy on behalf of one client. Neither can you pass one of the clients to another member of your firm. The rules make it quite clear that your firm cannot act for clients whose interests conflict.

13. Any decision to act, or not to act, for co-defendants should be recorded with a brief note of the reasons.

STEP BY STEP GUIDE – ACTING FOR TWO CLIENTS – AVOIDING CONFLICT

In order to minimise the potential for conflicts when you already act for Client 1 (C1) and are asked to act for Client 2 (C2) you should take the following steps:

Take instructions from C1. When doing so you should:

1. Advise C1 that you are also asked to act for C2 and that you can only do so if there is no conflict.
2. Ask C1 if he is aware of any conflict; if he states that there is, or might be, a conflict, ask C1 for full details.

    (1) If these amount to a conflict, you cannot act for C2.

3. If they do not, inform C1 of this and that you will be able to act for C2.
4. Inform C1 that if at any stage you come into possession of information which is confidential to C1, but which is relevant to C2, you will have a duty to disclose it to C2 at which stage you will need his consent to disclose it to C2.

Take instructions from C2. When doing so you should:

5. Advise C2 that you also act for C1 and that you can only act for C2 if there is no conflict.

6.   Inform C2 that if he tells you anything which is relevant to C1, you will have a duty to disclose it to C1.
7.   Ask C2 if he is aware of any conflict; if he states that there is, or might be, a conflict, you should not act for C2.

   (1)   If C2 states that there is not a conflict, inform C2 that if at any later stage you come into possession of information which is confidential to C2, but which is relevant to C1, you will have a duty to disclose it to C1, at which stage you will need his consent to disclose it to C1.

If at any stage you do receive confidential information in relation to one client ('the first client') which is relevant to the other client ('the second client'):

1.   You must inform the first client of this and seek his consent to disclose it to the second client.
2.   You should make it clear that there is no obligation upon him to give consent.
3.   If he does not consent to such disclosure, you must cease to act for the second client to whom you are required to disclose the information.
4.   You must not disclose your reasons for ceasing to act.
5.   You can only continue to act for the first client if the duty of confidentiality to the second client is not put at risk.

Form of undertaking recommended by the Law Society for children's video evidence

UNDERTAKING

Form of undertaking recommended by the Law Society for use by solicitors when receiving recorded evidence of a child witness prepared to be admitted in evidence at criminal trials in accordance with section 54 of the Criminal Justice Act 1991:

I/We acknowledge receipt of the recording marked 'evidence of . . .'

I/We undertake that whilst the recording is in my/our possession I/we shall:

(a) not make or permit any other person to make a copy of the recording;
(b) not release the recording to [*name of the accused*];
(c) not make or permit any disclosure of the recording or its contents to any person except when in my/our opinion it is necessary in the course of preparing the prosecution, defence, or appeal against conviction and/or sentence;
(d) ensure that the recording is always kept in a locked, secure container when not in use;
(e) return the recording to you when I am/we are no longer instructed in the matter.

Witness care

NATIONAL STANDARDS OF WITNESS CARE

The Law Society has formally recognised the various responsibilities which you owe to witnesses in a National Statement which was produced by the Trial Issues Group (TIG) (which has been replaced by the National Criminal Justice Board[1] (NCJB)). Implementation of the statement is co-ordinated by the Local Criminal Justice Boards[2] (LCJBs) (which have replaced local TIGs), incorporating the National Standards into Local Service Agreements on Witness Care.

The National Standards include some timescales for the defence, during which it is expected that a particular action will be taken. These actions have been carefully phrased so that a solicitor is only asked to do something which it is in his power to do, rather than something for which he depends upon the co-operation of the client or defence witnesses. Likewise, only timescales which are realistic for all solicitors have been adopted.

LCJBs may choose to set their own timescales. Although TIG accepted that a solicitor who chose to agree to a shorter timescale did so only on behalf of that solicitor's firm, the Law Society was concerned that this may have the effect of pressurising other firms in the area. The Law Society recommended that solicitors instead concentrate on keeping within the timescales negotiated for them by the Law Society in the National Standards which, unless varied locally, would automatically become part of any local agreement.

The No Witness, No Justice programme brings the police and prosecution together to support prosecution victims and witnesses of crime at each stage of the process from the point that a statement is taken by the police, to the conclusion of a case when the witness will be notified of the result of the case. In many areas, witness units have been established under this programme.

The detailed standards

The National Standards make various demands on the police, CPS, barristers and the courts as well as on defence solicitors. Under the terms of the agreement, you are required to look after your own witnesses.

1. When taking statements, note details of witnesses' availability and record details of any special needs the witnesses have including standby arrangements (e.g. permitting witnesses to wait at known locations near the court where they can be contacted by telephone, mobile phone or pager) for child, expert/professional, intimidated and vulnerable witnesses. Note: this includes those with disabilities

who may require communication aids or assistance with access to court facilities. Contact the court customer services officer for assistance for disabled court users.

2. Immediately identify difficulties which witnesses have in expressing themselves through differences in languages, mannerisms or expressions.

3. Where a witness is under a mental disability, consider how their special needs can be addressed, for example by arranging for the attendance and assistance of a key worker or support worker as appropriate.

4. Give the witness a copy of the leaflet entitled 'Witness in Court' (available at **www.homeoffice.gov.uk/cpd/pvu/witness.pdf**), deal with any queries and encourage the witness to inform you immediately of any change in his availability for court. Note: you may wish to draw the witness's attention to the availability of the Witness Service. There is a service in all Crown Courts and magistrates' courts. The Witness Service provides an opportunity for a witness to get used to the court environment and the procedure. It can be useful both in terms of witness care and in relaxing the witness to enable him or her to give evidence more effectively. Prosecution witnesses are increasingly being referred to the Witness Service and defence witnesses should be equally well looked after.

5. If children are witnesses in cases involving cruelty, sexual abuse or violence, give them and their parents or carers an information pack called The Young Witness Pack and the video *Giving Evidence – what's it really like?*[3]

6. At the time of taking a statement, enquire whether the witness has been or is at risk of being subjected to intimidation and, if so, take necessary steps, for example informing the police and indicating to the court that circumstances make it necessary to prioritise the case. Where intimidation is an issue, the witness at risk should be provided with the name and telephone number of a police contact, additional to the officer in the case who works during normal office hours.

7. Where interpreters are required for a hearing, establish that they are familiar with the particular dialect or regional variation of the language which the witness uses. Interpreters should be familiar with the terms used in court proceedings. Note: there are also different forms of sign languages for deaf people.

8. Decide the order in which witnesses should be called to give evidence and consider whether it is possible to stagger their attendance so that any inconvenience to them can be minimised. The court's agreement should be obtained to the staggering of witnesses.

9. Within four working days of being informed of a trial date or the appearance of a case in a warned list, the defence should inform a defence witness of this and of the time they are required to attend court.

10. Defence advocates and, when permitted, those from the instructing solicitor's office who attend the Crown Court should meet their witnesses at an agreed time.

11. Unless it is necessary for evidential purposes, witnesses should not be required to disclose their addresses in open court.

12. Deal with any queries about court procedures raised by witnesses. Action should be taken to ensure that witnesses understand the procedure for claiming their expenses.

13. In the event of witnesses having to wait for more than two hours (one hour in the magistrates' court) from the time they are required to attend court to the time they are called to give evidence, they should be informed of the reason for the delay and told how long they may have to wait.

If a case is to be adjourned part-heard, the court should provide the defence with sufficient time to ascertain the availability of witnesses so that the case can be adjourned to a date that is, so far as is possible, convenient to the witnesses.

The defence solicitor and the CPS are also required to communicate with each other about the case:

1. When undertaking a review of the full file, the prosecution should decide which statements can appropriately be tendered in evidence under CJA 1967, s.9.
2. Within seven working days from entering a not guilty plea in the magistrates' court, the defence should serve on the court and the prosecutor copies of the defence statements in their possession which can be appropriately tendered in evidence under CJA 1967, s.9.
3. In cases to be tried in the magistrates' court, any additional witness statements should be served on the other party and the court as quickly as possible and in any event within seven working days of possession.
4. In cases to be tried in the magistrates' court, the defence and prosecution should make admissions of fact in writing within seven working days of knowledge of those facts.
5. If the defence or prosecution advocate has proposed a section 9 statement or section 10 admissions, the defence solicitor or the CPS should inform the other party within four working days.

NO WITNESS, NO JUSTICE

In many areas, witness units have now been established under the No Witness, No Justice project. This brings together the police and the CPS to provide for the needs of witnesses and victims from the beginning to the end of a case.

WITNESS CHARTER

The Office for Criminal Justice Reform (OCJR) is currently developing proposals for a Witness Charter which will include new standards of care for all non-professional witnesses. The Witness Charter will update the National Standards of Witness Care. The National Standards were aimed at CJS agencies rather than the witnesses themselves and there were few mechanisms or the necessary infrastructure in place to deliver them and in practice compliance has been poor. The National Standards are also out of date and there are now gaps.

The new Witness Charter will take account of recent developments such as the introduction of Witness Service staff and volunteers in every court in England and Wales, the roll out of Witness Care Units as part of the national No Witness, No Justice project, and the use of special measures to give evidence by vulnerable or intimidated witnesses.

NOTES

1. The National Criminal Justice Board is made up of CJS ministers, agency heads and senior policy officials as well as the Chair of the Criminal Justice Council.

2.   There are 42 Local Criminal Justice Boards which work at local level supporting the work of the NCJB by reviewing the operation of the criminal justice system in their area and working to make improvements. Membership is restricted to local chief officers of the police, CPS, courts, prisons, the Probation Service and YOTs.

3.   The Young Witness Pack and the video *Giving Evidence – What's it Really Like?* are both available from NSPCC Publications, tel. 020 7825 7422; e-mail: publications@nspcc.org.uk.

APPENDIX 6

Professional skills

[References in square brackets are to the LSC Transaction Criteria.]

COMMUNICATION SKILLS

When writing to clients, it is advisable to:

(a) use short sentences;
(b) write in short paragraphs;
(c) use few long words;
(d) be logical in the order in which you present things;
(e) avoid legal jargon.

You should also let your client feel he has your complete attention. Interruptions undermine the relationship; have a system in place to minimise them, e.g. take no telephone calls unless they are very urgent and nobody else can deal with them.

Listening

1. Approach things with an open mind.
2. Do not interrupt unless:

    (a) the conversation goes off the topic;
    (b) you need to clarify something.

3. Pay attention: to concentrate and comprehend.
4. Encourage the person who is talking.
5. Do not jump in and answer for the person.
6. Summarise the points being made.
7. Invite feedback.

Advise your client what is in store for him in terms of the various stages of the court procedures [54] (including whether he will have to give evidence). See your client 'through the system'. Central to your client's concern are the questions, 'Will I get bail?', 'Will I be found guilty?' [54.2], 'If I am found guilty/plead guilty what will I get?' [54.5]. Always be realistic; that way you will gain your client's confidence which is the essential basis of your relationship.

Talk to your client in a language he understands; avoid legal jargon. Make allowances for your client's nervousness.

Talking

1. Be calm.
2. Take your time.
3. Be logical in the order in which you present things: do not topic hop.

4. Use clear understandable language.
5. Speak in manageable chunks.
6. Tailor what you say to the understanding of the receiver.
7. Avoid interruptions, noises, distractions.
8. Do not talk over anyone else.
9. Summarise the points you are making.
10. Invite comment and feedback.
11. Check out non-verbal signs.

INTERVIEWING A WITNESS

To minimise the risk of preventing, obstructing, influencing, distorting or displacing the witness's account, interviewing should be a two-phase process:

(a) uninterrupted free narration by the witness;
(b) probing, to expand and to test the details of the narration and subsequent responses.

Free narration

Invite the witness to give the fullest possible account at his own pace, reporting everything in his mind or mind's eye, editing out nothing and including even the apparently inconsequential. The witness must not be interrupted when narrating. If the witness stops momentarily or for even longer, you must resist the urge to interrupt.

A free-narrative phase elicits approximately 35 per cent of the total accurate information gained from the interview as a whole.

Interruption

Interruption:

(a) prevents completion of what the witness wanted to say;
(b) disrupts concentration, the essential requirement for effective and fuller retrieval;
(c) discourages concerted effort at retrieval, resulting in more superficial responses;
(d) leads the witness to give shorter, less detailed, responses to fit the reduced talking time.

Create a detailed image in your mind's eye of what is being asserted. Re-create, e.g. by role play, to test out the reality of what is being asserted.

Probing

1. Pause after each question and after the witness's answer to remove pressure, help recollection of thoughts and facilitate retrieval.
2. Key individuals must be identified when reference is made to them.
3. Any verbal exchanges which took place should be referred to. Both sides of the conversation should be reported.
4. If an outcome is described, or a reaction, then the triggering cause should also be stated.
5. Refer to sensations, feeling and emotions.

Do not topic hop. Move logically from one topic to another, leaving a topic only when it has been exhaustively probed. After a series of connected topics it is wise to give a staged summary, checking back with the witness the sum total of his replies before moving on.

Ask open-ended questions (e.g. 'how', 'why') or closed identificatory questions ('who', 'what', 'when', 'where', 'how', 'which') with minimal supportive prompts ('and', 'then') to give maximum latitude for responding and encourage expansion, creating more detail for probing.

Avoid leading, option or multiple questions. They trigger short, frequently affirmative answers and involve less concentrated retrieval.

Use closed confirmatory questions (prompting answers of 'yes', 'no') with care, particularly resisting using these early in the interview.

On completion of the interview give an overall summary, having invited feedback on its accuracy.

DELEGATION

Subsidiary work should be delegated, if appropriate:

1. Ensure that the delegate's workload enables the task to be reasonably carried out.
2. Explain the purpose of the task and the context in which it is to be carried out: the key results to be obtained and the time allowed for it.
3. Clarify the scope of the authority given and any limitations, for example whether any advice should be given as to the likely length of sentence if the client asks.
4. Enable competence and confidence with appropriate training.
5. Remain accountable: delegation is not abrogation and you remain responsible for the task that you have delegated.
6. Phase the process so that as confidence is gained you progressively hand over control of the task.
7. Let go! Let them get on with the job and do not make on-the-spot requests for detailed information.
8. Monitor and supervise without interfering.
9. Accept that a reasonable number of errors will be made and provide support.
10. Remain available and interested.

Where the file is transferred to another office, department or fee earner within the same firm, the client should be given:

(a) an explanation of the reasons for the transfer [80.1];
(b) the name of the person taking over the case and their supervisor [80.2];
(c) an opportunity to comment or raise any issues [80.3].

An appropriate record must be kept when clients are referred to other organisations [81].

Working with interpreters

REGISTERED PUBLIC SERVICE INTERPRETERS (RPSIS)

RPSIs are those who have met the criteria for appearing in the National Register, namely:

(a) an appropriate level of educational attainment (i.e. a degree or equivalent);
(b) a high level of fluency in both the written and oral form of English and of the other language;
(c) a relevant interpreting qualification (such as the Diploma in Public Service Interpreting);
(d) a body of relevant interpreting experience at the appropriate quality standard;
(e) relevant references;
(f) personal suitability.

RPSIs agree to abide by a code of conduct, which sets out the standards which the public services expect of interpreters admitted to the National Register. In order to maintain these standards, public services and clients who are dissatisfied with the performance of an interpreter recruited through the Register are requested to supply details to the Institute of Linguists. Any disciplinary action will be decided upon by the disciplinary panel as described in the Code. The code of conduct is registered with the Office of Fair Trading (Registration No. RMS/21 51).

COMPETENCE

RPSIs are expected to:

(a) have a written and spoken command of both languages, including any specialist terminology, current idioms and dialects;
(b) understand the relevant procedures of the particular discipline in which they are working;
(c) maintain and develop their written and spoken command of English and other languages;
(d) be familiar with the cultural backgrounds of both parties.

PROCEDURE

RPSIs will:

(a) interpret truly and faithfully what is said, without anything being added, omitted or changed; in exceptional circumstances a summary may be given if requested, and consented to by both parties;

(b)   disclose any difficulties encountered with dialects or technical terms, and if these cannot be satisfactorily remedied, withdraw from the assignment;

(c)   not enter into the discussion, give advice or express opinions or reactions to any of the parties;

(d)   intervene only:

- to ask for clarification;
- to point out that a party may not have understood something;
- to alert the parties to a possible missed cultural inference; or
- to ask for accommodation for the interpreting process (for instance if someone is speaking too quietly or too fast);

(e)   not delegate work, nor accept delegated work, without the consent of the client;

(f)   be reliable and punctual at all times;

(g)   state (in criminal trial) if they have been involved in interpreting at the police station on the same case.

ETHICAL AND PROFESSIONAL

RPSIs will:

(a)   respect confidentiality at all times and not seek to take advantage of any information disclosed during their work;

(b)   act in an impartial and professional manner;

(c)   not discriminate directly or indirectly, on the grounds of race, colour, ethnic origin, age, nationality, religion, gender or disability;

(d)   disclose information, including any criminal record, which may make them unsuitable in any particular case;

(e)   disclose immediately if the interviewee or immediate family is known or related;

(f)   disclose any business, financial, family or other interest which they might have in the matter being handled;

(g)   not accept any form of reward, whether in cash or otherwise, for interpreting work other than payment by the employer.

FINDING AN INTERPRETER

The Institute of Linguists maintains the National Register of Public Service Interpreters (the National Register). The Council for the Advancement of Communications with Deaf People (CACDP) maintains the National Directory of Sign Language Interpreters (the National Directory). Wherever possible interpreters used in court should be chosen from the National Register or National Directory.

The National Register contains Registered Public Service Interpreters (RPSIs) at one of two levels. Interim level is awarded to interpreters who have work experience but are not yet qualified or who have appropriate qualifications but not yet sufficient experience. Full level interpreters are both appropriately qualified (holding the Diploma in Public Service Interpreting or an equivalent qualification) and can demonstrate evidence of adequate work experience. An entry on the Register specifying that they have taken the legal training option demonstrates an understanding of court procedures. In order to provide interpreters for rare languages, there is a further small category of 'non-assessed' interpreters. An assessment has been made of the quantity and quality of their experience as interpreters but not of their qualifications.

Similarly, for sign language interpreting, CACDP is the national assessment and awarding body.

REGISTERED QUALIFIED AND TRAINEE SIGN LANGUAGE INTERPRETERS

Registered Qualified Sign Language Interpreters (RQSLIs) are those who have passed the CACDP professional interpreting examination and are required to abide by the code of ethics and complaints procedure. Registered Trainee Sign Language Interpreters (RTSLIs) are those who have passed CACDP stage 3 (advanced) examination in British sign language, are attending a recognised interpreting training programme and are also bound by the code of ethics and complaints procedure. The National Directory contains further details and includes the interpreters' code of ethics and complaints and disciplinary procedure.

The solicitor's preferred choice should be an RPSI or CACDP registered interpreter. Details of RPSIs can be obtained by subscribing to the National Register. Contact the National Register of Public Service Interpreters Ltd, Saxon House, 48 Southwark Street, London SE1 1UN, tel. 020 7940 3166; **www.nrpsi.co.uk**. For CACDPs contact CACDP, Block 4, Durham University Science Park, Stockton Road, Durham DH1 3U2, tel. 0191 383 1155; **www.cacdp.org.uk**. Their register is updated annually.

Geographical considerations alone should not preclude the engagement of an RPSI or Registered Sign Language Interpreter in preference to an unregistered interpreter. If an interpreter from the National Register or National Directory is not available, the solicitor should aim to instruct an interpreter who as far as possible meets the National Register criteria which are set out in this appendix.

WORKING WITH AN INTERPRETER

Before the interview

1. Give the interpreter as much advance notice as possible.
2. Provide clear information about the proposed assignment when you first contact the interpreter, including:

   (a) the date and time you need the interpreter;
   (b) clear instructions, with a map if necessary, for reaching the venue;
   (c) transport arrangements: details of available parking space, suitable public transport, or specific arrangements if work is to be carried out during unsociable hours;
   (d) the name and telephone number of the person the interpreter is to contact on arrival or in case of delay;
   (e) the name of the client involved, to ensure that your client is not known personally to the interpreter, placing his impartiality at risk;
   (f) the language and/or dialect you need: if you are unsure, contact an interpreter in the language you think might be right, and ask for advice; if your client is present, it may be helpful to ask the interpreter to cross-check the language match over the telephone;
   (g) an outline of the subject matter, to allow the interpreter to research any terminology or procedures in advance, time permitting; the interpreter should refuse an assignment which is beyond his competence.

3. Consider whether you need the interpreter to translate a letter from you to your client, setting out the time, date and place of the proposed appointment and giving travel instructions.
4. Confirm the above arrangements in writing where possible.

5. You may need to consult your client who, depending on the nature of the case, may wish to speak through an interpreter of the same sex.
6. Make proper accommodation for the interpreter. Arrange the seating so that you and your client face each other. The interpreter should be seated in between and to one side so that he can hear easily, without preventing you from talking directly to your client; the interpreter must not be perceived as being on one 'side' or the other. Provide the interpreter with work space to write notes (e.g. dates, addresses, numbers) if necessary.
7. Provide water for refreshment.
8. Allow for rest breaks.

During the interview

Always face your client, using direct speech. The interpreter should not be asked to interview, nor expected to know what information to look for, nor how to process the information received.

1. Introduce yourself to your client. Allow the interpreter to introduce himself to your client, and to explain the interpreter's role: that is, to give an impartial, complete and confidential rendition of everything that is said.
2. Establish how your client's name should be recorded for formal documents and how your client wishes to be addressed.
3. It may be helpful to explain who you are and what your job is. Ensure your client understands the function of any other professionals who may be involved.
4. Explain fully structures and procedures which your client may be unfamiliar with.
5. The interpreter may intervene if required, and explain the reasons for doing so to both parties, such as:
   (a) to clarify something which has been said before interpreting it;
   (b) to alert one of the parties that, in spite of accurate interpretation, the other might not have fully understood what has been said;
   (c) to alert both parties to a missed cultural inference: knowledge of a piece of information may incorrectly have been assumed;
   (d) to ask for accommodation to the interpreting process – for instance, if someone is speaking too quietly or too fast.
6. Ask your client if you are not sure of relevant attitudes, perceptions or cultural norms. Do not ask the interpreter.
7. Different cultures approach conflict resolution and the exchange and presentation of information in different ways. You may need to alter your interviewing techniques to accommodate differing forms of communication.
8. At the end of every two or three sentences (never in the middle of a sentence) the interpreter needs to interpret.
9. Express yourself clearly and unambiguously.
10. Use appropriate language. For example, jargon or popular language can be difficult to interpret accurately. Avoid using double negatives or using a question as a statement; avoid where possible use of paired, redundant phrases e.g. 'will and testament' or 'freely and voluntarily'.
11. For the communication to be effective, check mutual understanding regularly by asking open questions.
12. At the end of the interview, clearly summarise what has been decided and point out the next steps to be taken.

After the interview

1. Check with your interpreter that working procedures were effective and satisfactory.
2. Complete any necessary forms to ensure payment of the interpreter.

Further information

For comprehensive information on working with interpreters see A. Corsellis, *Non-English Speakers and the English Legal System*, (Institute of Criminology, University of Cambridge, 1994). Further information about registration, professional etiquette and disciplinary procedures is available from the Institute of Linguists, tel. 020 7359 7445.

Information about Interpreters

Record to be attached to client's file

Name of client: _____

Name of court: _____

Unique case reference no: _____

A. Action to be Taken

Information to be sent to (*enter 'court' or 'interpreter'*)			
For (*type of hearing*)			
On (*date*)			

B. Details of Person for Whom an Interpreter is Required

Use a different form for each defendant/witness

1. Defendant/defence witness (*delete as appropriate*) _____

2. Country/region of origin: _____

3. Name: _____

4. Sex: _____

5. Age: _____

6. Best language: _____

7. Dialect if any: _____

   For deaf/deafened people note whether British or other sign language or lip speaking required.

8. Language of literacy   Fluent/modest/elementary/nil

9. Knowledge of English   Nil/a few words/modest

10. Above checked via interpreter Y/N

11. Preferences in selection of an interpreter:

(note both information and strength of preference 1–5)

Sex

Age

Religion

Ethnic origin

Other

C. Briefing of Interpreter Required

12.
Date			
Time			
Place of the hearing			

13. **Subject content**
(the interpeter will be helped by having a sight of the copy of the statement made to the solicitor by the person named above, as well as copies of any prosecution witness statements which are likely to be put to him/her in cross-examination)

14. **Technical contect**
(the case may involve technical matters such as medical or forensic evidence, psychiatric reports, or financial transactions)

15. **Procedures**
(where other than common ones may be involved)

16. **Terminology**
(technical, formal or slang terms not commonly understood. It may be useful for a glossary to be compiled in both languages, checked and passed on to maintain consistency during a case)

17. **Contact point at solicitor's firm**

Name:

Address:

Tel:

Fax:

18. **Terms of engagement**   Legal Services Commission/Central Funds/Private
(the solicitor should make it clear to the interpreter what the terms of engagement are and when s/he is not responsible for the interpreter's fees)

D. Record of Interpreters Involved in the Case to Date

Date (*interpreter used*)			
Agency (*who instructed interpreter*)			
Place (*where interpreter used*)			
Interpreter (*name and NRPSI no.*)			

E. Record of Legal Translators Involved in the Case to Date

(DPSI holders are assessed as being competent to translate straightforward, short texts. A more complex and lengthy text, such as an extradition document, may well have to be referred to a qualified specialist and perhaps a legally qualified one.)

Date			
Agency			
Name and address of translator			

F. Information Given to Non-English Speaker
(enter Y/N against each item, and date of hearing it refers to)

Method
(enter either 'T' if text in own language or 'E' if explanation via interpreter)

i) Date, time and place of hearing:			
ii) Purpose of the hearing:			
iii) The procedures to be used:			

293

Standards of Competence for the Accreditation of Solicitors and Representatives Advising at the Police Station

(Source: Solicitors Regulation Authority]

The standards of competence are in three parts as follows:

Part 1: Underpinning knowledge – Details the knowledge and understanding that the solicitor or representative will need to have in order to be competent when giving advice in the police station.

Part 2: Underpinning skills – Details the skills which the solicitor or representative will need in order to represent effectively the client in the police station and which should be demonstrated as the solicitor or representative undertakes the activities detailed in the units of performance in Part 3.

Part 3: Standards of performance – Details the standards of performance that the solicitor or representative should demonstrate at each stage of the process of representing the client. In order to demonstrate competent performance the solicitor or representative will need the knowledge and skills detailed in Parts 1 and 2. The solicitor or representative's understanding of how and the reasons why each of the performance criteria should be demonstrated in a police station situation may be examined in the written test. The standards of performance will be used to assess the candidate's performance in the critical incidents test.

PART 1   UNDERPINNING KNOWLEDGE

1.1   The role of defending the client

The solicitor or representative must be able to demonstrate a practical understanding of:

1.1.1. ethical rules and principles relevant to advising and assisting a client at the police station

1.1.2. a solicitor's or representative's authority to act for a person detained in the police station

1.1.3. a solicitor's or representative's role and aims when acting for such a client with regard to the probing of the immigration officer's assessment of a client's immigration status, representations to be made to the immigration officer and the purpose of the advice to be given to the client

1.1.4. a solicitor's or representative's role and aims when acting for such a client with regard to the probing of the prosecution case, representations to be made to the police and the purpose of the advice to be given to the client

1.1.5. the effect that detention can have on a client's behaviour in the police station and appropriate responses to typical behaviour

1.1.6. how to identify a client's vulnerability

1.1.7. how to identify inappropriate behaviour by the police and when and how to respond to it

1.1.8. the need for accurate records to be made of the information obtained from the police, the instructions obtained from the client, actions taken and advice given to the client

1.1.9. the need to give consideration to any conflict of interests and the appropriate course of action where a conflict, or significant risk of a conflict of interests is identified.

1.2 An understanding of criminal law and procedure

The solicitor or representative must be able to demonstrate a practical understanding of the:

1.2.1. basic sequence of events in criminal cases from the client's arrest/arrival at the police station, to conviction and sentence and the critical factors at each stage

1.2.2. definition of an arrestable offence

1.2.3. definition of a serious arrestable offence and the significance of an offence being so classified

1.2.4. different ways by which crimes may be tried

1.2.5. meaning of the terms: burden of proof, actus reus, mens rea, intentionally, recklessly, maliciously, dishonestly, knowing or believing, possession

1.2.6. defence of self-defence

1.2.7. modes of participation in crime of sole and joint principal and accomplice

1.2.8. law and procedure relating to young suspects and defendants

1.2.9. implications of the Human Rights Act 1998 for advice and assistance at the police station.

1.3 An understanding of relevant immigration law and procedure

The solicitor or representative must be able to demonstrate a practical understanding of:

1.3.1. the basis upon which a person can be detained under the Immigration Act or other similar legislation

1.3.2. the meaning of the terms: overstayer; illegal entrant; asylum seeker; deportee; refugee; exceptional leave to remain

1.3.3. the main Immigration Act offences

1.3.4. the basic sequence of events in immigration cases from the client's arrest/arrival at the police station, to interview, the decision of the immigration officer and detention/release, and the critical factors at each stage.

1.4 An understanding of the common crimes

The solicitor or representative must be able to demonstrate that they are able to determine the components or elements of any crime, and defences that may relate to such a crime. In particular the solicitor or representative must be able to demonstrate an awareness of the components of the following common crimes, together with their specific defences sufficient to enable advice to be given to a client about the strengths and weaknesses of the prosecution case including the elements which the prosecution have to prove:

1.4.1. assault occasioning actual bodily harm
1.4.2. possessing a controlled drug with intent to supply
1.4.3. handling stolen goods
1.4.4. possessing an offensive weapon
1.4.5. taking a motor vehicle
1.4.6. theft
1.4.7. affray
1.4.8. criminal damage
1.4.9. robbery
1.4.10. burglary.

1.5 An understanding of the rules of evidence

The solicitor or representative must be able to demonstrate a practical understanding of:

1.5.1. the legal and evidential burdens of proof as they relate to prosecution and defence
1.5.2. how facts are proved including the rule against hearsay and its exceptions
1.5.3. the evidential consequences of a suspect

> (i)   remaining silent
> (ii)   remaining selectively silent
> (iii) denying guilt at interviews
> (iv)   lying
> (v)   making a 'mixed' statement
> (vi)   making a confession

1.5.4. legal professional privilege
1.5.5. the evidential value of admissions made by a co-accused
1.5.6. the exclusion of an unreliable confession or evidence obtained unfairly (PACE s.76 and s.78).

1.6 A practical understanding of PACE and the codes of practice under PACE

The solicitor or representative must be able to demonstrate a practical understanding of PACE and the Codes of Practice and of their interpretation in the light of case decisions, and an understanding of the evidential consequences of a breach, as they relate to:

1.6.1. the search of the client's premises
1.6.2. arrest, voluntary attendance at the police station and search upon arrest
1.6.3. the duties of the custody office before and after the charge
1.6.4. responsibilities in relation to detained persons
1.6.5. detention, time limits of detention and reviews
1.6.6. searches of detained persons
1.6.7. the right to have someone informed when arrested
1.6.8. fingerprinting
1.6.9. the taking of intimate and other samples
1.6.10. the right to legal advice

1.6.11. charging
1.6.12. bail
1.6.13. the special treatment of juveniles and other vulnerable persons
1.6.14. the keeping of and entitlement to see the custody record
1.6.15. documentary evidence
1.6.16. cautions
1.6.17. the conduct and tape recording of interviews
1.6.18. identification procedures.

PART 2 UNDERPINNING SKILLS

Communication skills

The solicitor or representative must be able to communicate effectively with the client, the police officers involved and any third parties. The solicitor or representative must be able to:

2.1.1. use language appropriate for the recipient
2.1.2. identify if there is a need for an interpreter
2.1.3. express requests, objections, ideas and advice with precision, logic and economy
2.1.4. listen actively
2.1.5. speak effectively and assertively
2.1.6. communicate in a manner and form that takes account of ethnic, cultural or other forms of diversity.

Negotiating skills

The solicitor or representative must be able to demonstrate negotiating skills. The solicitor or representative must be able to:

2.2.1. identify the issues to be resolved
2.2.2. assess the relative strengths and weaknesses of the parties' positions
2.2.3. identify the strategy and tactics adopted by the other party
2.2.4. explain the benefits that would result from an acquiescence to his or her request
2.2.5. generate alternative approaches to the issues
2.2.6. make accurate records of the negotiation and the outcome.

Interviewing and advising skills

The solicitor or representative must be able to elicit effectively the relevant information from the client in order to be able to offer appropriate advice. The solicitor or representative must be able to:

2.3.1. allow the client to explain his or her position
2.3.2. elicit relevant information
2.3.3. gain the trust and confidence of the client
2.3.4. assist the client to be able to decide upon the best course of action
2.3.5. agree on the action to be taken by both the client and the representative
2.3.6. deal with the above in a manner which takes proper account of ethnic, cultural and other forms of diversity
2.3.7. deal with any ethical problems which may arise when advising the client
2.3.8. accurately record the information elicited and the advice given.

PART 3   STANDARDS OF PERFORMANCE

The solicitor or representative must act in accordance with relevant ethical rules and principles at all times.

Unit 1: Respond to the request to attend

Element 1

Obtain information about the detained person and his or her circumstances.

PERFORMANCE CRITERIA:

3.1.1.   Details about the detained person are obtained
3.1.2.   The relationship between the detained person and the third party is established where appropriate
3.1.3.   Information about the circumstances of the arrest and any other people involved is sought
3.1.4.   Information about whether a criminal investigation is being conducted, is sought
3.1.5.   Details about the location of the detained person are obtained
3.1.6.   Reasons for concern regarding the detained person's well being, vulnerability or police conduct are identified
3.1.7.   An appropriate assessment of the authority to act for the detained person is made
3.1.8.   All information obtained is accurately recorded.

RANGE STATEMENT

The initial request to attend might be received from a friend or relative, existing or former client, an appropriate adult, the duty solicitor service, or the detained person choosing from a list at the police station.

Element 2

Consult with the custody officer by telephone.

PERFORMANCE CRITERIA

3.2.1.   The custody officer is informed of the solicitor's or representative's status
3.2.2.   Information is sought regarding the client and associated suspects, the alleged offence and the circumstances of the arrest
3.2.3.   Information is sought regarding the evidence in support, detention, bail and charging decisions, the police officers involved, the police investigation and the officer's assessment of the client and actions taken
3.2.4.   Where appropriate, information is sought regarding the immigration officer involved and as to whether a criminal investigation is being conducted
3.2.5.   An appropriate response is given to non disclosure of the information requested
3.2.6.   Access to the client is sought and an appropriate response is given to a refusal to allow access.

Element 3

Consultation with the client by telephone, if access is obtained.

PERFORMANCE CRITERIA

3.3.1. The client is informed of the representative's status
3.3.2. The client is reminded that the conversation might not be private
3.3.3. The client is directly questioned about admissions, treatment and police responses to requests
3.3.4. Information is sought to enable an assessment about the client's vulnerability to be made
3.3.5. The client's right to free legal advice service is explained
3.3.6. The client is advised to exercise the right to silence if questioned prior to the solicitor's or representative's attendance.

Element 4

Decide what action to take and communicate this decision.

PERFORMANCE CRITERIA

3.4.1. An assessment of the solicitor's or representative's competence to advise on the case is made
3.4.2. If the case is outside the solicitor's or representative's competence appropriate action is taken
3.4.3. An assessment of the need to make a personal visit is made
3.4.4. The urgency of the need for advice is determined
3.4.5. The custody officer and client are informed of the proposed course of action.

Unit 2: Consult with the appropriate officers at the police station

Element 1

Consult with the custody officer.

PERFORMANCE CRITERIA

3.5.1. The custody officer is informed of the solicitor's or representative's status if this information has not been given previously
3.5.2. Information about the client, the allegation and the investigation are sought
3.5.3. A copy or sight of the custody record is sought and an appropriate response is given to a refusal to allow access to the custody record
3.5.4. A private consultation of adequate duration with the client is sought and an appropriate response is given to a refusal to allow such consultation
3.5.5. The solicitor's or representative's presence during the police interview of the client is sought and an appropriate response given to a refusal to allow such attendance.

Element 2

Consult with the investigating officer.

PERFORMANCE CRITERIA

3.6.1. The investigating officer is informed of the representative's status if this information has not been given previously

3.6.2. Information about the strength and nature of the prosecution case is sought and an appropriate response is given to a refusal to disclose such information

3.6.3. Information regarding the purpose of the interview is sought

3.6.4. The proper arrangement of the interview room is sought

3.6.5. The solicitor's or representative's presence at the interview is sought and an appropriate response given to a refusal to allow such a presence

3.6.6. The investigating officer's consideration of the client's possible vulnerability and fitness for interview is confirmed.

Unit 3: Consult with the client

Element 1

Introduction to and assessment of the client.

PERFORMANCE CRITERIA

3.7.1. The client is informed of the solicitor's or representative's status, if this information has not been given previously

3.7.2. The client's trust and confidence are sought

3.7.3. An assessment is made of the client's vulnerability and fitness for interview

3.7.4. Complaints of maltreatment of the client by the police or immigration service are ascertained together with any response made to such complaints

3.7.5. Full records are kept of the consultation with the client.

Element 2

Inform and advise the client.

PERFORMANCE CRITERIA

3.8.1. The client is informed about the offence(s) alleged, what the prosecution would need to prove, the evidence in support, the strengths and weaknesses of the police case and prosecution evidence, the likely procedures to be followed in the event of the client being charged

3.8.2. Instructions are taken from the client and any information obtained is kept confidential

3.8.3. Reasoned and considered advice is given to the client concerning the answering of questions, the right to silence, the making of a written statement under caution, or the signing of a written record of any comment made to the police

3.8.4. Where relevant, instructions are taken to establish the client's immigration status, and advice is given as to what action the police and/or immigration service may take, and as to the appropriate action to be taken by the client

3.8.5. An explanation is given of how the information gathered has been used to formulate the advice

3.8.6. An explanation of the conduct of a tape-recorded interview and its implications is given to the client

3.8.7. The solicitor's or representative's role during the interview is explained to the client

3.8.8. Where appropriate an assessment is made of the solicitor's or representative's position with regard to the representation of more than one detained person.

Unit 4: Monitoring of and intervening during the interview

Element 1

Ensure the proper conduct of the interview.

PERFORMANCE CRITERIA

3.9.1. An opening statement is made as appropriate
3.9.2. Representations are made to the police or immigration officer if the interview room is not satisfactorily arranged and an appropriate response is made if these representations are ignored
3.9.3. Improper behaviour by or questions from the police or immigration officer is recognised and responded to appropriately
3.9.4. Attempts to undermine a decision by the client to exercise a right to silence are recognised and responded to appropriately
3.9.5. Appropriate action is taken to ensure that the interview is accurately recorded
3.9.6. The time at which the interview should cease is recognised and responded to appropriately
3.9.7. Full and accurate records of the interview are made.

Element 2

Advise the client during the interview.

PERFORMANCE CRITERIA

3.10.1. The client is advised without stopping the interview when appropriate
3.10.2. The interview is stopped in order to give the client legal advice in private, when appropriate
3.10.3. The client is made to understand the questions put and is allowed to answer freely.

Unit 5: Representing a vulnerable client.

Element 1

Identify a vulnerable client and ensure appropriate action is taken.

PERFORMANCE CRITERIA

3.11.1. The representative identifies a vulnerable client
3.11.2. Appropriate representations are made to the police or immigration service to ensure that suitable provisions are made to prevent the client from being disadvantaged
3.11.3. The client is advised about the role of an appropriate adult or an interpreter, as appropriate, and the need to ensure that confidentiality is maintained.

Element 2

Working with an appropriate adult or interpreter.

3.12.1. The appropriate adult or interpreter is made aware of his or her role
3.12.2. The interpreter is made aware of his or her duty to be impartial and to keep information confidential.

RANGE STATEMENT

The client might be vulnerable due to age, mental disorder or disability, a difficulty in understanding English, or a hearing or speech disability.

Unit 6: Identification procedures

Element 1

Advising the client on identification procedures.

PERFORMANCE CRITERIA

3.13.1. Details of the witnesses' descriptions of the suspect to the police are sought and an appropriate response is given to a refusal to disclose this information
3.13.2. The client is given appropriate advice on the advantages and disadvantages of different identification procedures
3.13.3. The client is advised of the right to request an identification parade and the advantages and disadvantages of doing so
3.13.4. The client is advised of the consequences of not agreeing to take part in any identification procedure.

Element 2

Ensure that identification procedures are conducted fairly.

PERFORMANCE CRITERIA

3.14.1. Representations are made to the police and precautions taken to ensure that the identification procedure is conducted fairly
3.14.2. Appropriate advice is given to the client on participation in the form of identification chosen
3.14.3. A written record is kept of the identification procedure.

RANGE STATEMENT

The identification procedures on which advice might be given are identification parades; group identification; video film identification; confrontation; fingerprinting; identification by body samples, swabs, impressions.

Unit 7: Representing the client after the interview or identification procedure

Element 1

Ensure that improper questioning does not take place.

PERFORMANCE CRITERIA

3.15.1. Appropriate representations are made to the police and at reviews that the client should be charged or released without further questioning
3.15.2. Attempts are made to ensure that the client is not questioned further in the representative's absence.

Element 2

Ensure that after charge bail is given to the client where appropriate.

PERFORMANCE CRITERIA

3.16.1. Appropriate representations to the police after charge about bail
3.16.2. The client is information about bail decisions.

Element 3

Advising the client.

PERFORMANCE CRITERIA

3.17.1. An explanation is given to the client about charging and bail decisions
3.17.2. The client is advised how to respond to subsequent approaches by the police to question him or her in the solicitor's or representative's absence
3.17.3. The client is referred to a specialist immigration advisor where appropriate having regard to the nature and complexity of the case and the knowledge and experience of the solicitor or representative.

APPENDIX 9

Specified offences

(CJA 2003, Sched.15)

Serious specified offences are marked with an asterisk (offences carrying 10 years or more).

PART 1   SPECIFIED VIOLENT OFFENCES

*1. Manslaughter.
*2. Kidnapping.
*3. False imprisonment.
*4. An offence under section 4 of the Offences Against the Person Act 1861 (soliciting murder).
*5. An offence under section 16 of that Act (threats to kill).
*6. An offence under section 18 of that Act (wounding with intent to cause grievous bodily harm).
 7. An offence under section 20 of that Act (malicious wounding).
*8. An offence under section 21 of that Act (attempting to choke, suffocate or strangle in order to commit or assist in committing an indictable offence).
*9. An offence under section 22 of that Act (using chloroform, etc. to commit or assist in the committing of any indictable offence).
*10. An offence under section 23 of that Act (maliciously administering poison etc. so as to endanger life or inflict grievous bodily harm).
 11. An offence under section 27 of that Act (abandoning children).
*12. An offence under section 28 of that Act (causing bodily injury by explosives).
*13. An offence under section 29 of that Act (using explosives etc. with intent to do grievous bodily harm).
*14. An offence under section 30 of that Act (placing explosives with intent to do bodily injury).
 15. An offence under section 31 of that Act (setting spring guns etc. with intent to do grievous bodily harm).
*16. An offence under section 32 of that Act (endangering the safety of railway passengers).
 17. An offence under section 35 of that Act (injuring persons by furious driving).
 18. An offence under section 37 of that Act (assaulting officer preserving wreck).
 19. An offence under section 38 of that Act (assault with intent to resist arrest).
 20. An offence under section 47 of that Act (assault occasioning actual bodily harm).
*21. An offence under section 2 of the Explosive Substances Act 1883 (causing explosion likely to endanger life or property).
*22. An offence under section 3 of that Act (attempt to cause explosion, or making or keeping explosive with intent to endanger life or property).
*23. An offence under section 1 of the Infant Life (Preservation) Act 1929 (child destruction).
*24. An offence under section 1 of the Children and Young Persons Act 1933 (cruelty to children).

* 25. An offence under section 1 of the Infanticide Act 1938 (infanticide).
* 26. An offence under section 16 of the Firearms Act 1968 (possession of firearm with intent to endanger life).
* 27. An offence under section 16A of that Act (possession of firearm with intent to cause fear of violence).
* 28. An offence under section 17(1) of that Act (use of firearm to resist arrest).
* 29. An offence under section 17(2) of that Act (possession of firearm at time of committing or being arrested for offence specified in Schedule 1 to that Act).
* 30. An offence under section 18 of that Act (carrying a firearm with criminal intent).
* 31. An offence under section 8 of the Theft Act 1968 (robbery or assault with intent to rob).
* 32. An offence under section 9 of that Act of burglary with intent to –

    (a) inflict grievous bodily harm on a person; or
    (b) do unlawful damage to a building or anything in it.

* 33. An offence under section 10 of that Act (aggravated burglary).
* 34. An offence under section 12A of that Act (aggravated vehicle-taking) involving an accident which caused the death of any person.
* 35. An offence of arson under section 1 of the Criminal Damage Act 1971.
* 36. An offence under section 1(2) of that Act (destroying or damaging property) other than an offence of arson.
* 37. An offence under section 1 of the Taking of Hostages Act 1982 (hostage-taking).
* 38. An offence under section 1 of the Aviation Security Act 1982 (hijacking).
* 39. An offence under section 2 of that Act (destroying, damaging or endangering safety of aircraft).
* 40. An offence under section 3 of that Act (other acts endangering or likely to endanger safety of aircraft).
  41. An offence under section 4 of that Act (offences in relation to certain dangerous articles).
  42. An offence under section 127 of the Mental Health Act 1983 (ill-treatment of patients).
  43. An offence under section 1 of the Prohibition of Female Circumcision Act 1985 (prohibition of female circumcision).
* 44. An offence under section 1 of the Public Order Act 1986 (riot).
  45. An offence under section 2 of that Act (violent disorder).
  46. An offence under section 3 of that Act (affray).
* 47. An offence under section 134 of the Criminal Justice Act 1988 (torture).
* 48. An offence under section 1 of the Road Traffic Act 1988 (causing death by dangerous driving).
* 49. An offence under section 3A of that Act (causing death by careless driving when under influence of drink or drugs).
* 50. An offence under section 1 of the Aviation and Maritime Security Act 1990 (endangering safety at aerodromes).
* 51. An offence under section 9 of that Act (hijacking of ships).
* 52. An offence under section 10 of that Act (seizing or exercising control of fixed platforms).
* 53. An offence under section 11 of that Act (destroying fixed platforms or endangering their safety).
* 54. An offence under section 12 of that Act (other acts endangering or likely to endanger safe navigation).
* 55. An offence under section 13 of that Act (offences involving threats).

∗56. An offence under Part II of the Channel Tunnel (Security) Order 1994 (S.I. 1994/570) (offences relating to Channel Tunnel trains and the tunnel system).

57. An offence under section 4 of the Protection from Harassment Act 1997 (putting people in fear of violence).

58. An offence under section 29 of the Crime and Disorder Act 1998 (racially or religiously aggravated assaults).

59. An offence falling within section 31(1)(a) or (b) of that Act (racially or religiously aggravated offences under section 4 or 4A of the Public Order Act 1986).

∗60. An offence under section 51 or 52 of the International Criminal Court Act 2001 (genocide, crimes against humanity, war crimes and related offences), other than one involving murder.

∗61. An offence under section 1 of the Female Genital Mutilation Act 2003 (female genital mutilation).

∗62. An offence under section 2 of that Act (assisting a girl to mutilate her own genitalia).

∗63. An offence under section 3 of that Act (assisting a non-UK person to mutilate overseas a girl's genitalia).

∗63A. An offence under section 5 of the Domestic Violence, Crime and Victims Act 2004 (causing or allowing the death of a child or vulnerable adult).

64. An offence of:

(a) aiding, abetting, counselling, procuring or inciting the commission of an offence specified in this Part of this Schedule,

(b) conspiring to commit an offence so specified, or

(c) attempting to commit an offence so specified.

65. An attempt to commit murder or a conspiracy to commit murder.

PART 2   SPECIFIED SEXUAL OFFENCES

∗66. An offence under section 1 of the Sexual Offences Act 1956 (rape).

67. An offence under section 2 of that Act (procurement of woman by threats).

68. An offence under section 3 of that Act (procurement of woman by false pretences).

69. An offence under section 4 of that Act (administering drugs to obtain or facilitate intercourse).

∗70. An offence under section 5 of that Act (intercourse with girl under thirteen).[1]

∗71. An offence under section 6 of that Act (intercourse with girl under 16).

72. An offence under section 7 of that Act (intercourse with a defective).

73. An offence under section 9 of that Act (procurement of a defective).

∗74. An offence under section 10 of that Act (incest by a man).[1,2]

75. An offence under section 11 of that Act (incest by a woman).

∗76. An offence under section 14 of that Act (indecent assault on a woman).

∗77. An offence under section 15 of that Act (indecent assault on a man).

∗78. An offence under section 16 of that Act (assault with intent to commit buggery).

∗79. An offence under section 17 of that Act (abduction of woman by force or for the sake of her property).

80. An offence under section 19 of that Act (abduction of unmarried girl under eighteen from parent or guardian).

81. An offence under section 20 of that Act (abduction of unmarried girl under sixteen from parent or guardian).

82. An offence under section 21 of that Act (abduction of defective from parent or guardian).

83. An offence under section 22 of that Act (causing prostitution of women).
84. An offence under section 23 of that Act (procuration of girl under twenty-one).
85. An offence under section 24 of that Act (detention of woman in brothel).
*86. An offence under section 25 of that Act (permitting girl under thirteen to use premises for intercourse).
87. An offence under section 26 of that Act (permitting girl under sixteen to use premises for intercourse).
88. An offence under section 27 of that Act (permitting defective to use premises for intercourse).
89. An offence under section 28 of that Act (causing or encouraging the prostitution of, intercourse with or indecent assault on girl under sixteen).
90. An offence under section 29 of that Act (causing or encouraging prostitution of defective).
91. An offence under section 32 of that Act (soliciting by men).
92. An offence under section 33 of that Act (keeping a brothel).
93. An offence under section 128 of the Mental Health Act 1959 (sexual intercourse with patients).
*94. An offence under section 1 of the Indecency with Children Act 1960 (indecent conduct towards young child).
95. An offence under section 4 of the Sexual Offences Act 1967 (procuring others to commit homosexual acts).
96. An offence under section 5 of that Act (living on earnings of male prostitution).
*97. An offence under section 9 of the Theft Act 1968 of burglary with intent to commit rape.
98. An offence under section 54 of the Criminal Law Act 1977 (inciting girl under sixteen to have incestuous sexual intercourse).
*99. An offence under section 1 of the Protection of Children Act 1978 (indecent photographs of children).
100. An offence under section 170 of the Customs and Excise Management Act 1979 (penalty for fraudulent evasion of duty etc) in relation to goods prohibited to be imported under section 42 of the Customs Consolidation Act 1876 (indecent or obscene articles).
101. An offence under section 160 of the Criminal Justice Act 1988 (possession of indecent photograph of a child).
*102. An offence under section 1 of the Sexual Offences Act 2003 (rape).
*103. An offence under section 2 of that Act (assault by penetration).
*104. An offence under section 3 of that Act (sexual assault).
*105. An offence under section 4 of that Act (causing a person to engage in sexual activity without consent).
*106. An offence under section 5 of that Act (rape of a child under 13).
*107. An offence under section 6 of that Act (assault of a child under 13 by penetration).
*108. An offence under section 7 of that Act (sexual assault of a child under 13).
*109. An offence under section 8 of that Act (causing or inciting a child under 13 to engage in sexual activity).
*110. An offence under section 9 of that Act (sexual activity with a child).
*111. An offence under section 10 of that Act (causing or inciting a child to engage in sexual activity).
*112. An offence under section 11 of that Act (engaging in sexual activity in the presence of a child).
*113. An offence under section 12 of that Act (causing a child to watch a sexual act).

114. An offence under section 13 of that Act (child sex offences committed by children or young persons).

*115. An offence under section 14 of that Act (arranging or facilitating commission of a child sex offence).

*116. An offence under section 15 of that Act (meeting a child following sexual grooming etc).

117. An offence under section 16 of that Act (abuse of position of trust: sexual activity with a child).

118. An offence under section 17 of that Act (abuse of position of trust: causing or inciting a child to engage in sexual activity).

119. An offence under section 18 of that Act (abuse of position of trust: sexual activity in the presence of a child).

120. An offence under section 19 of that Act (abuse of position of trust: causing a child to watch a sexual act).

*121. An offence under section 25 of that Act (sexual activity with a child family member).

*122. An offence under section 26 of that Act (inciting a child family member to engage in sexual activity).

*123. An offence under section 30 of that Act (sexual activity with a person with a mental disorder impeding choice).

*124. An offence under section 31 of that Act (causing or inciting a person with a mental disorder impeding choice to engage in sexual activity).

*125. An offence under section 32 of that Act (engaging in sexual activity in the presence of a person with a mental disorder impeding choice).

*126. An offence under section 33 of that Act (causing a person with a mental disorder impeding choice to watch a sexual act).

*127. An offence under section 34 of that Act (inducement, threat or deception to procure sexual activity with a person with a mental disorder).

*128. An offence under section 35 of that Act (causing a person with a mental disorder to engage in or agree to engage in sexual activity by inducement, threat or deception).

*129. An offence under section 36 of that Act (engaging in sexual activity in the presence, procured by inducement, threat or deception, of a person with a mental disorder).

*130. An offence under section 37 of that Act (causing a person with a mental disorder to watch a sexual act by inducement, threat or deception).

*131. An offence under section 38 of that Act (care workers: sexual activity with a person with a mental disorder).

*132. An offence under section 39 of that Act (care workers: causing or inciting sexual activity).

133. An offence under section 40 of that Act (care workers: sexual activity in the presence of a person with a mental disorder).

134. An offence under section 41 of that Act (care workers: causing a person with a mental disorder to watch a sexual act).

*135. An offence under section 47 of that Act (paying for sexual services of a child).[3]

*136. An offence under section 48 of that Act (causing or inciting child prostitution or pornography).

*137. An offence under section 49 of that Act (controlling a child prostitute or a child involved in pornography).

*138. An offence under section 50 of that Act (arranging or facilitating child prostitution or pornography).

139. An offence under section 52 of that Act (causing or inciting prostitution for gain).
140. An offence under section 53 of that Act (controlling prostitution for gain).
* 141. An offence under section 57 of that Act (trafficking into the UK for sexual exploitation).
* 142. An offence under section 58 of that Act (trafficking within the UK for sexual exploitation).
* 143. An offence under section 59 of that Act (trafficking out of the UK for sexual exploitation).
* 144. An offence under section 61 of that Act (administering a substance with intent).
* 145. An offence under section 62 of that Act (committing an offence with intent to commit a sexual offence).
* 146. An offence under section 63 of that Act (trespass with intent to commit a sexual offence).
147. An offence under section 64 of that Act (sex with an adult relative: penetration).
148. An offence under section 65 of that Act (sex with an adult relative: consenting to penetration).
149. An offence under section 66 of that Act (exposure).
150. An offence under section 67 of that Act (voyeurism).
151. An offence under section 69 of that Act (intercourse with an animal).
152. An offence under section 70 of that Act (sexual penetration of a corpse).
153. An offence of—

   (a) aiding, abetting, counselling, procuring or inciting the commission of an offence specified in this Part of this Schedule,
   (b) conspiring to commit an offence so specified, or
   (c) attempting to commit an offence so specified.

NOTES

[1] An attempt to commit this offence is not a serious offence.
[2] Girl/woman must be under 13 for this to be a serious offence.
[3] Only a serious offence if the child is under 16.

APPENDIX 10

Suggested Guidance for Bail Decision-Takers

(Law Commission Report No. 269: Bail and the Human Rights Act 1998 Part XIII)

13.1 In producing this report, we hope that it may be of assistance to those providing training to decision-takers and their advisers, and that courts may find it useful to refer to it, at least until the issues discussed have become the subject of reported decisions in the higher courts. In summary we first set out our conclusions on the general principles applicable to the refusal of bail, and then give some guidance on how decision-takers might apply various provisions of the Bail Act, so as to comply with the ECHR.

ECHR PRINCIPLES APPLICABLE TO THE REFUSAL OF BAIL

13.2 A defendant should be refused bail only where detention is necessary for a purpose which the ECtHR has recognised as legitimate in that detention may be compatible with the defendant's right to release under Article 5(3). Those recognised purposes are to avoid a real risk that, were the defendant released,

(1) he or she would

    (a) fail to attend trial; or

    (b) interfere with evidence or witnesses, or otherwise obstruct the course of justice; or

    (c) commit an offence while on bail; or

    (d) be at risk of harm against which he or she would be inadequately protected; or

(2) a disturbance to public order would result.

13.3 Detention will be necessary only if that risk could not be adequately addressed, so that detention would no longer be necessary, by the imposition of appropriate bail conditions.

13.4 The court refusing bail should give reasons for finding that detention is necessary. Those reasons should be closely related to the individual circumstances pertaining to the defendant, and be capable of supporting the court's conclusion.

13.5 An English court exercising its powers in a way which is compatible with the Convention rights should refuse bail only where it can be justified under both the Convention, as interpreted by the ECtHR, and domestic legislation.

APPLICATION OF THE EXCEPTIONS TO THE RIGHT TO BAIL IN ENGLISH LAW IN A WAY WHICH COMPLIES WITH THE ECHR

13.6   The exceptions in paragraph 2(a) and (c) and paragraph 7 of Part I and paragraph 2 of Part II of Schedule 1 to the Bail Act 1976 can be readily applied in a manner which is compatible with the Convention without any guidance from us being necessary or desirable.

13.7   The remaining exceptions provided for in Parts I and II of Schedule 1 to the Bail Act 1976 and in section 25 of the Criminal Justice and Public Order Act 1994 may be applied in a way which complies with the ECHR. We offer the following guidance as an aid to taking such decisions.

1.   The risk of offending on bail

13.8   Pre-trial detention for the purpose of preventing the defendant from committing an offence while on bail can be compatible with Article 5(1)(c) and (3) of the ECHR, provided it is a necessary and proportionate response to a *real risk* that, if released, the defendant would commit an offence while on bail. Previous convictions and other circumstances may be relevant, but the decision-taker must consider whether it may properly be inferred from them that there is a real risk that the defendant will commit an offence.

2.   Defendant on bail at the time of the alleged offence

13.9   A defendant should be detained under paragraph 2A only where the court is also relying on another paragraph of Part I of Schedule 1 to the Bail Act. A decision to withhold bail *solely* because the circumstances in paragraph 2A exist would not only infringe Article 5, but would also be unlawful under sections 3 and 6 of the HRA.

13.10   The fact that the defendant was on bail at the time of the alleged offence should not, therefore, be regarded as an independent ground, but as one of the considerations which the court should take into account when considering withholding bail because, for example, of a real risk that the defendant will commit an offence while on bail. Thus, courts should not refuse bail under paragraph 2A alone, but should do so only where such a decision may properly be based on one of the other grounds for refusal of bail, such as paragraph 2(b).

3.   Detention for the defendant's own protection

13.11   A refusal of bail for the defendant's own protection, whether from harm by others or self-harm, can be compatible with the Convention where

- detention is *necessary* to address a *real risk* that, if granted bail, the defendant would suffer harm by others or self-harm, against which detention could provide protection, and
- there are exceptional circumstances in the nature of the alleged offence and/or the conditions or context in which it is alleged to have been committed.

13.12   Given the absence of authority, we can presently see no reason why a decision of a court to order detention because of a risk of *self*-harm should not be compatible with the ECHR even where the circumstances giving rise to the risk are unconnected with the alleged offence, provided that the court is satisfied that there is a real risk of self-harm, and that a proper medical examination will take place rapidly so that the

311

court may then consider exercising its powers of detention under the Mental Health Act 1983.

4. Detention because of a lack of information

13.13 The refusal of bail by a court because it has not been practicable to obtain sufficient information for the taking of a full bail decision for want of time since the institution of proceedings against the defendant can be compatible with Article 5 provided that

- detention is for a short period, which is no longer than necessary to enable the required information to be obtained, and
- the lack of information is not due to a failure of the prosecution, the police, the court, or another state body to act with 'special diligence'.

Where these tests are met, the general principles applicable to the refusal of bail that we identified in paragraphs 13.2–13.5 above will not apply.

13.14 After that short period of time has passed, a lack of information that is not due to a failure of a state body to act with 'special diligence' may be taken into account as a factor militating in favour of detention, in support of the existence of another Convention-compliant ground for detention.

5. Detention following arrest under section 7

Section 7(5) hearings

13.15 Paragraphs 6 of Part I and 5 of Part II of Schedule 1 to the Bail Act provide that a defendant arrested pursuant to section 7 need not be granted bail. The general words of these paragraphs should not be construed as overriding the effect of the limitations imposed by section 7(5) on when bail can be refused.

13.16 Thus, where a defendant, arrested under section 7(3), is brought before a justice of the peace under section 7(4) to be dealt with under section 7(5), paragraphs 6 of Part I and 5 of Part II of Schedule 1 should be read as subject to the provisions of section 7(5).

13.17 Although a literal reading of section 7(5) could lead to the conclusion that the mere fact that a condition has been breached could justify detention, that approach would not comply with the ECHR. Even where one of the threshold conditions for detention or the imposition of new conditions contained in section 7(5) is met, the defendant should be detained, or granted bail subject to additional conditions, only where it is necessary to do so for one of the purposes identified in paragraph 13.2 above.

13.18 A justice hearing section 7(5) proceedings is not required to hear oral evidence in every case, but should take account of the quality of the material presented. If the material includes oral evidence, the defendant must be given an opportunity to cross-examine. Likewise, a defendant should be permitted to give relevant oral evidence if he or she wishes to do so.

13.19 Article 5 does not require that the whole of the prosecution file be disclosed to the defence prior to such a hearing. It is sufficient if disclosure is provided of the material the defendant needs in order to enjoy 'equality of arms' with the prosecution in relation to the issue to be decided by the court.

OTHER BAIL HEARINGS CONCERNING DEFENDANTS WHO HAVE BEEN ARRESTED UNDER SECTION 7

13.20   The courts should not refuse to grant a defendant bail *simply* because he or she has been arrested under section 7. These provisions should be applied so that bail is refused only where this is necessary for one of the purposes identified in paragraph 13.2 above. The circumstances leading to the defendant being arrested under section 7 may properly be taken into account as a possible reason for concluding that detention is necessary for such a purpose.

6.   Section 25 of the Criminal Justice and Public Order Act 1994

13.21   Section 25 can be interpreted compatibly with the Convention as meaning that, where the defendant would not, if released on bail, pose a real risk of committing a serious offence, this constitutes an 'exceptional circumstance' so that bail may be granted. This construction achieves Parliament's purpose of ensuring that, when making bail decisions about defendants to whom section 25 applies, decision-takers focus on the risk the defendant may pose to the public by re-offending.

13.22   There may be other 'exceptional circumstances' which may permit bail to be granted.

13.23   Even if 'exceptional circumstances' do exist, bail may, nonetheless, be withheld on an ECHR-compatible ground if this is deemed to be necessary in the individual case.

CONDITIONAL BAIL

1.   Conditional bail as an alternative to custody

13.24   A court cannot detain a person pursuant to an aim which complies with the ECHR where there is another way to achieve that aim which will interfere with the defendant's liberty to a lesser extent. Thus, a defendant must be released, if need be subject to conditions, unless (i) that would create a risk of the kind which can, in principle, justify pre-trial detention, and (ii) that risk cannot, by imposing suitable bail conditions, be averted, or reduced to a level at which it would not justify detention.

2.   Conditional bail as an alternative to unconditional bail

13.25   A court should only impose bail conditions for a purpose which the ECtHR recognises as capable of justifying detention.

13.26   A bail condition should be imposed only where, if the defendant were to break that condition or be reasonably thought likely to do so, it may be necessary to arrest the defendant in order to pursue the purpose for which the condition was imposed.

13.27   Decision-takers should state their reasons for imposing bail conditions and specify the purposes for which any conditions are imposed.

13.28   Decision-takers should also be alert to ensure that any bail conditions they impose do not violate the defendant's other Convention rights, such as those protected by Articles 8–11.

GIVING REASONS FOR BAIL DECISIONS

13.29   It is of particular importance that magistrates' clerks make, and retain for the file, a note of the gist of the arguments for and against the grant of bail, and the oral reasons given by the bench for their decision.

13.30   Standard forms should be completed accurately and show that a decision has been taken in a way that complies with the Convention.

CHALLENGES TO THE LEGALITY OF PRE-TRIAL DETENTION

1.   The right to challenge pre-trial detention

13.31   The procedural safeguards required by the ECHR of a domestic court that makes decisions on the lawfulness of detention are satisfied by our domestic law and procedure. In particular:

(1)   It is unlikely that Article 5(4) would be infringed simply because the defendant was not present at a bail hearing, provided that he or she was represented. Nevertheless, the court should not hear a bail application to a conclusion in the absence of a defendant where the defendant's presence is essential to fair proceedings. Indeed, we have been informed that magistrates treat defendants as entitled to be present.

(2)   It is not necessary to hear **sworn evidence** in the great majority of cases. Courts should, in particular cases, consider whether fairness requires the calling of evidence on oath for the determination of the application, as a failure to call such evidence may cause a particular decision to fall foul of Article 5(4).

(3)   A court hearing bail proceedings should take account of the quality of the material presented. If the material includes oral evidence, the defendant must be given an opportunity to cross-examine. Likewise, the defendant should be permitted to give relevant oral evidence if he or she wishes to do so.

(4)   *Ex parte Lee* recognises an ongoing duty of **disclosure** from the time of arrest. The Court of Appeal emphasised that at the stage before committal there are continuing obligations on the prosecutor to make such disclosure as justice and fairness may require in the particular circumstances of the case, that is, where it could reasonably be expected to assist the defence when applying for bail. If this requirement is observed, together with the Attorney General's guidelines to prosecutors, Article 5(4) can be complied with.

(5)   The duty of disclosure does not require that the whole of the prosecution file be disclosed to the defence prior to such a hearing. It is sufficient if disclosure is provided of the material the defendant needs in order to enjoy 'equality of arms' with the prosecution in relation to the matter to be decided by the court.

(6)   If the defendant requests that the bail hearing be held in public, it should be held **in public** unless there is a good reason not to do so.

2.   Repeated applications

13.32   Article 5(4) gives a detained person the right, in certain cases, to make further court challenges to the legality of his or her detention despite having already made one or more such challenges. With the passage of time, the circumstances which once were considered by a court to justify detention may have changed.

13.33   Part IIA of Schedule 1 to the Bail Act 1976 is capable of being interpreted and applied compatibly with Article 5(4). In hearings to which that provision applies, courts should be willing, at intervals of 28 days, to consider arguments that the passage of time constitutes, in the particular case before the court, a change in circumstances relevant to the need to detain the defendant, so as to require the hearing of all the arguments on the question of bail. It may be, for example, that the time served on remand may have reduced the risk of the defendant absconding.

13.34   If the court finds that the passage of time does amount to a relevant change of circumstances then a full bail application should follow in which all the arguments, old and new, can be put forward and taken into account.

Standards of Competence for the Accreditation of Solicitors Representing Clients in the Magistrates' Court

(Source: Solicitors Regulation Authority)

The standards of competence are in three parts as follows:

Part 1: Underpinning knowledge – This sets out the knowledge and understanding that a court duty solicitor must have in order to be competent when advising, assisting and representing a client in the magistrates' court and youth court.

Part 2: Underpinning skills – This sets out the skills that a court duty solicitor requires in order to advise, assist and represent a client in the magistrates' court and youth court, and which a duty solicitor should demonstrate in undertaking the activities set out in the units of performance in Part 3.

Part 3: Standards of performance – This sets out the standards of performance that a duty solicitor should demonstrate at each stage of the process of advising, assisting and representing a client as duty solicitor in the magistrates' court or youth court. In order to demonstrate competent performance, a duty solicitor will need the knowledge and skills set out in Parts 1 and 2.

PART 1   UNDERPINNING KNOWLEDGE

1.1   An understanding of the role and duties of a duty solicitor

The solicitor must be able to demonstrate a practical knowledge and understanding of:

1.1.1   a solicitor's duty to his or her client
1.1.2   a solicitor's duty to the court
1.1.3   the role and obligations of, and limitations on, a solicitor acting as duty solicitor as set out in the general criminal contract
1.1.4   the eligibility of defendants for legal aid
1.1.5   the special needs of, and procedures and laws concerning, vulnerable defendants, whether such vulnerability results from age, mental disorder or handicap, or otherwise
1.1.6   the requirements of, and facilities for, defendants who need, or who may need, an interpreter
1.1.7   the Law Society's Code for Advocacy
1.1.8   the implications of the Human Rights Act 1998 for the work of a court duty solicitor.

1.2 An understanding of relevant criminal law and procedure

The solicitor must be able to demonstrate a practical knowledge and understanding of:

1.2.1 the definition of crimes commonly dealt with in the magistrates' court, and of the means of discovering the definition of a crime where this is not known to the solicitor

1.2.2 the defences commonly available to defendants appearing in the magistrates' court, and of the means of discovering the requirements of a defence where these are not known to the solicitor

1.2.3 the different ways of classifying offences by reference to powers of arrest and mode of trial

1.2.4 the different modes of participation in a crime

1.2.5 the different methods of commencing criminal proceedings, and the legal requirements of those methods

1.2.6 the obligation of the prosecution to keep the decision to prosecute under review, and the power to discontinue a prosecution

1.2.7 the methods of funding advice, assistance and representation in respect of a person charged with a criminal offence

1.2.8 the sequence of events in criminal cases, whether indictable-only, either-way or summary-only, from charge or summons to conviction and sentence, and the relevant critical factors at each stage

1.2.9 the circumstances in which a prosecution may be dismissed for abuse of process

1.2.10 the restricted powers of single justices and justices' clerks

1.2.11 the obligations on the prosecution to disclose the evidence on which they intend to rely, and to disclose 'unused material', and the discretion or obligation on the defence to serve a defence statement

1.2.12 the special procedures and powers relevant to mentally disordered or handi-capped defendants.

1.3 An understanding of relevant immigration law and procedure

The solicitor must be able to demonstrate a practical knowledge and understanding of:

1.3.1 the main immigration offences

1.3.2 the meaning of the terms overstayer, illegal entrant, deportee, refugee, asylum seeker, exceptional leave to remain

1.3.3 the possible consequences of committing an immigration offence

1.3.4 the need, where appropriate, to refer the defendant to a specialist immigration law practitioner.

1.4 An understanding of criminal law and procedure as it relates to youths

The solicitor must be able to demonstrate a practical knowledge and understanding of:

1.4.1 the significance of age and gender for the procedures in and powers available to magistrates' and youth courts

1.4.2 the rules concerning the courts in which a youth may, or must, appear and/or be sentenced, the power or duty of a magistrates' court to remit a youth to the youth court, and the power of a magistrates' or youth court to commit a youth to the Crown Court

1.4.3   the obligations of parents and guardians of youths appearing in court, and the
        powers of the court in relation to them
1.4.4   the law and practice concerning sentencing of youths
1.4.5   the reprimand and final warning schemes, and their implications for sentence.

1.5   An understanding of rules of evidence

The solicitor must be able to demonstrate a practical knowledge and understanding
of:

1.5.1   the legal and evidential burdens of proof on the prosecution
1.5.2   the legal and evidential burdens of proof on the defence
1.5.3   the mechanisms by which evidence may be adduced, and the rules concerning
        different forms of evidence
1.5.4   the rules concerning admissibility of evidence
1.5.5   the court's discretion to exclude evidence
1.5.6   the circumstances in which inferences may be drawn under the Criminal
        Justice and Public Order Act 1994 and the Criminal Procedure and
        Investigations Act 1996, and the implications of the drawing of inferences
1.5.7   legal professional privilege
1.5.8   the evidential value of admissions made by a co-accused.

1.6   An understanding of law and practice concerning bail in the magistrates' court and the youth court

The solicitor must be able to demonstrate a practical knowledge and understanding
of:

1.6.1   the prima facie right to bail of an unconvicted defendant
1.6.2   the circumstances in which a court may withhold bail from an unconvicted
        defendant charged with an imprisonable or non-imprisonable offence
1.6.3   the law concerning bail in respect of convicted defendants
1.6.4   the power of a court to require a security, to accept a surety, and to impose
        conditions
1.6.5   the availability of facilities such as bail information schemes, duty psychiatric
        schemes, and bail hostels
1.6.6   the powers of the court to remand youths to local authority accommodation
        (with or without a security requirement), and to make a custodial remand
1.6.7   the consequences of a grant of bail, including enforcement of the obligation to
        surrender and of conditions, variation of bail conditions and the prosecution
        right of appeal against the grant of bail
1.6.8   the consequences of a refusal of bail, including the power to commit the defen-
        dant to detention at a police station, the right to make further applications for
        bail in the magistrates' court, Crown Court and High Court
1.6.9   the law concerning custody time limits.

1.7   An understanding of law and procedure concerning sentencing in magistrates' courts, and enforcement of orders of the court

The solicitor must be able to demonstrate a practical knowledge and understanding
of:

1.7.1   sentencing procedures, including powers to order or dispense with pre-sentence
        reports

1.7.2   the circumstances in which a 'Newton hearing' should be held
1.7.3   the implications of a plea of guilty for sentence discount and mitigation
1.7.4   the Magistrates' Association Sentencing Guidelines, and relevant aggravating or mitigating factors
1.7.5   the sentencing powers of a magistrates' court, including custody and community penalty thresholds, maximum powers of sentence, and the power to commit to the Crown Court for sentence
1.7.6   the implications of the imposition of a custodial sentence, including the institution in which the sentence is likely to be served, and the likely length of time to be served
1.7.7   the powers of a magistrates' court to sentence, or otherwise deal with, a mentally disordered defendant
1.7.8   the powers of a magistrates' court to enforce financial penalties, and other penalties and orders of the court.

1.8   An understanding of law and procedure concerning appeals against and reviews of decisions of a magistrates' court

The solicitor must be able to demonstrate a practical knowledge and understanding of:

1.8.1   the power of a magistrates' court to review its own decisions
1.8.2   the right of a defendant, and the procedures applicable, to appeal against sentence or conviction to the Crown Court
1.8.3   the right of the defendant or prosecution, and the procedures applicable, to appeal by case stated to the Divisional Court
1.8.4   the availability of judicial review proceedings in respect of magistrates' court decision
1.8.5   the law and procedure concerning bail pending appeal
1.8.6   the right to challenge an alleged breach of a defendant's Convention rights under the Human Rights Act 1998.

PART 2   UNDERPINNING SKILLS

2.1   Communication skills

The solicitor must be able to communicate effectively with the client, the prosecutor, the court clerk, and other relevant persons. In doing so, the solicitor must be able to:

2.1.1   use language that is appropriate to the person who is being addressed
2.1.2   express him or herself clearly and assertively
2.1.3   listen actively
2.1.4   identify if there is a need for an interpreter
2.1.5   identify whether there are indications of vulnerability in respect of the client, whether resulting from age, mental disorder or handicap, or otherwise
2.1.6   communicate in a manner and form that takes account of ethnic, cultural and other forms of diversity
2.1.7   do the above when working under pressure resulting from acting for a number of clients on the same occasion
2.1.8   make an appropriate written record of information obtained, steps taken, advice given and decisions taken.

2.2 Interviewing and advising skills

The solicitor must be able to obtain relevant information from the client, the prosecutor and relevant others, and give appropriate advice to the client in a form that is likely to be understood by the client. The solicitor must be able to:

2.2.1 convey to the client in appropriate language the role of the duty solicitor
2.2.2 allow the client to explain his or her position
2.2.3 take appropriate steps in order to gain the trust and confidence of the client, taking into account ethnic, cultural and other forms of diversity
2.2.4 elicit relevant information from the client, the prosecutor, and other relevant persons
2.2.5 formulate appropriate advice by correctly identifying and analysing the legal and non-legal issues raised by the case
2.2.6 give appropriate advice to the client in a form that assists them to decide upon the best course of action
2.2.7 agree on the action to be taken by both the client and the solicitor
2.2.8 deal appropriately with any ethical issues that may arise when advising the client
2.2.9 do the above when working under pressure resulting from acting for a number of clients on the same occasion.

2.3 Advocacy skills

The solicitor must be able to advocate effectively on behalf of his or her client in the magistrates' court and youth court. The solicitor must be able to:

2.3.1 establish a suitable rapport with the court
2.3.2 use appropriate body language, and speak audibly, clearly, and at an appropriate pace, using appropriate language
2.3.3 present a coherent and persuasive case that is consistent with the client's instructions, and which takes proper account of ethnic, cultural and other forms of diversity
2.3.4 demonstrate that they have a practical understanding of substantive and procedural law applicable to the case
2.3.5 correctly apply the relevant law to the facts of the instant case
2.3.6 demonstrate that they understand and can apply relevant ethical rules, rules of etiquette and conventions
2.3.7 do the above when working under pressure resulting from acting for a number of clients on the same occasion.

PART 3   STANDARDS OF PERFORMANCE

Unit 1:   Gathering information

Element 1

Obtain information from the police and/or court and/or prosecutor.

PERFORMANCE CRITERIA

3.1.1 Defendants who wish to speak to the duty solicitor are identified
3.1.2 The location of such defendants is ascertained, in particular, whether or not they are in custody

3.1.3   Information as to the alleged offence(s), breach of court order, or other reason for the court hearing is obtained

3.1.4   Information about the prosecution case is sought

3.1.5   Information is sought about whether the client is likely to have any disability or vulnerability

3.1.6   Information about previous convictions, previous bail record, previous compliance with court orders (as appropriate) is sought

3.1.7   The attitude of the prosecutor to bail, acceptable pleas, bind-over, etc. (as appropriate) is ascertained

3.1.8   Information obtained is accurately recorded.

RANGE STATEMENT

The information contained in 3.1.3 to 3.1.6 may be sought or obtained before or after the duty solicitor has had a consultation with the client, depending on the availability of the prosecutor and on local arrangements.

Element 2

Consult with the client and take instructions.

PERFORMANCE CRITERIA

3.2.1   The client is seen in a confidential setting (where the available facilities permit)

3.2.2   The client is informed of the identity of the duty solicitor and of the duty solicitor's role, and of the confidentiality of solicitor/client communications

3.2.3   The client is informed that the services of the duty solicitor are free

3.2.4   The client is informed that they are not obliged to instruct the duty solicitor, and is asked whether they have a solicitor that they wish to instruct

3.2.5   The duty solicitor considers the level of service that he or she can provide in accordance with the terms of the general criminal contract, and the client is informed accordingly

3.2.6   Information is sought to enable an assessment to be made about any disability or vulnerability of the client, and to assess whether an interpreter will be required

3.2.7   The client is informed of the information that the duty solicitor has obtained in relation to the case.

3.2.8   General information regarding the client is obtained or confirmed, including the client's name, address, telephone number, date of birth, nationality, immigration status (if relevant), marital status, dependants, and financial circumstances (as appropriate)

3.2.9   Instructions relevant to the reason why they are appearing in court are taken

3.2.10 Information given and obtained is accurately recorded.

Unit 2:   Giving advice

Element 1

Inform and advise the client as to general procedure and venue.

3.3.1   Appropriate advice is given in respect of the client's vulnerability (if any), including the need for an interpreter, the presence in court of a parent or guardian etc

3.3.2 An assessment is made of the client's fitness to plead, and appropriate advice is given

3.3.3 An assessment is made, where relevant, of the client's immigration status and appropriate advice is given, including as to whether the client should instruct an immigration law specialist

3.3.4 Advice is given as to the procedure of the court hearing, when the client's case is likely to be called, and what decisions the court may make

3.3.5 Advice is given as to what is likely to happen after the court hearing, including arrangements for the client's representation

3.3.6 An assessment is made of the client's likely eligibility for legal aid, and the client is advised accordingly

3.3.7 An assessment is made of the decisions as to venue that may be made by the client or the court, and the client is advised as to the venue representations that may be made on behalf of the client and/or the venue choices that the client may make, and as to the power of the court to commit for sentence

3.3.8 Instructions are taken as to venue, and as to representations and applications to be made

3.3.9 Information given and obtained, and advice given and the reasons for that advice, is accurately recorded.

Element 2

Advise the client as to plea.

3.4.1 Consideration is given to whether sufficient information is available from the prosecution and from the client to advise on plea (including information as to the likely admissibility of prosecution evidence), and on whether a plea or indication of plea should be entered at this stage, and the client is advised accordingly

3.4.2 Where the client is appearing in respect of a summary-only offence, consideration is given to whether advice on plea should be delayed until disclosure has been requested from the prosecution, and the client is advised accordingly

3.4.3 Subject to paragraph 3.4.4, where the client is appearing in respect of an offence triable either-way, consideration is given to whether advice on plea or indication of plea should be delayed until advance information has been obtained from the prosecution, and the client is advised accordingly

3.4.4 Where the client is appearing in respect of an offence triable only on indictment, or an either-way offence that is governed by the notice of transfer provisions under s4 of the Criminal Justice Act 1987 or s53 of the Criminal Justice Act 1991 (or similar legislation), the client is advised of the implications of those provisions

3.4.5 Where the solicitor concludes that there is sufficient information to enable advice to properly be given on plea or indication of plea, the client is advised as to plea and, if relevant, is advised of the mitigation advantages of an early indication of a guilty plea

3.4.6 Where the solicitor concludes that it is appropriate to advise the client to plead guilty or to give an indication of a guilty plea, consideration is given to whether there is sufficient information available in relation to mitigation, and the client is advised accordingly

3.4.7 Where the solicitor concludes that it is appropriate to advise the client to plead guilty or to give an indication of a guilty plea, consideration is given to the need for a 'Newton hearing', and the client is advised accordingly

3.4.8   Instructions are taken as to the course of action that the client wishes to take, and the solicitor confirms with the client that they understand the consequences of their decision

3.4.9   Where appropriate, negotiations are conducted with the prosecutor as to acceptable pleas

3.4.10 Information given and obtained, and advice given and the reasons for that advice, is accurately recorded.

Element 3

Advise the client regarding bail (where relevant).

3.5.1   Consideration is given to whether an application for bail is relevant and appropriate, and the client is advised accordingly

3.5.2   Consideration is given to the relevant law governing bail, including the implications of the Human Rights Act 1998, and to the relevant bail facilities in the area concerned

3.5.3   Consideration is given to the known, or likely, prosecution objections to bail, and the likely attitude of the court

3.5.4   The client is advised regarding their prima facie right to bail (where applicable), as to securities, sureties and conditions (where relevant) and as to the consequences of non-compliance with bail obligations

3.5.5   Instructions are taken as to the client's objectives regarding bail, previous convictions and previous bail record (if any) and, where relevant, as to securities, sureties and conditions, and the client is advised as to the most suitable arguments for achieving their objectives

3.5.6   Instructions are taken as to whether a bail application is to be made and, if appropriate, as to what securities, sureties or conditions are to be offered

3.5.7   The client is advised, where appropriate, as to the consequences of refusal by the court to grant bail, including the place where the client is likely to be remanded, the power of the court to commit the defendant to detention at a police station, and the opportunities for further applications for bail to be made.

3.5.8   In the case of a client who is a juvenile, they are advised as to the power of the court to remand them to local authority secure accommodation or direct to prison (as appropriate)

3.5.9   The client is advised, where appropriate, as to the right of the prosecution to appeal against the grant of bail

3.5.10 Where the client is appearing for breach of the obligation to surrender to bail, or for breach of bail conditions, instructions are taken as to whether the client accepts the breach, and advice is given as to whether the prosecution are likely to be able to prove the breach, and as to the appropriate application or submission to be made

3.5.11 Appropriate negotiations are conducted with the prosecutor concerning bail and bail conditions

3.5.12 Where bail is refused, or conditions imposed, advice is given to as to appropriate courses of action available to the client

3.5.13 Information given and obtained, and advice given and the reasons for that advice, is accurately recorded.

Element 4

Advise the client as to sentence and other orders of the court.

3.6.1 Instructions relevant to mitigation and sentence are obtained from the client, including information about previous convictions and sentences, compliance with previous sentences and orders, reasons for and attitude to the offence, any consequences for the client of committing the offence, positive steps taken by the client (eg. in respect of any drug or alcohol abuse, reparation to the victim, practical expressions of remorse, etc.), and the likely consequences for the client and others of possible sentences

3.6.2 Consideration is given to the sentencing powers, and power to commit for sentence, available to the court given the nature and circumstances of the client and of the offence including, where relevant, the custody and community sentence thresholds

3.6.3 Consideration is given to the likely attitude of the court to sentence, to the relevant available mitigating factors, to the relevant aggravating factors and to the desirability of a pre-sentence and/or medical or other report

3.6.4 Instructions are taken as to the client's objectives regarding sentence, reasoned advice is given as to the way in which mitigation should be conducted, and agreement is sought as to the conduct of the mitigation plea

3.6.5 Advice is given as to the likely sentence range

3.6.6 In the case of enforcement proceedings, whether concerning fines imposed or other orders of the court, relevant instructions are obtained from the client as to whether they accept the non-compliance and, if so, the reasons for non-compliance, and (if relevant) the client's attitude to future compliance with the relevant order and (if relevant) their financial circumstances. Advice is given as to the appropriate representations to be made to the court, and agreement is sought as to such representations

3.6.7 When the court has made its sentence or enforcement decision, advice is given as to the implications for the client of the decision and as to appropriate courses of action available to the client if they wish to contest the decision

3.6.8 Information given and obtained, and advice given and the reasons for that advice, is accurately recorded.

RANGE STATEMENT

The elements in Unit 2 will not all apply in every case. Which element or elements will apply will depend upon the nature of the case concerned. The client must be advised as to sentence where they are advised to plead guilty or indicate a guilty plea, and may be advised as to sentence in other circumstances.

Unit 3: Appearing before the court

Element 1

Making or resisting a procedural application.

3.7.1 The court is informed, as appropriate, of the solicitor's name, the fact that they appear as duty solicitor, and the identity of the defendant or person for whom they appear

3.7.2 Where relevant, the solicitor makes the appropriate application, having regard to relevant law and facts, and in a coherent and persuasive manner, in accordance with the client's instructions

3.7.3   Where relevant, the solicitor resists an application made by the prosecution or other party, having regard to relevant law and facts, and in a coherent and persuasive manner, in accordance with the client's instructions

3.7.4   Where the application, or resistance to an application, is unsuccessful, the solicitor considers, and advises the client upon whether they have realistic grounds for challenging the decision

3.7.5   The decision of the court, and any reasons given, is accurately recorded.

Element 2

Making or resisting a venue application in either-way cases.

3.8.1   The solicitor indicates to the court that his or her client intends, or does not intend, to plead guilty (as appropriate)

3.8.2   Where the client does not indicate a guilty plea at the plea before venue procedure, and following any representations by the prosecutor, the solicitor makes appropriate representations to the court regarding venue, in accordance with his or her client's instructions, and by reference to the relevant statutory criteria and Mode of Trial guidelines

3.8.3   Where the court indicates that it believes that the case is suitable for summary trial, the solicitor (if necessary) reminds the client of their decision as to the desired trial venue

3.8.4   The decision of the court, and any reasons given, is accurately recorded.

Element 3

Making a bail application.

3.9.1   The solicitor confirms with the prosecutor the prosecutor's attitude to bail with, or without, conditions

3.9.2   The solicitor indicates to the court whether they will be applying for bail on behalf of their client

3.9.3   Following the presentation to the court of the prosecutor's objections to bail, the solicitor makes a coherent and persuasive application for bail, taking into account the relevant law and facts, the objections to bail put to the court by the prosecutor, the likely attitude of the court, and the client's instructions, and indicating (where relevant) appropriate conditions

3.9.4   Where the prosecution apply for a remanded defendant to be committed for detention in a police station, the solicitor makes appropriate representations regarding whether the defendant should be so committed and/or the period of such committal

3.9.5   Where the court grants bail with conditions, the solicitor advises the client as to any course of action open to them if they are dissatisfied with those conditions

3.9.6   Where the court denies bail, the solicitor considers the reasons given for refusal of bail, and advises the client as to the courses of action open to them to try to secure bail

3.9.7   The decision of the court, and any reasons given, and advice given to the client and the reasons for that advice, is accurately recorded.

Element 4

Making a plea in mitigation.

3.10.1 Where the client has pleaded guilty (in a summary-only case) or where the client has indicated that they intend to plead guilty (in an either-way case), the solicitor mitigates on behalf of his or [her] client, having regard to his or [her] client's instructions, as set out below

3.10.2 Where appropriate, the solicitor makes a coherent and persuasive application for an adjournment to enable a pre-sentence and, if appropriate, other reports to be prepared

3.10.3 Where appropriate, the solicitor makes a coherent and persuasive plea in mitigation, having regard to the client's instructions, the relevant law, and the relevant factors

3.10.4 The solicitor makes appropriate representations regarding any costs order that may be made by the court

3.10.5 Following the sentence of the court, the solicitor advises the client of the implications of the sentence, and (if appropriate) advises the client of their right of appeal

3.10.6 An accurate record is made of the decision of the court, and any instructions from and advice given to the client, including the reasons for such advice.

Element 5

Representations in enforcement proceedings.

3.11.1 In fine enforcement proceedings, the solicitor makes appropriate representations regarding his or her client's financial circumstances, the reasons for non-payment, and the appropriate order of the court, in accordance with the client's instructions and having regard to the relevant law

3.11.2 In other enforcement proceedings, the solicitor makes appropriate representations in accordance with the client's instructions and having regard to the relevant law

3.11.3 The solicitor makes appropriate representations regarding any costs order that may be made by the court

3.11.4 Following the order of the court, the solicitor advises the client of the implications of the order and, if appropriate, advises the client of their right of appeal

3.11.5 An accurate record is made of the decision of the court, and any instructions from and advice given to the client, including the reasons for such advice.

RANGE STATEMENT

The elements in Unit 3 will not all apply in every case. Which element or elements are relevant will depend upon the nature of the application, submission or representations made.

Grave crimes and obligatory minimum sentences

GRAVE CRIMES

Detention under section 91(3) of the Powers of Criminal Courts (Sentencing) Act 2000 is available for the following offences:

Offence	Statute	Sentence
Offences against person/ property – various		
Abduction of a woman by force or for the sake of her property	Sexual Offences Act 1956, s.17	14 years
Aggravated burglary	Theft Act 1968, s.10	Life
Aiding suicide	Suicide Act 1961, s.2	14 years
Arson	Criminal Damage Act 1971, s.1	Life
Assault with intent to rob	Theft Act 1968, s.8	Life
Attempted murder	Criminal Attempts Act 1981, s.4(1)	Life
Attempting to strangle with intent to endanger life	Offences Against the Person Act 1861, s.21	Life
Blackmail	Theft Act 1968, s.21	14 years
Buggery with a person under the age of 16 or with an animal	Sexual Offences Act 1956, s.12	Life
Burglary of dwelling	Theft Act 1968, s.9(3)(a)	14 years. NB does not include non-dwelling burglaries
Causing death by aggravated vehicle taking	Theft Act 1968, s.12A(5)	14 years, only for offences committed on or after 27 February 2004

Offence	Statute	Sentence
Causing death by dangerous driving	Road Traffic Act 1988, s.1	14 years for offences committed on or after 27 February 2004; 10 years, for offences committed before 27 February 2004 and only in relation to offenders who have attained 14 years
Causing death by careless driving while under the influence of alcohol or drugs	Road Traffic Act 1988, s.3	14 years for offences committed on or after 27 February 2004; 10 years, for offences committed before 27 February 2004 and only in relation to offenders who have attained 14 years
Child destruction	Infant Life (Preservation) Act 1929, s.1	Life
Criminal damage with intent to endanger life	Criminal Damage Act 1971, s.1(2)	Life
Demanding money with menaces	Theft Act 1968, s.21	14 years
Destroying property with intent to endanger life	Criminal Damage Act 1971, s.1	Life
Endangering safety of aircraft	Aviation Security Act 1982, s.3	Life
Endangering safety of railway passengers	Offences Against the Person Act 1861, s.32	Life
False imprisonment	Common law	
Female genital mutilation	Female Genital Mutilation Act 2003, ss.1–3	14 years
GBH with intent	Offences Against the Person Act 1861, s.18	Life
Handling stolen goods	Theft Act 1968, s.22	14 years
Hijacking	Aviation Security Act 1982, s.1	Life
Infanticide	Infanticide Act 1938, s.1	Life
Kidnapping	Common law	
Manslaughter	Offences Against the Person Act 1861, s.5	Life
Murder	Common law	

Offence	Statute	Sentence
Perverting the course of justice	Common law	
Placing object on railway with intent to obstruct or overthrow any engine	Malicious Damage Act 1861, s.35	Life
Robbery	Theft Act 1968, s.8	Life
Soliciting to murder	Offences Against the Person Act 1861, s.4	Life
Throwing corrosive liquid with intent to endanger life	Offences Against the Person Act 1861, s.29	Life
Throwing object with intent to endanger rail passengers	Offences Against the Person Act 1861, s.33	Life
Torture	Criminal Justice Act 1988, s.134	Life
Wounding with intent to cause grievous bodily harm	Offences Against the Person Act 1861, s.18	Life

Child prostitution or pornography

Offence	Statute	Sentence
Paying for sexual services of a child	Sexual Offences Act 2003, s.47	14 years if child under 14; life if child under 13
Causing or inciting child prostitution or pornography	Sexual Offences Act 2003, s.48	14 years
Controlling a child prostitute or a child involved in pornography	Sexual Offences Act 2003, s.49	14 years
Arranging or facilitating child prostitution or pornography	Sexual Offences Act 2003, s.50	14 years

Drugs

Offence	Statute	Sentence
Production	Misuse of Drugs Act 1971, s.4(2)	Class A: Life; Class B: 14 years
Supplying/offering to supply/ being concerned in the supply	Misuse of Drugs Act 1971, s.4(3)	Class A: Life; Classes B and C: 14 years
Possession with intent to supply	Misuse of Drugs Act 1971, s.5(3)	Class A: Life; Classes B and C: 14 years
Cultivation of cannabis	Misuse of Drugs Act 1971, s.6(2)	14 years

Explosives

Offence	Statute	Sentence
Causing explosion likely to endanger life	Explosive Substances Act 1883, s.2	Life
Attempting to cause explosion	Explosive Substances Act 1883, s.3	Life
Possession of explosive substance with intent	Explosive Substances Act 1883, s.3	Life

Offence	Statute	Sentence
Making or possessing explosive substance	Explosive Substances Act 1883, s.4	14 years

Firearms

Possession of prohibited weapon	Firearms Act 1968, s.5(1)(a), (ab), (aba), (ac), (ad), (af) or (c) or (1A)(a)	10 years; only for offenders who have attained 16 by the date of offence and are subject to the minimum mandatory sentence under Firearms Act 1968, s.51A
Possession with intent to endanger life	Firearms Act 1968, s.16	Life
Using a firearm with intent to resist arrest	Firearms Act 1968, s.17(1)	Life
Possession of a firearm at time of commission of offence or arrest for scheduled offence	Firearms Act 1968, s.17(2)	14 years
Possession with intent to commit an indictable offence or to resist arrest	Firearms Act 1968, s.18	14 years

Sex offences

Arranging commission of a child sex offence	Sexual Offences Act 2003, s.14	14 years
Assault by penetration	Sexual Offences Act 2003, s.2	Life
Assault of a child under 13 by penetration	Sexual Offences Act 2003, s.6	Life
Causing child under 13 to engage in sexual activity	Sexual Offences Act 2003, s.8	14 years; life if subsection (2) applies
Causing person with a mental disorder impeding choice to engage in sexual activity	Sexual Offences Act 2003, s.31	14 years; life if subsection (3) applies
Causing a person with a mental disorder to engage in or agree to engage in sexual activity by inducement, threat or deception	Sexual Offences Act 2003, s.35	14 years; life if subsection (2) applies
Child sex offences	Sexual Offences Act 2003, s.13	5 years
Facilitating commission of a child sex offence	Sexual Offences Act 2003, s.14	14 years
Incest by man with girl under 13	Sexual Offences Act 1956, s.10	Life

Offence	Statute	Sentence
Inciting a child under 13 to engage in sexual activity	Sexual Offences Act 2003, s.8	14 years; life if subsection (2) applies
Inciting a person with a mental disorder impeding choice to engage in sexual activity	Sexual Offences Act 2003, s.31	14 years; life if subsection (3) applies
Indecent assault upon a female	Sexual Offences Act 1956, s.14	10 years
Indecent assault upon a male	Sexual Offences Act 1956, s.15	10 years
Inducement, threat or deception to procure sexual activity with a person with a mental disorder	Sexual Offences Act 2003, s.34	14 years; life if subsection (2) applies
Rape	Sexual Offences Act 1956, s.1	Life
Rape	Sexual Offences Act 2003, s.1	Life
Rape of a child under 13	Sexual Offences Act 2003, s.5	Life
Sexual activity with a child family member	Sexual Offences Act 2003, s.25	5 years
Sexual activity with a person with a mental disorder impeding choice	Sexual Offences Act 2003, s.30	14 years; life, if subsection (3)applies
Sexual assault	Sexual Offences Act 2003, s.3	10 years
Sexual assault of a child under 13	Sexual Offences Act 2003, s.7	14 years
Trafficking for sexual exploitation	Sexual Offences Act 2003, ss.57–59	14 years
Unlawful sexual intercourse with a girl under the age of 13	Sexual Offences Act 1956, s.5	Life

Note: an attempt or conspiracy to commit any of the above offences will also be a grave crime (Criminal Attempts Act 1981, s.1 and Criminal Law Act 1977, s.1 respectively).

OBLIGATORY MINIMUM SENTENCES

1. **Murder.** Life and see CJA 2003, Sched.21 for starting points for minimum sentences and for aggravating and minimum factors.
2. **Firearms.** Firearms Act 1968, s.51A. Minimum term for offences committed at dates shown:

22 January 2004–6 April 2007
21 and over	5 years
18–21	No minimum
Under 18	3 years

In respect of offences under Firearms Act 1968, s.51A: namely offences under s.5(1)(a), (ab), (aba), (ac), (ad), (ae), (af) or (c), or an offence under s.5(1A)(a):

'5.

(1) A person commits an offence if, without the authority of the Defence Council, he has in his possession, or purchases or acquires, or manufactures, sells, or transfers –

    (a)   any firearm which is so designed or adapted that two or more missiles can be successively discharged without repeated pressure on the trigger;

    (ab)   any self-loading or pump-action rifled gun other than one which is chambered for .22 rim-fire cartridges;

    (aba)   any firearm which either has a barrel less than 30 centimetres in length or is less than 60 centimetres in length overall, other than an air weapon, a muzzle loading gun or a firearm designed as signalling apparatus;

    (ac)   any self-loading or pump-action smooth-bore gun which is not an air weapon or chambered for .22 rim-fire cartridges and either has a barrel less than 24 inches in length or is less than 40 inches in length overall;

    (ad)   any smooth-bore revolver gun other than one which is chambered for 9 mm rim-fire cartridges, or a muzzule-loading gun;

    (ae)   any rocket launcher, or any mortar, for projecting a stabilised missile, other than a launcher or mortar designed for line-throwing or pyrotechnic purposes or as signalling apparatus;

    (af)   any air rifle, air gun or air pistol which uses, or is designed or adapted for us with, a self-contained gas cartridge system;

    (c)   any cartridge with a bullet designed to explode on or immediately before impact, any ammunition containing or designed or adapted to contain any such noxious thing as is mentioned in paragraph (b) above and, if capable of being used with a firearm of any description, any grenade, bomb (or other like missile), or rocket or shell designed to explode as aforesaid

(1A) Subject to section 5A of this Act, a person commits an offence if, without the authority of the Secretary of State, he has in his possession, or purchases or acquires, or sells or transfers –

    (a)   any firearm which is disguised as another object

    (b)   any rocket or ammunition not falling within paragraph (c) of subsection (1) of this section which consists in or incorporates a missile designed to explode on or immediately before impact and is for military use;

    (c)   any launcher or other projecting apparatus not falling within paragraph (ae) of that subsection which is designed to be used with any rocket or ammunition falling within paragraph (b) above or with ammunition which would fall within that paragraph but for its being ammunition falling within paragraph (c) of that subsection;

    (d)   any ammunition for military use which consists in or incorporates a missile designed so that a substance contained in the missile will ignite on or immediately before impact;

    (e)   any ammunition for military use which consists in or incorporates a missile designed on account of its having a jacket and hard-core, to penetrate armour plating, armour screening or body armour;

(f)   any ammunition which incorporates a missile designed or adapted to expand on impact;

(g)   anything which is designed to be projected as a missile from any weapon and is designed to be, or has been, incorporated in –

    (i)   any ammunition falling within any of the preceding paragraphs; or

    (ii)   any ammunition which would fall within any of those paragraphs but for its being specified in subsection (1) of this section'

6 April 2007–28 May 2007

21 and over	5 years
18–21	No minimum
Under 18	3 years

In addition to those offences also Firearms Act 1968, s.51A(1):

'51A.

(1)   (a) ...

    (iii)   an offence under any of the provisions of this Act listed in subsection (1A) in respect of a firearm or ammunition specified in section 5(1)(a), (ab), (aba), (ac), (ad), (ae), (af) or (c) or section 5(1A)(a) of this Act

(1A) The provisions are –

(a)   section 16 (possession of firearm with intent to injure);

(b)   section 16A (possession of firearm with intent to cause fear of violence);

(c)   section 17 (use of firearm with criminal intent);

(d)   section 18 (carrying a firearm in a public place);

(e)   section 20(1) (trespassing in a building with a firearm)'

and Violent Crime Reduction Act 2006, s.28 (using someone to mind a weapon).

From 28 May 2007

21 and over	5 years
Under 21	3 years

3.   **Domestic burglary.** PCC(S)A 2000, s.111.

Minimum of 3 years required if:

(a)   burglary committed on or after 1 December 1999;

(b)   at the time of the burglary defendant 18 or over;

(c)   defendant had on date of burglary twice previously been convicted of domestic burglary;

(d)   each such burglary on or after 1 December 1999;

(e)   defendant was convicted of first burglary before he committed the second.

Unless there are particular circumstances which relate to any of the offences and which make it unjust to do so in all the circumstances; or a hospital order is made.

The minimum sentence may be reduced by 20 per cent for a guilty plea.

4.   **Drug trafficking.** PCC(S)A 2000, s.110.

Minimum of 7 years required if convicted of Class A drug trafficking:

(a) offence committed after 1 October 1997;
(b) at the time of the offence defendant 18 or over;
(c) defendant has been convicted on two separate previous occasions of Class A drug trafficking

unless there are particular circumstances which would make it unjust to do so; or a hospital order is made.

The minimum sentence may be reduced by 20 per cent for a guilty plea.

Drug trafficking excludes simple possession.

It includes offences under:

- Misuse of Drugs Act 1971, ss.4(2), (3), 5(3) and 20;
- Customs and Excise Management Act 1979, ss.50(2), 68(2) or 170;
- Drug Trafficking Act 1994, ss.49, 50 or 51;
- Criminal Justice (International Cooperation) Act 1990, ss.12 and 19;
- inciting, attempting or conspiring to commit any of these offences or aiding, abetting, counselling or procuring the commission of any of them.

A conviction that has been followed by a conditional or absolute discharge does not count for these purposes.

APPENDIX 13

Available sentences

SUMMARY: AVAILABLE PRIMARY SENTENCES

Sentence	Age (last birthday)									
	10–11	12–13	14	15	16	17	18	19	20	21 or over
Discharge	*	*	*	*	*	*	*	*	*	*
Compensation order	*	*	*	*	*	*	*	*	*	*
Community sentence[1]							*	*	*	*
Curfew order					*	*				
Drug rehabilitation					*	*				
Reparation order	*	*	*	*	*	*				
Supervision	*	*	*	*	*	*				
Attendance centre	*	*	*	*	*	*				
Referral order	*	*	*	*	*	*				
Action plan order	*	*	*	*	*	*				
Rehabilitation order					*	*				
Community punishment order					*	*				
Rehabilitation and community service order					*	*				
Detention and training		†	†	*	*	*				
Detention in YOI							*	*	*	
Detention (PCC(S)A 2000, s.91)	*	*	*	*	*	*				
Custody for life							*	*	*	
Imprisonment										*

335

	Age (last birthday)									
	10–11	12–13	14	15	16	17	18	19	20	21 or over
Detention in default or for contempt							*	*	*	

[1] Available requirements: unpaid work; activity programme; prohibited activity; curfew; exclusion; residence; mental health treatment; drug rehabilitation; alcohol treatment supervision; attendance centre.
[†] If persistent offender.
[*] The order is available.

APPENDIX 14

Sample instructions to expert – publicly funded case

It is prudent in this publicly funded case to apply to the Legal Services Commission for authority. A request for authority involves the calculation of the work to be carried out pursuant to the advocate's advice or our letter of instruction.

The LSC may grant authority up to a maximum fee only. When deciding on a maximum fee carefully consider how much time you may spend on this case and build in a margin for error. This firm may only be paid sums up to the maximum fee by the LSC; further payments are discretionary and if we do not receive payment, neither will you!

A list of the documents provided by us to enable you to make an assessment is attached, marked Schedule A. When calculating your maximum fee, remember that your assessment should generally include the following:

(a) perusal of all documents listed in Schedule A;
(b) attendance on client if necessary;
(c) viewing prosecution exhibits at source;
(d) perusal of required scientific journals and authorities;
(e) preparation of report.

Your maximum fee should be calculated on Schedule B which we intend to submit to the LSC. Please make any further comments for the LSC in an accompanying letter.

Please retain the papers referred to in Schedule A until we notify you of the LSC's decision. If our application is refused, please return them. If our application is accepted we will tell you the maximum fee allowed, which must not be exceeded.

If you receive formal notification from us to proceed and it is necessary to examine any prosecution exhibits, please contact us and we will ask the CPS to authorise you to make arrangements to do so with the laboratory and police officer in charge of the case.

Please send us three copies of your report including your curriculum vitae and let us have a note of your charges to date.

Please let us also have details of your availability for the next three months. If the case is not concluded within that period, we will request your availability dates at three-monthly intervals.

Please remember these terms of service requirements when calculating your maximum fee and contact us if you have any queries about them.

At the end of the case we will require all case papers to be returned to us.

SCHEDULE A: DOCUMENTS SENT TO EXPERT

Name of expert:

Name of client: **File no:**

Charge sheet	[. . .]
Advance disclosure	[. . .]
Custody record	[. . .]
Tape/transcript	[. . .]
Defendant's statement	[. . .]
Medical report	[. . .]
Photographs	[. . .]
Advocate's opinion	[. . .]
Witness(es) statement(s)	[List]
Depositions	[List]
Notice(s) of additional evidence	[List]

We confirm that the documents indicated have been forwarded to the expert.

Dated: Signed:

SCHEDULE B: EXPERT CALCULATION OF MAXIMUM FEE

Name of expert:
Qualifications:
Years of experience:
Calculation of fees: Specify under individual heading
Perusal documents: Schedule A
View prosecution exhibits at source:
Attend client:
Perusal journals and authorities:
Prepare report:
Maximum fee:

Dated: Signed:

APPENDIX 15

Finding a defence expert

ORGANISATIONS THAT YOU MAY FIND HELPFUL

The Council for the Registration of Forensic Practitioners

Tavistock House, Tavistock Square, London WC1H 9HX. Tel: 020 7383 2200; fax: 020 7383 0888; e-mail: info@crfp.org; www.crfp.org.uk.

The Council for the Registration of Forensic Practitioners (CRFP) has established the first and only register of currently competent forensic practitioners in the UK which relies upon peer review. CRFP publishes the register, ensures through periodic revalidation that forensic practitioners keep up to date and maintain competence and deals with registered practitioners who fail to meet the necessary standards. CRFP has a code of conduct which defines the essential standards and values that apply to every forensic practitioner.

The register contains many specialities including: anthropology; archaeology; drugs; fingerprint development; fingerprint examination; fire scene examination; firearms; forensic computers; human contact traces; incident reconstruction; marks; medicine and paediatrics; odontology; particulates; questioned documents; road transport; scene examination; scene examination volume crime; toxicology; veterinary science. There are in excess of 2,000 registered forensic practitioners.

The register is published on the CRFP website for anyone to consult and is updated daily **www.crfp.org.uk/register.asp**. Applicants for registration have their current competence individually assessed by an external assessor from their own speciality. The assessor looks at the quality of the applicant's work. CRFP is a regulatory council, not a professional association. Its focus is the public interest rather than representing the interests of forensic practitioners.

The Law Society Directory of Expert Witnesses and CD

This is published every July by Sweet & Maxwell and can be ordered from the Law Society distributors, Prolog, tel: 0870 850 1422.

The Academy of Experts

3 Gray's Inn Square, London WC1R 5AH. Tel: 020 7430 0333; fax: 020 7430 0666; e-mail: admin@academy-experts.org; **www.academy-experts.org**.

It has a free online search directory of accredited experts.

British Academy of Forensic Sciences

Enquiries to: Dr Denise Syndercombe Court, BAFS, Haematology, Barts and The London, 4 Newark Street, London E1 2AT. Tel: 020 7882 2276; e-mail: y.d.syndercombe-court@qmul.ac.uk; or to the administrator, Sandra Dawson, PO Box 6314, London N1 0DL. Tel: 020 7837 0069; e-mail: Sandra@admin4u.org.uk; www.bafs.org.uk. A body to 'encourage the study, improve the practice and advance the knowledge of legal, medical and forensic science'. It keeps a list of experts, including forensic pathologists.

Forensic Access

The Health Centre, Bath Road, Thatcham, Berkshire RG18 3HD. Tel: 01635 862123; fax: 01635 869020; e-mail: Science@forensic-access.co.uk; www.forensic-access.co.uk. Provides a forensic consultancy for solicitors.

The Forensic Science Service

Trident Court, 2920 Solihull Parkway, Birmingham Business Park, Birmingham B37 7YN. Tel: 0121 329 5200; fax: 0121 788 3470; **www.forensic.gov.uk**. Open to prosecution and defence alike. It has a marketing division in Birmingham which solicitors can telephone to find out about the facilities it offers and its charges. Where work is conducted by the FSS for the prosecution and the defence in the same case, the work is carried out in different laboratories which do not disclose confidential information to each other.

LGC Forensics

Formerly the laboratory of the Government Chemist, LGC is a large private provider of chemical analysis and diagnostic services, including DNA profiling, digital crime units, questioned documents, forensic analysis and toxicology. LGC acquired Forensic Alliance in 2005. Together they provide a complete range of services across all areas of mainstream forensic science, with a staff of over 1,000. For customer care tel: 01235 551800; **www.forensic-alliance.com**; **www.lgc.co.uk**.

The Forensic Science Society

Clarke House, 18a Mount Parade, Harrogate, North Yorkshire HG1 1BX. Tel: 01423 506068; fax: 01423 566391; **www.forensic-science-society.org.uk**. An international body whose object is to advance the study of forensic science. It runs a directory of independent consultants.

DIFFERENT AREAS OF EXPERTISE

Which expert you choose will depend upon the area of expertise that is required: forensic biology; forensic chemistry; firearms; document examination; fingerprints; photographs; accountancy; or professional practice.

Forensic biology

Biological evidence is material that originates from a living source and is most relevant to the investigation of offences against the person. Examples are:

(a)   hair and textiles fibres;
(b)   bloodstains on clothing and weapons;
(c)   semen on underwear, bedding and swabs;
(d)   saliva;
(e)   clothing.

An experienced forensic biologist should be able to help the defence in a number of ways:

1.   Ascertain whether material was cut or torn, how recently the damage was done and whether a particular knife could have caused it.
2.   Ascertain the number of matching fibres found on your client's clothing, the number and type of each different fibre at the scene and how representative of them the fibres found on your client's clothing are.
3.   It might be that the absence of fibres is of significance.
4.   You would need to look for an alternative source of the fibres.
5.   You would also need to look at the chain of custody of the exhibit to ensure that it has not become contaminated.
6.   Check the chain of custody of an exhibit from the moment the police take possession of it until it is examined at the laboratory.
7.   The distribution of blood and size of the splashes will tell a forensic scientist a lot about what actually happened.
8.   Human hair can be distinguished from animal hair.
9.   Dyes, colourings, rinses, spray or lacquers help to identify the owner in comparison with a control sample.
10.   There is a two-way transfer of hair and fibres when woolly hats, balaclavas or masks are worn.
11.   Residue from the scene of the crime may be found in the offender's hair.

Once a scientist has found a match between a suspect and the profile of samples taken from a crime scene, a calculation will be made to estimate the rarity of that profile – the random occurrence ratio. This calculation is made by using information stored in a database of DNA measurements created by other DNA work done in the laboratory. It results in a statement 'it is estimated that the frequency with which the DNA characteristics in the profile is likely to be found in the population at large is one in . . .'.

Forensic chemistry

This is the area of expertise which is used in relation to offences against property, analysing and comparing material from a non-biological source. These are some examples:

• paint;
• oil;
• glass;
• footwear impressions;
• fire debris;
• tyre marks;
• blood, urine and breath alcohol specimens.

341

Forensic pathology

A Memorandum of Good Practice regarding the early release of bodies in cases of suspicious death has been agreed with the Home Office (see **Appendix 1**) and other criminal justice agencies. It sets out steps which the solicitor should take.

Document examination

Document examination can involve:

(a) disguised handwriting;
(b) ink analysis;
(c) typewriting analysis;
(d) photocopying analysis;
(e) electrostatic deposition analysis of indented handwriting.

FURTHER INFORMATION

Forensic Practice in Criminal Cases (L. Townley and R. Ede, Law Society Publishing, 2003) gives information about:

- drugs, toxicology and related areas of expertise;
- footwear impressions and instrument marks;
- contact traces and other particulates: fibres, glass, paint;
- DNA, blood, hair;
- firearms;
- traffic accident investigators;
- questioned document examiners;
- fingerprints;
- forensic physicians;
- forensic odontologists;
- forensic pathologists;
- forensic psychiatry and forensic psychology;
- forensic linguistics;
- veterinary science;
- fire investigators;
- forensic accountancy;
- computer crime;
- facial mapping, closed circuit TV, video and image enhancement;
- forensic anthropology;
- forensic archaeology.

Bar Council's guidance on drafting defence statements

THE PREPARATION OF DEFENCE CASE STATEMENTS PURSUANT TO THE CRIMINAL PROCEDURE AND INVESTIGATIONS ACT 1996

Guidance on the duties of counsel (as approved by the PCCC on 24 September 1997)

1   It is becoming increasingly common for solicitors to instruct counsel to draft or settle Defence Case Statements, required under section 5 of the Criminal Procedure and Investigations Act 1996. Often these instructions are given to counsel with no or little previous involvement in the case shortly before the expiry of the time limit.

2   The relevant legislation is set out at sections 12–82 et seq. of the 1997 edition of Archbold. In summary, however:

   (i)   The time limit for compliance is short – 14 days from service of prosecution material or a statement that there is none. The permitted grounds for an extension of time are limited; [See the Defence Disclosure Time Limit Regulations 1997 made pursuant to the Act: Archbold Supplement, para. 12–3.]

   (ii) The contents of the Defence Case Statement are obviously of great importance to the defendant. An inaccurate or inadequate statement of the defence could have serious repercussions for the defendant, if the trial judge permits 'appropriate' comment;

   (iii) Whilst it will be the natural instinct of most defence counsel to keep the Defence Case Statement short, a short and anodyne statement may be insufficient to trigger any obligation on the prosecution to give secondary disclosure of prosecution material.

3   Normally it will be more appropriate for instructing solicitors to draft the Defence Case Statement, since typically counsel will have had little involvement at this stage.

4   However, there is nothing unprofessional about counsel drafting or settling a Defence Case Statement, although it must be appreciated that there is no provision in the current regulations for graduated fees allowing for counsel to be paid a separate fee for his work. This most unsatisfactory situation (which has arisen, as a result of the 1996 Act, since the graduated fees regulations were negotiated) is being addressed urgently by the Fees and Legal Aid Committee. A barrister has no obligation to accept work for which he will not be paid. The absence of a fee will justify refusal of the instructions of counsel who are not to be retained for the trial and are simply asked to do no more than draft or settle the Defence Case Statement. Where counsel is retained for the trial, Rule 502(b) of the Code of Conduct deems instructions in a legally aided matter to be at a proper fee and

counsel would not be justified in refusing to draft or settle a Defence Case Statement on the sole ground that there is no separate fee payable for this work.

5   Many members of the Bar will nevertheless feel that, in the interests of their lay client and/or of good relations with instructing solicitors, they cannot refuse work, even where they would otherwise be entitled to do so. Those who do so need to recognise the crucial importance of:

(i)   Obtaining all prosecution statements and documentary exhibits;

(ii)   Getting instructions from the lay client, from a properly signed proof and preferably a conference. Those instructions need to explain the general nature of the defence, to indicate the matters on which issue is taken with the prosecution and to give an explanation of the reason for taking issue. They must also give details of any alibi defence, sufficient to give the information required by Section 5(7) of the 1996 Act;

(iii) Getting statements from other material witnesses;

(iv)   Ensuring that the client realises the importance of the Defence Case Statement and the potential adverse consequences of an inaccurate or inadequate statement;

(v)   Getting proper informed approval for the draft from the client. This is particularly important, given the risks of professional embarrassment if the client seeks to disown the statement during the course of the trial, perhaps when the trial is not going well or when under severe pressure in cross-examination. Counsel ought to insist on getting written acknowledgement from the lay client that:

(a)   he understands the importance of the accuracy and adequacy of the Defence Case Statement for his case;

(b)   he has had the opportunity of considering the contents of the statement carefully and approves it.

This may often mean having a conference with the lay client to explain the Defence Case Statement and to get informed approval, although in straightforward cases where counsel has confidence in the instructing solicitor, this could be left to the solicitor. Where the latter course is taken, a short written advice (which can be in a standard form) as to the importance of obtaining the written acknowledgement before service of the statement should accompany the draft Defence Case Statement. A careful record should be kept of work done and advice given.

(vi)   If there is inadequate time, counsel should ask the instructing solicitor to apply for an extension of time. This needs to be considered at a very early stage, since the application must be made before the expiry of the time limit.

6   It follows that counsel ought not to accept any instructions to draft or settle a Defence Case Statement unless given the opportunity and adequate time to gain proper familiarity with the case and to comply with the fundamental requirements set out above. In short, there is no halfway house. If instructions are accepted, then the professional obligations on counsel are considerable.

APPENDIX 17

Plea and case management hearing form: guidance notes and template

HOW TO USE THE FORM

The parties should complete only one form for each case. **The form should be used in every Crown Court centre, without any local exception or variation.**

The form may be completed in manuscript or electronically.

Questions 1 to 14 must be answered in every case. Questions 15 to 35 need only be answered if they are relevant.

The advocate may be asked by the court to expand upon or explain an entry, or to account for the absence of an entry, where one is required. The judge will record on the template any orders made and, if practicable, issue a copy to the parties before the hearing ends.

The parties must obtain a copy of that record and comply with the orders made by the date given.

Accessing the form

The current version of the form is available on the Court Service website at **www.hmcourts-service.gov.uk/HMCSCourtFinder**. Please note that the form will be updated from time to time. When you open the file, a box will appear with the options of disabling or enabling macros. Choosing 'enable macros' will produce a fully operational e-form. Choosing 'disable macros' may cause some of the functions to be lost, including the option of altering the number of defendants or using a screen reader.

Next will appear the box giving the option of a screen reader. This is software which translates text into speech.

The next box asks for the number of defendants in the case. This can be altered later by clicking on 'Add Def' in the toolbar at the top of the screen.

Once this question has been answered, the form that is produced is ready for completion.

The space available to answer any question expands to accommodate the text inserted.

The Tab button can be used to jump to the next box. Alternatively, the arrow keys will move the cursor backwards or forwards.

Transmitting the form

If you complete the form on the screen, it can still be printed off and used in hard copy. Alternatively, it can be e-mailed; the process for this differs depending on whether Outlook is available.

In order to send the form by e-mail, click on the 'e-mail' button on the toolbar at the top of the screen and follow the instructions. If the document is to be e-mailed using Outlook, that programme must be open at the time. Following the instructions will produce an e-mail window with the form attached. If Outlook is not used, the file must be saved and can then be attached in the usual way.

THE NEED FOR AN EFFECTIVE PCMH

The public, and all those concerned in or affected by a criminal case, have a right to expect that the business of the courts will be conducted fairly but also efficiently and effectively. Delays cost money and adversely impact on the quality of justice. The plea and case management hearing offers the best, and often the only, opportunity for the judge properly and effectively to manage the case before it is listed for trial. Other hearings – formerly called 'mentions'– are expensive and should actively be discouraged; nearly everything formerly done at a 'mention' can – and should – be done in some other way (usually by telephone or on paper or by an exchange of e-mail, as permitted by CPR 3.5(2)(d)). An effective PCMH is therefore vital.

Advocates should attend the hearing fully prepared to deal with the issues that are likely to arise, and the listing officer should consider reasonable requests to list the PCMH to enable trial counsel to attend.

Since an effective PCMH can only take place after the defence have had a proper opportunity to consider the papers, it is suggested that at least four weeks should elapse between the service and listing of the PCMH.

The short guidance given here is intended to be followed in every case but, of course, it is not possible to cover exhaustively all the situations which may be relevant to achieving an effective PCMH. See also Consolidated Criminal Practice Direction (CCPD) IV.41, Management of Cases to be Heard in the Crown Court; V.56 Case Management in Magistrates' Courts and Criminal Case Management Framework (available online at **www.cjsonline.gov.uk/framework**).

CONTENTS OF THE FORM

Date of trial and custody time limits

The date of trial should normally be fixed at the PCMH (or before). Any application to extend the custody time limit is best dealt with at the PCMH, when the reasons for fixing a case beyond the time limits will be clear; otherwise there will be the avoidable expense of another hearing.

1, 2 and 3   Details of case and parties

This section must be fully completed. The parties must be able to contact one another as must case progression officers and the court. Any change in the details must immediately be notified to the other parties and to the court. See CPR 3.4.

4   Compliance with the directions given by magistrates' courts

The standard/specific directions given by magistrates' courts should be complied with (CPR 3.5(3)). The court will need to know which orders have not been complied with, and why.

5 Credit for guilty plea

Defendants are entitled to be given the advice that credit is given for guilty pleas and the earlier the plea is entered, the greater is the credit given. The judge needs to know that this advice has been given.

6 Trial in absence

Defendants need to be warned that if they waive their right to attend, the trial may proceed in their absence. No one can engineer an adjournment simply by absconding. Those who claim to be ill must support that claim by medical evidence to the effect that they are unfit to attend their trial; it is unlikely that a medical certificate merely suggesting that they are unfit to work will be sufficient. See CCPD, I.13; CPR 3.8(2)(a).

7 The pleas which the defendant is offering

Recording in writing pleas offered to alternative offences which the prosecution is initially unwilling to accept will be advantageous to the defendant if the prosecution subsequently changes its position. In such circumstances, it will be easier for a defendant to claim maximum credit if that offer has been recorded. Pleas offered to counts on the indictment must similarly be recorded before credit is claimed.

8 Allocation of the case

Most courts have a system to identify before the PCMH those cases which require allocation to a particular judge; this question is intended to seek out those cases which have been missed.

9 Fitness to plead

This is self-explanatory but the judge will need assistance to fix a timetable for the service of experts' reports and for the issue to be tried.

10 Disclosure and defence statement

The parties must identify any outstanding disclosure points. The defence must serve a detailed defence statement setting out the issues in the trial; any failure to do so may be the subject of adverse comment at the trial and the judge may issue a warning to this effect, under the Criminal Procedure and Investigations Act 1996, s 11(3) Pending service of a defence statement, question 10.4 allows the defence to give some notification of the defence. The practice of appending long 'shopping lists' to vague and unspecific defence statements has no legal foundation; any application for further disclosure should be made by way of formal application under the Criminal Procedure and Investigations Act 1996, s.8 (as amended). The judge will expect reference to and compliance with the Disclosure Protocol: A Protocol for the Control and Management of Unused Material in the Crown Court.

11 and 12 Timetable of further evidence and expert evidence

Advocates should have available proper information as to what remains to be served, together with a realistic timetable for compliance. Parties should be prepared to provide realistic time estimates and not rely on a standard time period of, for example,

28 days if this has little bearing on the true amount of time likely to be required. The court needs detailed and accurate information as to when the evidence will be available. These enquiries should be made before the hearing. Failure to do so is likely to cause unnecessary adjournments. Consideration should be given to CPR 33.5 and whether (now or later) the experts should be asked to confer to identify the real areas of dispute.

13 Witness list (see also 36)

The mere fact of warning a witness to attend may cause him or her anxiety. Furthermore, the warning of witnesses is time consuming and expensive. The court may decline to order the attendance of witnesses unless their presence is really necessary. Consideration should therefore also be given to those witnesses in respect of whom a summons is required. See CPR Part 28 for rules on witness summonses. Thought should always be given to the staggering of witnesses to eliminate or reduce waiting times. The witnesses' availability must be known at the PCMH to ensure that the trial date is convenient.

14 Certificate for a litigator

Attendance by a litigator is not a matter of right and should always be justified by reference to the facts of the particular case.

15 Admissions

Properly drafted admissions can save a great deal of court time and proposals should be made in most cases.

16 Case summary

Case summaries should have been provided before the PCMH in all Class 1 cases and in any other case of complexity, but they may be needed in other cases as well.

17 Special measures

In accordance with CPR Part 29, special measures applications should have been made by the parties and considered by the court before the PCMH, but this question serves to remind advocates and judges of any outstanding applications.

18 Young and other vulnerable defendants

The needs of young and other vulnerable defendants must be identified in advance of the trial so that the necessary arrangements can be made. See CCPD III.30.

19 Reporting restrictions

Reporting restrictions need to be carefully considered and balanced against the rights of the press and other interested parties. The judge is likely to require assistance before making any order. See CCPD I.3.

20 Third party material and applications to produce documents

Such applications must comply with CPR Part 28. Careful thought needs to go into identifying the witness to be served, the material sought and the reason that it is said to be relevant to an issue in the case. Any person whose right of confidentiality might be adversely affected must also be identified and information provided as to how and by whom they are to be notified, how they are to be permitted to make representations and when and by whom any rulings are to be made. It is important that such applications are made no later than the PCMH to avoid adjournments at a later stage arising out of delayed applications.

21 Defendant's interviews

Inaccuracies within transcriptions and likely submissions as to admissibility must be identified. Furthermore, the police may interview suspects at length, producing bundles of transcripts, the volume of which may make them unsuitable to put before a jury. The parties must consider producing summaries. The production of the first draft is primarily the responsibility of the advocate for the prosecution. If practicable, interviews should be available in electronic form, so that editing, pagination and copying can be done without delay. Further guidance is given in CCPD IV.43.

22 Video evidence

These four questions, each of which raises a separate point, are self explanatory but failure to address them is a frequent source of adjournments. Accuracy, admissibility and quality are not the same. Errors of transcription or material on the tape that is indistinct or unclear, or which is alleged to be inadmissible, must be dealt with at PCMH. Editing takes time. It should not be done on the morning of the trial or the day beforehand. Only if these issues are addressed in advance can child witnesses be called as soon as they arrive at court. It is unacceptable to prolong the anxiety of vulnerable witnesses simply because these issues have not been resolved at PCMH. See also CPR Part 29 for rules on special measures directions; and CCPD IV.40.

23 Witness interviews

The issues raised in this question differ from those raised in question 22. There is a growing practice of recording interviews with witnesses before setting out their evidence in a written witness statement. If this is done, then, subject to the disclosure test, the video or audio recording should be disclosed as unused material. The prosecution advocate therefore needs to know if any witness was interviewed in this way (which may not be clear from the papers served). It will normally suffice for the video or audio recording itself to be disclosed. Transcripts are expensive and any claim for a transcript needs to be justified.

24 and 25 CCTV and electronic equipment

The prosecution have duties to consider disclosure only of CCTV footage in their possession. If the defence seek footage from third parties, it is for them to do so, rather than the prosecution. Furthermore, much CCTV footage is in a format (e.g. multiplex) which is unsuitable for showing in court without adaptation or editing. This must be sorted out before the trial. Many courts have simple VHS video and DVD playback facilities and the parties must ensure that the material which they want to play is compatible with the court equipment (if not, they must provide their own).

26   Cross-examination on sexual history

The Youth Justice and Criminal Evidence Act 1999, s.41 enacts an important principle and compliance with its requirements is vital to ensure that those who complain that they are victims of rape (and other sexual offences) receive the protection which the law affords to them. In accordance with CPR Part 36, applications should be made and considered – by the trial judge if possible – at or before the PCMH. Applications made on the day of the trial are strongly to be discouraged.

27 and 28   Bad character and hearsay

CPR 34.5 and 35.6 provide for detailed applications to be made in the prescribed forms. Questions 27 and 28 therefore only seek to identify any outstanding issues (or potential future applications).

29   Admissibility and legal issues

Issues of admissibility and legal issues should, where possible, be identified before the trial, so that the parties can exchange skeleton arguments and the judge can properly prepare for the hearing. See also the Criminal Justice Act 1987, s.7; and the Criminal Procedure and Investigations Act 1996, ss.31 and 40.

30   Timetable of the trial

If there are to be preliminary points taken, then consideration must be given to when a jury will be required and arrangements made to stagger the attendance of witnesses. No one should be asked to attend for a 10.30am start only to find that there is a lengthy legal argument before the case can even be opened. See CPR 3.10, which deals with, amongst other things, timetabling and witness arrangements.

31   PII claims

If a claim is to be made on notice, then the necessary arrangements must be made. See CPR Part 25.

32   Jury bundle

If a jury bundle will be needed at the trial, then its content will need to be agreed before the trial. Any outstanding issues need to be identified.

33   Concurrent family proceedings

It is important to identify those cases where there are concurrent family proceedings, so that the Designated Family Judge can be alerted.

34   Special arrangements

Any requirements for an interpreter or for those with a disability must be identified in advance, so that proper arrangements can be made. See CPR 10.5(1)(h) and 12.1(1)(e).

35   Linked criminal proceedings

These need to be identified, if possible with the court reference numbers.

TEMPLATE FOR ORDERS MADE AT PLEA AND CASE MANAGEMENT HEARING

*delete as appropriate

PCMH question	Description of order/ work required	Order made
1	Trial date [*fixed for] [*warned for week commencing] Estimated length of hearing	
9	The defence to serve expert evidence (fitness to plead)	
9	The prosecution to serve expert evidence in response (fitness to plead)	
10	The defence to serve any defence statement by	
10	Was a warning given that inferences may be drawn from failure to comply?	
10	The prosecution to make further disclosure by	
10	The defence to make any application under CPIA 1996, s.8 for disclosure by	
11	The prosecution to serve further evidence by	
12	The prosecution to serve expert evidence by	
12	The defence to serve any expert evidence on which they rely by	
13	Defence to serve a list of witnesses required at trial by	
13	Record any ruling that the judge has made that the attendance of any witness on that list is not required	
14	Certificate for litigator granted for [*the first day] [*the whole trial]	
15	Prosecution to serve schedule of facts for agreement by	
16	Prosecution to serve case summary or note of opening by	
17	Prosecution to apply for special measures directions by	
17	Prosecution to apply for special measures directions by	
17	Defence to apply for special measures directions by	
19	Reporting restrictions made in terms attached	
20	Prosecution to seek disclosure of third party material by	
20	Defence to seek disclosure of third party material by	
20	Person adversely affected [give name] to be notified by	
21	Defence to notify editing required of defendant's interview by	
21	Prosecution to respond to same by	
21	Prosecution to prepare summaries for agreement by	
22	Prosecution to serve video tape of vulnerable witness by	
22	Prosecution to serve [*transcript][*summary] of evidence by	
22	Defence to notify editing required of defendant's interview by	
22	Prosecution to respond to same by	
23	Prosecution to serve tapes of witness interviews by	
23	Prosecution to transcribe tapes of witness interviews by	
24	Prosecution to serve or disclose CCTV footage by	
24	Prosecution to serve edited version of CCTV footage by	
25	Prosecution to confirm that court equipment compatible with tape by	

PCMH question	Description of order/ work required	Order made
26	Defence to serve application to cross-examine on sexual history by	
27	Prosecution to serve further bad character application by	
27	Defence to serve further bad character application by	
28	Prosecution to serve further hearsay application by	
28	Defence to serve further hearsay application by	
29	Defence to serve skeleton argument on legal points to be taken by	
29	Prosecution to respond by *Other orders * *	

Judge's signature: Date:

Index

SA